Stephen

Rock
Hudson

Other titles by David Bret also published by Robson Books:

The Piaf Legend
The Mistinguett Legend
Maurice Chevalier
Marlene Dietrich – My Friend
Morrissey: Landscapes of the Mind
Maria Callas: The Tigress and the Lamb
George Formby
Piaf: A Passionate Life
Errol Flynn: Satan's Angel
Gracie Fields: The Authorised Biography
Valentino: A Dream of Desire
Living on the Edge: The Freddie Mercury Story
Tallulah Bankhead
Elvis: The Hollywood Years
Morrissey: Scandal and Passion

Rock
Hudson

DAVID BRET

 ROBSON BOOKS

First published in Great Britain in 2004 by Robson Books, The Chrysalis Building, Bramley Road, London W10 6SP

An imprint of Chrysalis Books Group plc

British Library Cataloguing in Publication Data
A catalogue record for this title is available from the British Library.

ISBN 1 86105 855 1

Typeset by SX Composing DTP, Rayleigh, Essex
Printed by Creative Print & Design (Wales), Ebbw Vale

This book is for Henry and *Les Enfants de Novembre*

N'oublie pas . . .
La vie sans amis c'est comme
un jardin sans fleurs.

Contents

Acknowledgements

Writing this book would not have been possible, had it not been for the inspiration, criticisms and love of that select group of individuals whom I still regard as my true family and *autre coeur*: Barbara, Irene Bevan, Marlene Dietrich, Roger Normand and Dorothy Squires, *que vous dormez en paix*; René and Lucette Chevalier, Jacqueline Danno, Betty Paillard and Gérard, Annick Roux, Tony Griffin, Terry Sanderson, Hélène Delavaux, John and Anne Taylor, Axel Dotti, François and Madeleine Vals, Caroline Clerc, Charley Marouani, and those *hiboux* and *amis de foutre*, who happened along the way. Very special thanks to Professor Ronald L Davis. Also heartfelt appreciation to Peter Burton, to the munificent Melanie Letts and to Jane Donovan, Gillian Holmes and Clive Hebard for their excellent work on the script and for unearthing more than a few 'Bretisms' and for generally bullying me into shape. Indeed, to the entire Robson team for yet another sterling production. Last but not least, especial thanks to my agent, David Bolt, and to my wife, Jeanne, still the keeper of my soul!

And a final *chapeau-bas* for Rock, for having lived.

David Bret

Introduction

Why didn't Rock tell me he had the virus? I might have been able to help. Improbable as it seems, right up to the very end he truly believed he would beat that thing. He wished to remain proud, brave, to hold his head up high for my sake. He did this by appearing in several episodes of *Dynasty*. I advised him to rest, but he reckoned working enabled him to forget the monster that was slowly devouring him. Rock Hudson was an exceptional man, one to whom I owe the most beautiful moments of my life.

This was Marc Christian, the last of Rock Hudson's stereotyped lovers – with few exceptions his small army of conquests were big, blond and above all macho – addressing a live audience (by then not quite so ignorant of AIDS) on the French television programme *Stars à la Barre*, four years after the actor's death from an AIDS-related illness.

At a press conference of 2 November 1985, however, just one month after Rock passed away, Christian's attitude – and public opinion – had been less sympathetic. Then the young man had announced that he would be suing the Hudson estate, Rock's manager and best friend Mark Miller, and two unspecified doctors for a staggering $14 million because, Christian claimed, they had conspired to endanger his life by keeping the true nature of Rock's illness from him while he and Rock had continued having unprotected sex.

There was outrage amongst both gay and anti-gay activists across the United States when Christian eventually won his case – though not without considerable reduction in damages after Rock's lawyers launched a Pyrrhic appeal.

A surprisingly shy, sensitive and intensely private man, Rock Hudson gave but a handful of in-depth interviews that were frequently vetted by the actor before being submitted for publication. I have drawn heavily on these original, unexpurgated conversations for this book – namely the ones with David Castell, Joan Mac Trevor, Gordon Gow, Gérard Néves and several others whom Rock found he could trust (for dates *see* Bibliography). Important too are the revelations of Sara Davidson and Rock's wife, Phyllis Gates.

On 24 August 1983, two years before his death, Rock came close to baring his soul when granting an unprecedented interview to Professor Ronald L Davis, Director of the Southern Methodist University of Dallas' Oral History Collection on the Performing Arts – being permitted to use the tapes freely was an enormous privilege, and large segments of the interviews form the series of statements and confessions accompanying my text. The tapes and transcripts of the interview are currently housed in the archives of the SMU's DeGolyer Institute.

As an actor, few would deny that Rock Hudson's abilities were limited in comparison with contemporaries such as Montgomery Clift, Marlon Brando, William Holden and even James Dean. Complicated lengths of dialogue are said to have confused him, his emotional approach to a role was considerable but his intellectual standing, certainly during his formative years, was virtually non-existent, and during his earlier films he frequently fluffed his lines, requiring many takes for the simplest scene. In addition, his on-screen movements were cumbersome, even wooden at times.

On the other hand he was a consummate professional. With Rock there were never any on-set tantrums, he rarely challenged the director's or producer's instructions and hardly ever fought with co-stars, making him not only a delight to work with but a joy to be around once the cameras had stopped rolling. And his most important quality, something that positively lights up the screen even in his most banal pictures, was his absolute, completely natural and limitless charisma.

I leave the last word to Sheridan Morley, a hugely respected literary and theatrical figure, who met Rock several times during his later years and spoke to me of him only with the utmost reverence:

> He had been programmed by the studios to be charming, but charm came naturally to Rock Hudson. He really was the last of the great gentleman stars, there's absolutely no doubting that. Rock Hudson wasn't just a nice man – he was a very nice man.

This, then, is the story of that charming, very nice man.

1

The Gentle Giant

'He's just a great big, amiable boy. That's the first thing that struck me about him, and I imagine it's what appeals to the mother in all women.'

Yvonne de Carlo, co-star

He was born Roy Scherer Jr on 17 November 1925 in Winnetka, a suburb of Chicago, Illinois, and his was an excessively crowded and miserable childhood. His parents were Roy, sr, a garage owner, and Kay (Katherine Wood), a strong-willed, domineering woman, luckless in her choice of partners, but to whom Rock would remain inextricably close, despite her frequent meddling in his personal life. 'Kay was mother, father and sister to me,' he often said. 'And I was son and brother to her, regardless of who she was married to.'

When Roy was five, at the height of the Depression that gripped America in the wake of the Wall Street Crash, his father was declared bankrupt and he, Kay and their son were forced to move in with Kay's parents, James and Mary Ellen Wood. They were already sharing their tiny one-bedroom bungalow in Winnetka's Center Street – one of the city's poorest districts – with Kay's brother, his wife and their four children, who upon the Scherers' arrival were forcibly relocated to the attic.

Over the next few months, Roy's stalwart Catholic grandmother held the family together by the skin of her teeth through an endless

1

series of heated arguments, mostly over money. Mary Ellen also went against her daughter's wishes by having Roy re-baptised a Catholic one day while Kay was at work. Although Kay overruled her by insisting that he was the only child in the household who would not attend a Catholic school or church.

Roy Scherer, sr put up with these unbelievably frustrating living arrangements for over a year before packing his bags and heading for California in search of work. Initially, Kay coped with having to fend for herself. For a while she worked as a housekeeper for a local dignitary, sharing a room and a bed with Roy in servants' quarters that were just as cramped as Grandmother Wood's bungalow until she had saved enough money to put down a bond on a two-room apartment above a local drugstore. Rock later said that the only thing worth remembering about the place was that, while he lived there, he learned to play the piano by ear.

However, the arrangement only lasted until the summer of 1932 when, short of cash once more and taking her son with her rather than leave him with her interfering mother, Kay travelled by bus to California, where she discovered her husband living rough and working as a doughnut-seller. Much as she pleaded with him, though, Scherer refused to return with her to Illinois, and Roy would not see his father again for many years. More than this, on the journey home, Kay met a young marine named Wallace Fitzgerald – a loutish, womanising individual – with whom she very quickly became involved.

The pair were married in February 1934, immediately after Kay's divorce from Roy Scherer, and a few months later – more financially secure than Scherer had ever been – Fitzgerald left the Navy to work at a local electricity plant and Kay took a job as a waitress, reluctantly leaving her son with her parents. The union was doomed from the outset and by 1941 the Fitzgeralds had divorced, remarried and divorced again.

Wallace Fitzgerald legally adopted Roy and gave him his name, though precious little affection. 'He took all my toys away and used to beat me regularly, saying he wanted to make a man out of me,' Rock recalled, three decades later. Fitzgerald's major source of disappointment in his stepson centred around Roy's acute lack of interest in matters academic, despite his eventual enrolment at the prestigious New Trier High School – 'Drop-dead gorgeous but thick as two bricks,' was how Tallulah Bankhead described him after their first meeting in 1953 – and with the exception of swimming he was not much interested in sports, either.

All Roy ever wanted to be was an actor, as he explained in his now legendary 1983 interview with Professor Ronald L Davis of Dallas' Southern Methodist University:

> I knew I wanted to be an actor when I was a little boy – but living in a small town in the Middle West, I didn't say so because that's just sissy stuff. I once asked my stepfather if I could have drama lessons. When I said I wanted to be an actor – Crack! – and that was that!

This 'sissy' tag of his childhood would haunt and persecute him for years, though at the time this and his desperately unhappy home life only made Roy more determined to achieve his goal. So, encouraged by his mother, he decided at the age of ten that he would pay for his own acting lessons by taking a weekend job with a local butcher, plucking chickens and running errands . . . and spending every last cent not on evening classes but on cinema tickets and movie magazines.

Roy's greatest inspiration was camp-icon Jon Hall (1913–79), the muscle-bound star of such colourful films, with implausible plots, as *Cobra Woman* (1944) and *Ali Baba and the Forty Thieves* (1944) – who frequently appeared on the screen wearing as little as the all-powerful Hays Office would allow without inciting so-called 'moral turpitude'. When Roy witnessed the mouthwateringly attractive, loin-clothed Hall diving in and out of the water in the 1937 film *The Hurricane* – unaware that some of the actor's more hair-raising stunts had called for the services of a stunt double – his mind was made up. 'I'd always been a diver,' he recalled, 'so I had to be an actor and go to Tahiti and be like Jon Hall!'

But not only did Roy want to be like his idol – for at the age of twelve, he later claimed, he had already become aware of his sexuality, having developed a crush on Jon Hall, among others.

*

At the end of 1940, Roy's mother bought a run-down property on Winnetka's Ash Street, and hired a small team of poorly paid navvies to renovate the place and convert it into a boarding house. With her second marriage to Wallace Fitzgerald already on the rocks, Kay was probably hoping that the new venture would repair the rift between them and, as an added incentive to keep the short-tempered Fitzgerald calm, his prime source of irritation – Roy – was dispatched to live with an aunt.

This temporary measure lasted until the summer of 1941, during which time Roy hardly saw his mother at all, but when Kay brought him back to Ash Street that summer, the situation had improved – Wallace Fitzgerald was gone for good.

Fitzgerald's departure, however, did not result in Roy seeing much more of his mother, for Kay was now compelled to support her meagre income from the boarding house by working as a part-time telephone operator at the Great Lakes Naval Training Centre some twenty miles out of Winnetka. Added to this was Roy's misery of having to stay on at school for an extra six months because of his abysmal grades. Instead of graduating in the summer of 1943, he did not leave New Trier High until early in 1944. Three weeks later – to be closer to his mother – Roy enlisted with the Navy and was sent on a training course as an apprentice aircraft repairman. The boot camp was at the same training centre that employed Kay.

By now, aged eighteen, Roy had attained his full height of six feet four inches – though people meeting him for the first time often declared he was taller and expressed astonishment that such an imposing specimen had weighed less than six pounds at birth – and though he was thin and reed-like, photographs taken at the time reveal him to have been a good deal better-looking than Jon Hall had ever been, his handsome features marred only by a crooked eye-tooth.

'Fitz', as his pals nicknamed him, proved hopeless as a marine. He was posted to Samar, in the Philippines, on the SS *Lew Wallace*, and for two years worked for the Aviation Repair Overhaul Unit. Much of his time was spent unloading fighter planes from aircraft carriers, and on one occasion he accidentally switched on both engines of the bomber he was repairing, causing the machine to career across the runway and crash into another stationary plane. He is also said to have been unusually timid for his size, terrified of being reprimanded by superiors for botched repair-work (which he was, time and time again). Despite this, he wasn't too timid to go looking for men or to engage in a number of affairs with fellow marines. These naturally were very clandestine, but all the more thrilling, he later confessed, on account of the tremendous risks involved. And when the war ended and Roy was transferred to the base's laundry unit, he indulged in several more.

Roy returned to Winnetka in May 1946, but instead of staying with his mother, after two weeks working as a piano remover, and still bent on becoming an actor, he joined his father in California. Roy Scherer had remarried and was living in Long Beach with his new wife and adopted daughter – he had set himself up in an electrical appliances business, and when Roy was refused a place at the University of California on account of his below-standard high school grades, Scherer, sr offered him a job as a door-to-door vacuum cleaner salesman. Roy was so shy and lacking in patter that in his first month he did not make a single sale. Then, just as he was thinking of taking the bus back to Illinois he discovered paradise – the uncloseted, bohemian, gay community.

Taking a room in a lodging house and a job as a truck driver with a company owned by a friend of his father's, Roy divided his spare time between touting for work outside the various studio gates – leaning against the tail-plate of his truck, chain-smoking, looking studious but ungainly, and subsequently always ending up ignored – and hustling for sex on the exclusively gay section of the beach. He became a frequent visitor to the men-only bars on Ocean Boulevard, and in one of these met his first serious lover: Ken Hodge was the wealthy ex-producer of the Lux Radio Theater.

Blond, debonair, and fifteen years his senior, Hodge was Roy's first mentor – a man who recognised his screen potential in that, though Roy was possessed of no acting ability whatsoever, he certainly had the looks and appeal to melt female hearts and bring money to the box office and Roy's own depleted bank account.

For several weeks the couple resided in a luxurious apartment at the Chateau Marmont. Then they moved to Hollywood, where Hodge rented a small bungalow.

Hodge was so besotted with his lusty young lover that he pledged Roy all the financial support he might need to launch his acting career. He installed him at a gymnasium where, in less than a year, Roy filled out, increasing his weight to a staggering 220 pounds of solid muscle. Then Hodge took his protégé to a tailor and kitted him out with a suit – until now Roy had always bought his clothes off the peg, and since he had never been able to find a pair of trousers long enough, he had often worn these at half-mast. Hodge also paid for Roy's first photographic shoot. Pictures of his 'discovery' were quickly dispatched to studio executives, and the pair spent their evenings attending parties and receptions at which these would be present.

At one, in Culver City, Roy was introduced to David O Selznick's talent scout and the former agent of Lana Turner – the infamous Henry Willson. Without telling Ken Hodge, who would almost certainly have advised him otherwise, Roy agreed to attend an audition at Willson's house in Stone Canyon.

Not long before Roy met him, Henry Willson had commented upon the thousands of letters he was receiving every week, telling the acid-tongued columnist Hedda Hopper, 'I'm what you might call a Salvation Army worker at heart. The kids in this business know it and that's why they come to me looking for work.' But even Hopper, accustomed to having free rein when it came to exposing Tinsel Town's hypocrisy, would never have risked printing the truth of this man, who (quoted by Jimmie Hicks, *Films In Review*, May 1975) said of his most bankable asset:

> He was the moviegoer's ideal of the typical American boy. He had size, good looks, strength, and a certain shyness that I thought would make him a star like Gable. He had the kind of personal charm that makes you think you'd enjoy sitting down and spending time with him.

A bitchy, overweight and wildly promiscuous homosexual in his early forties, with almost certain Mafia connections, Willson's power was such that he only had to reach under his desk and stroke some young wannabe's thigh and, with the promise of almost certain imminent fame by way of Willson's seemingly limitless web of contacts, the aspiring actor would hop straight on to the casting couch. And if the young man happened to be rampantly hetero-sexual, Willson would bide his time until the actor had started to make a name for himself, then pounce – threatening to expose his homosexuality to the press and, if he still refused to yield, mounting a devious, extremely virulent smear campaign that ensured he would never work again.

On the plus side – and this was the key to his almost 100 per cent success rate – Willson was a whizz at inventing hugely marketable names that often took precedence over their owners' limited acting abilities. Thus Arthur Gelien had become Tab Hunter, Francis Durgin had become Rory Calhoun, and Merle Johnson had made a huge impact as Troy Donahue. Additionally, another hopeful unwillingly seduced by Willson, Robert Mosely, had had his name changed to Guy Madison on account of his fondness for Dolly Madison cakes! Willson's further discoveries included John Smith (Robert Van Orden), Nick Adams (Nicholas Adamschock), John Saxon (Carmen Orrico) and Rip (Elmore) Torn – stars who appeared on the surface so naturally wholesome, handsome and athletic that girls swooned while young, impressionable men across America emulated their every gesture.

In 1957, thinly disguised as the character Tex Warner, Henry Willson would play third lead in the Elvis Presley film *Loving You*, portrayed by closeted gay actor Wendell Corey. In his pursuit of archetypal rebel-hero Deke Rivers (Presley), Warner famously suggests while drooling over him, 'Maybe a special name, like Rock or Tab.' This, and the film's wealth of gay innuendo and double entendre, was scriptwriter and director Hal Kanter's revenge on Willson for 'negotiating' a deal with *Confidential* magazine (of which more later) wherein a Hudson exclusive would be spiked (abandoned) in favour of outing Presley's leading lady in the film, Lizabeth Scott, as a lesbian. Few people at the time, however, were aware of Rock's or Tab Hunter's homosexuality, and such in-jokes would have gone way over the heads of Hudson and Presley fans and the general public.

When Ken Hodge learned that Roy had begun seeing Henry

Willson behind his back and that Roy was more than willing to
allow Willson to have his way with him as often as he liked so long
as he achieved his acting goal, he refused to have any more to do
with him. Without even bothering to say goodbye, he headed back to
Long Beach.

Roy coped with his 'loss' by flinging himself headlong into his
new venture. Willson sent him to Lester Luther, one of Hollywood's
top voice coaches: Luther helped rid him of his Midwestern drawl and
the stammer that Roy claimed was prominent only when he was
feeling nervous – in other words, most of the time – and subjected him
to several weeks of 'bawling' sessions, where Roy was ordered to yell
and scream non-stop for thirty minutes at a time. This ruptured his
vocal chords so that when they healed his voice was half a tone lower
and as butch as the rest of him. Roy received drama lessons from
Florence Cunningham, and he was taught how to stand, sit and walk
by Universal's athletics coach, the no-nonsense ex-boxer Frankie
Van. Like many people of great height, Roy had a tendency to stoop:
Van corrected this by giving him a hard punch to the middle of the
back every time he did so, and the young man is said never to have
complained. On top of this, he was enrolled for lessons in horse-
riding, fencing, tap-dancing, even ballet and deportment, all at
considerable expense to Henry Willson, whose only immediate
recompense was several months exclusivity – or so he was led to
believe at the time – on his exciting discovery's sexual favours.

One trait which Willson and his training team could not rid Roy
of was his acute lack of faith in his abilities, an unwillingness to let
himself go except within the privacy of his home, a problem which
would burden him for the rest of his life. In 1972 Ken Martin, a
reporter from the British *TV Times*, would upset him with an only too
true observation:

> His manner confirms that he lacks self-confidence. He tries too
> hard to make a good impression: he times his brief answers to
> questions as if playing drawing-room comedy. You write down
> his reply and look up to see that he's still waiting for you to
> show appreciation of his wit. If you miss the joke, he takes a
> studied, disappointed drag at a cigarette, of which he smokes

too many. You can't help thinking what a great person he would be if he would relax and enjoy – and stop worrying about his image.

Over the years there have been numerous theories as to how Roy Fitzgerald became Rock Hudson, though the most widely believed is that the 'Rock' came from 'hard as' after a top Hollywood actress grabbed a handful at a reception – the 'Hudson' came when Henry Willson stabbed the telephone directory with a pin. Many years later Rock would claim that his 'boner' had been brought about by the attentions of an actor standing nearby, and he often joked with friends, 'I wanted to be called Geraldine Fitzgerald, but Hollywood already had one of those!'

Henry Willson was now faced with the invidious task of trying to place an inexperienced, untalented but devilishly attractive young man into a suitable vehicle. Rock failed five successive screen tests largely on account of his nervousness and wooden stance. Though by no means backwards in coming forwards when chatting up prospective bed mates, he was intensely shy in front of the camera and even five years later when he was a massive star, near-contemporaries James Dean and Montgomery Clift would still be calling him 'lumpish'. Then in early 1948 Rock was introduced to renegade director Raoul Walsh.

Walsh, then in his early sixties, prided himself with the fact that he was the quintessential rebel who had never been officially recognised by the Academy or even the studio system. 'He didn't want to know about such subtleties as psychological nuances and profound probings into character,' said his friend Jesse Lasky Jr, the son of the Hollywood pioneer. 'His target was the solar plexus rather than the cerebellum, and his films never missed the mark.'

When a boy, Walsh had run away from home, and after a period as a cabin boy had worked on cattle drives, breaking in horses, before appearing in his first film as an extra in 1909. Six years later he had appeared in D W Griffith's legendary *Birth of a Nation*, and several minor roles had followed before he made his directorial debut in 1928 with *Sadie Thompson*. The next year Walsh had acquired his trademark eye-patch after losing an eye in a driving mishap when a jack rabbit had jumped through his windscreen, and since 1930 he had directed such luminaries as James Cagney, Errol Flynn and Marlene Dietrich. He went on to enjoy a successful career until advancing blindness forced him into retirement in 1964.

Probably on account of his own contrary nature – 'He was your archetypal hard-bitten Johnny Opposite, an absolute son-of-a-bitch to cross,' Marlene Dietrich told me – Walsh decided to take Rock under his wing, arguing that there must have been something good about him for everyone else to consider him so bad. He is on record as telling Henry Willson, 'The kid's green, but he's juicy. Even if he can't do anything, he'll make damned pretty scenery!' Walsh subsequently offered him a small, unbilled role as a Jewish fighter-pilot in *Fighter Squadron* (1948), first filmed as *The Dawn Patrol* in 1930 with Richard Barthelmess and Douglas Fairbanks Jr, and again in 1938 under the same title with Errol Flynn and David Niven. This new version, far inferior to the other two, starred Edmund O'Brien and Robert Stack. Rock appeared in twelve scenes and had about a dozen lines. Later, he would recall:

I'm often asked by young actors, 'How do you approach a scene?' So I tell them, 'You just do it!' That was Raoul Walsh's attitude, you just do it! When he said that to me, it made it so simple in my head. 'Don't try to act,' Raoul said. 'Remember, up on the screen you're magnified forty times. Be natural. Underplay it and you'll look great!'

Rock did not put Walsh's theory into immediate practice while attempting to pronounce his lines in *Fighter Squadron*. One of the lines – 'Pretty soon you're going to have to get a bigger blackboard!' – a tongue-twister that might have foxed an experienced thespian, required forty takes before the scriptwriter changed it in desperation to, 'Pretty soon you'll have to write smaller numbers!' When Jack Warner, the feisty head of the studio, whose on-set fights with Errol Flynn and Bette Davis were notorious, heard about Rock's 'fuck-ups', he told Walsh in no uncertain terms to fire the 'Midwest hick' the moment the picture finished shooting. Walsh, always a law unto himself, refused to do this and the wily Warner exacted his revenge

– seizing Rock's bungled takes he ensured that these were used in drama classes, teaching hopefuls how not to act!

What Rock lacked in artistic ability, however, he more than made up for in charisma, and a feigned innocence in his early years, which, combined with his natural raw sex appeal, virtually set the screen alight. Neither did he have any intention, during this formative period, of becoming a studio pawn. Tyrone Power, Basil Rathbone, Robert Taylor and any number of others, primarily gay, had followed the dictates of their employers by entering into largely unsuccessful 'lavender' marriages, while the truly brave ones – rebels such as Valentino and Flynn – had stood up to these tyrants and more or less slept with anyone they pleased.

Rock informed Raoul Walsh and several other confidants who were aware of his sexuality that he would never marry, though within a short time he would have modified this to 'Not before I'm thirty,' doubtless anticipating that by this time he would have progressed to that section of the entertainment world – the legitimate stage – where same-sex relationships were more tolerated, or that maybe by the time he reached thirty the impossible might have happened: Hollywood might no longer be blighted by double-standards homophobia. Rock certainly struck out against convention when Walsh offered him a one-year's trial contract worth $9,000: Rock refused to appear in another film until he had taken further acting lessons, and so that Walsh would not accuse him of not earning the money he was paying him out of his own pocket, Rock spent a month decorating and refurbishing the director's house!

Walsh would nurture a lifelong fondness for Rock Hudson, and some years later film critic Jimmie Hicks (*Films In Review,* May 1975) would quote him as saying:

Because he had all the physical requirements for stardom and although he was practically inarticulate, you could sense his deep-rooted desire and self-expression. He seemed so anxious to please and so eager to be accepted and liked. And of course he knew how little he knew about acting, but he was so willing to learn. It's difficult to define, but there was always a quality about this fellow that made you want him to win.

Henry Willson, meanwhile, had no intention of ending up with an expensive failure on his hands, albeit a decidedly pretty one. First he approached MGM, hoping that the fearsomely tetchy Louis B Mayer might take him on. Mayer was well aware of Willson's recruitment techniques, however, and would have nothing to do with an actor who in his eyes was little more than a male prostitute. Neither would Twentieth Century Fox's David O Selznick.

William Goetz, on the other hand, Mayer's rival son-in-law, whose International Studios had recently merged with Universal, was in the midst of his 'Stars for Tomorrow' campaign and, having already signed up the (then) dubious talents of Tony Curtis, Jeff Chandler and Barbara Rush, he decided to give Rock a chance. Reimbursing Willson and Raoul Walsh with the $10,000 they claimed to have spent on Rock above and beyond his contract, Goetz offered Rock a seven-year contract with a starting salary of $150 a week, and reinvented his past, as had happened earlier with 'Irish' Australian Errol Flynn. Movie magazines were informed that Universal's newest recruit was a former Los Angeles postman who had broken into films by writing a letter to a top talent scout, which he had then delivered personally, knocking the man for six with his looks, charm and tremendous acting skills. No such thing had happened, of course, not that this prevented these publications from receiving dozens of letters from Los Angeles residents who distinctly remembered Rock delivering mail to them!

During this period Rock sanctioned – ordered to do so by Henry Willson – every story, fabricated or otherwise, about his youth, though he detested anyone so much as suggesting that his had been the classic rags-to-riches story. In 1980 he would snarl at John Kobal, founder of the famous photographic collection, for broaching the subject during an interview:

Let's face it, there's no such thing as a Cinderella story. Lana Turner discovered sitting on a stool, sipping a chocolate soda? Bullshit. Everybody loves the idea that people can be discovered and a lot of other people like to say, 'I'm the person who discovered so-and-so.' It's a fucking ego trip! I always wanted to be an actor. Always!

Rock celebrated his new contract 'windfall' by renting a small house in the fashionable Sherman Oaks, moving there with his new lover, Bob Preble, another Willson discovery who, after breaking away from his clutches, had managed to sign a contract with Twentieth Century Fox, though his career as a film star would never amount to much. An educated man in his early twenties, Preble later said in an interview that he had been appalled by Rock's lack of refinement, the fact that he had 'never ever heard of Mozart' and never drunk wine 'apart from the cooking stuff'. He was of course exaggerating and being grossly unfair.

Since 1985, Preble varied the story of his relationship with Rock Hudson. In one interview he declared that, as a straight man, he had initially felt apprehensive about having a homosexual room-mate; in another that, sexually, he and Rock had 'done a little experimenting'; and in a third interview Preble attempted to divert public attention away from his own bisexuality – understandably when one considers the vituperative backlash against the early eighties San Francisco gay community at the dawn of the AIDS epidemic – by telling his interviewer of how he had attempted and failed 'to turn Rock around a little' by fixing him up on dates with women who were known to be 'easy'.

Between 1950 and 1953, however, there seems very little doubt that Rock and Preble were an item. The Universal and Twentieth Century Fox chiefs knew this and so did the press, who attempted to out them – as they had Cary Grant and Randolph Scott a generation earlier – in a magazine spread headed 'Bachelors' Bedlam'. The couple were coerced into being photographed doing odd jobs about the house and garden, and posing with Rock's new red convertible. But the shot that raised the most eyebrows amongst the film community was the one of Rock in bed, naked from the waist up, with Preble towering above him with a clock in his hand. The caption read: 'Rip Van Hudson Invariably Sleeps Through The Alarm – Which Awakens Bob In The Next Room!'

Cynics were not slow in pointing out that the house only had one bedroom and that though there were two single beds in this, these had been pushed together and covered by one large continental quilt. Hot on the heels of this exposé, another movie magazine named

Rock as Hollywood's most eligible bachelor and asked its female readers, 'So, you'd like to be Mrs Hudson? Here's how to handle Hollywood's Big Rock!' The feature included a 'beefcake' shot from the forthcoming *Iron Man*, one of thirteen B-movies that Rock appeared in during the eighteen months between *Fighter Squadron* and *Bend of the River*, the one that would really get him noticed.

The order in which these films were made – six were released in 1950 alone – is not known, and Rock's contribution ranges from one-liners to third-billing, depending on the director's whim. In *Tomahawk*, for instance, he was originally given a single line – 'Male detail approaching!' – which he pronounced at Fort Phil Kearney just as the cavalry were approaching. The take had to be shot so many times on account of Rock cracking up with a fit of the giggles, and director George Sherman was so taken by him that his part (Corporal Hanna) was enlarged. Though had Sherman known that Rock had fallen for Alex Nicol, one of the leads, he might not have been so enthusiastic.

Nicol showed up again in *Air Cadet*, directed by Joseph Pevney. 'From now on, mister, you'll only address an upper-classman when you're asked to,' Rock bellows at an over-enthusiastic raw recruit, though not without offering him a cursory once over, while another cadet (James Best) coyly observes, 'You've gotta drop anything you're doing if an upper-classman comes around!' Sadly, both Best and Rock exit the picture far too soon and do not get to participate in the homoerotic pool scene, and henceforth the story centres around the rivalry between Russ Coulter (Richard Long) and smarmy superior, Jack Page (Stephen McNally), who bullies Coulter the way he did his brother, until he cracked up and committed suicide. Matters are complicated when Coulter falls for Page's estranged wife (Gail Russell), though all ends well when Page gets into difficulties during an aerial exercise and the young man saves his life.

Billed as a 'tense drama' and filmed on location at San Antonio's Randolph Air Base, much of the tension occurred once the cameras had stopped rolling. Rock was originally given fourth billing, but he was demoted to seventh when news of his alleged 'indiscretions' with other actors reached the producer's office and he was politely requested not to report to the set again – hence the sudden, inexplicable disappearance of his character, Rock's best thus far in his career.

Rock pleaded with Henry Willson to intervene, unaware that his manager had enough on his plate already dealing with an irate Gail Russell, the much more important female lead. Russell, recovering from a recent suicide attempt, had just figured out that her husband, Willson discovery Guy Madison, liked having sex with men and that he had actually bedded one of the actors from *Air Cadet*! Willson knew that this was almost certainly Rock, and as most of the catfights between Madison and Russell were taking place on the lot when he came to pick her up after shooting, Willson thought it prudent to let his golden boy stew. Russell reacted by hitting the bottle: her marriage crumbled as the suicide bids multiplied, and in 1961 she finally succumbed to an overdose of pills, aged 36.

Meanwhile, in July 1950, some two years before his big break, Rock was 'spotted' by British journalist Eve Perrick, then working as film critic with the *Daily Express*. Perrick had actually been on vacation in Hollywood when she had dropped in on a publicist friend at Universal, and he had given her his ticket for the gala premiere of *Winchester '73*. The stars were James Stewart and Shelley Winters, but by sheer coincidence Perrick had found herself sitting next to one of the film's bit-parts, Young Bull, though until he introduced himself after the screening, she had been unaware of his identity. She is also reported to have uttered the classic Tallulah Bankhead one-liner, albeit without suggestive intent, 'I'm sorry, but I didn't recognise you with all your clothes on!' Perrick was, however, willing to stake her reputation by declaring how 'horribly wrong' her Hollywood contemporaries were in suggesting that Rock would never make it to the top.

What nonsense. I recognise a Film Star when I see one. I can remember the early days of Robert Taylor, Ray Milland, Clark Gable and Gregory Peck, when a film star was a Film Star and not a transferred character from the stage. They came one size larger than life, had dark eyes, darker hair and looked like –

why, exactly like Mr Hudson. There is no doubt about it: Mr H
is a star. I'd never seen him before: neither had the people round
me. They didn't know who the heck he was – but he was
obviously something pretty terrific. They passed their pro-
grammes to be autographed, then puzzled over the signature.
Then the mob of film fans in search of a prey grew to such
terrifying proportions that Rock had to hide in the manager's
office . . . About his acting ability, however, Rock has some
misgivings. 'I don't like myself on the screen. I can't make love
very well – I just go in and mash the make-up!' Never mind, Mr
Hudson. Were I fifteen years younger, I'd sigh for you anyway.

The real star of Anthony Mann's compelling portmanteau of sibling
rivalry was the infamous 'one-in-a-thousand' perfect Winchester,
which, as the action begins, is the coveted prize in a Dodge City
shooting contest – even the legendary Wyatt Earp (Will Geer) would
give his shooting hand to own one, and for such a trophy, we are told,
an Indian would sell his soul. The gun is won by sharpshooter Lin
McAdam (James Stewart), who narrowly beats his opponent, Dutch
Henry Brown (the magnificently sinister Stephen McNally again),
who is, in reality, Lin's brother Michael, who had killed his father.
Brown now steals the gun and heads off across the perilous Sioux
country, where he loses it in a card game to Indian-trader Joe Lamont
(John McIntire). Lamont is in turn scalped by Young Bull, the Sioux
chief – Rock, displaying a pleasing expanse of shaved chest and
trying hard to hold in his stomach, sporting pigtails, war paint, a false
nose and dispatching his lines robotically with a distinct Midwestern
twang – an on-screen participation that is nevertheless lamentably
brief before he is killed during an attack on a cavalry detachment.
Young Bull's gun is subsequently found by a young officer (Tony
Curtis in an early role, at around the time he appeared in another
Hudson film, *I Was a Shoplifter*, 1950) though it soon ends up back
in the hands of the evil brother until he is dispatched by the hero, who
also gets the girl (Winters), the saloon trollop who had been passed
from man to man like an unwanted parcel throughout the film.

Iron Man, directed by Joseph Pevney and starring Jeff Chandler
and Evelyn Keyes, was not the visual treat for gay fans that

Winchester '73 had been – Rock only strips off in a couple of scenes, and briefly. However, because it was a film with a 'manly' theme about coalminers becoming boxers after narrowly missing being buried alive, with the emphasis on fighting and not romance, Rock was not ordered to shave his chest, and one of the publicity shots of Tommy 'Speed' O'Keefe, bare-chested and flexing his muscles, sold many thousands of copies to fans of both sexes.

Tommy always fights clean and is well respected, as opposed to his friend Coke Mason (Chandler), who fights like a man possessed as soon as he steps into the ring. The crowds flock to Coke's bouts only to boo and hopefully witness his comeuppance. The film also has its moments of gay innuendo, as usual scripted to go over the heads of general cinemagoers, though fifty years on it is blatantly obvious that Speed's awe of the luckless Coke is such that he gives the impression that he might be interested in their friendship progressing beyond the platonic, if indeed it has not already done so. 'Ain't he the sweetest player you ever saw?' he quips, while he and a buddy watch Coke playing squash – in shorts that are so revealing that the Hays Office censors came close to cutting the entire scene. And a little later, Speed expresses his disinterest in the fairer sex when a bejewelled good-time girl tells him he is divine – one of the gay buzzwords of the day. 'I know,' he responds, allegedly off the cuff and bringing hoots of derision from the other females in his company. 'But I'm in training!'

While making *Iron Man*, Rock is known to have had a fling with Jeff Chandler, one that ended abruptly when Rock learned that the prematurely greying actor was into cross-dressing, and also somewhat boastful of his sexual conquests. Neither would he be shocked by Chandler's early death at 42, following routine minor surgery in 1961. Such was Chandler's unpopularity in Hollywood circles by this time that several tabloid newspapers suggested he had actually been murdered on the operating table.

Iron Man resulted in Rock being seconded to Anthony Mann, who had directed *Winchester '73* but not shown much interest in him then. Mann (1906–67) was not an adherent of the popular 'grit and spit' realism applied to Westerns at this time by the likes of Curtiz or Ford: his forte was the exploration of his characters psyches and innermost thoughts. It was Mann who, in *Bend of the River* (1952), brought out the hitherto untapped hard streak in James Stewart. Gone for good was the soft-spoken, milk-drinking pacifist hero of *Destry Rides Again* (1939), replaced by the tough, cynical and frequently ruthless frontiersman. Glyn McLyntock is the former borders raider who has escaped the hangman's noose and is now scouting for a pioneers' wagon-train, which is heading towards new life in Oregon territory. En route he rescues a killer, Garrett Cole (Arthur Kennedy), from a lynch mob, setting in motion a power struggle between the two that ends only with the inevitable to-the-death shoot-out. Rock played Trey Wilson, though viewing the film retrospectively one wonders what all the subsequent fuss was about: Mann does not give him a great deal to do other than pose and pout, and it is not until the penultimate scene, when he is slightly wounded and loses the hat that has obscured his features for most of the film, that he captivates – his cheery smile lighting up an until now dull screen as he is comforted by the leading lady (Julia Adams), before being reunited with his own sweetheart.

This one brief scene bore all the requisite ingredients to turn Rock into an overnight sensation. It was certainly applauded by the audience at the premiere in Portland, Ohio, the actual location of the film's middle section, taking even Henry Willson by surprise, for he had hired a team of 'shriekers' to ensure that his protégé received as much attention as possible. These mingled with the genuine fans outside the theatre just as the stars were on their way out, suddenly rushing forwards and chanting 'We want Rock!' as the actors emerged. James Stewart was visibly shaken and offended that 'this Chicago upstart' had stolen his thunder, so much so that he declared he would never speak to Rock again, let alone work with him. Rock was just as stunned to unexpectedly find himself surrounded by dozens of photographers and succumbed to an attack of nerves, very nearly collapsed, and had to be escorted to his car by police officers!

Media hype, and not the genuine acting talent that would come later by way of confidence in his abilities, had placed Rock Hudson firmly on the ladder towards celluloid glory, but before he progressed much further he was brought back to earth with a bump, as he explained to Ron Davis:

It went to my head. I was floating! I went back to the hotel that night and got drunk. I couldn't sleep! I got up at the crack of dawn, went out in front of the hotel so the people on their way to work could see me, but no one recognised me. I took a walk. My picture was in the window of practically every store, beauty parlour, supermarket, cleaners and still no one recognised me . . . Nobody knew who I was! It was sad, but I learned a great lesson. Mob scenes and cheering fans don't mean a damned thing. It's temporary. If you try to grab on to it, you get nothing but air in your hands.

Scarlet Angel (1952*),* set in 1860s New Orleans and directed by Sidney Salkow, was almost a precursor of Rock's later, more acclaimed comedies – though one would assume the humour to have been largely unintentional. Rock played Frank 'Panama' Truscott, the captain of the *Atlantic Star*. The Scarlet Angel of the title is not Roxy McClanahan (Yvonne de Carlo), though it might as well be – they do not come more hard-bitten than she – but the tawdry saloon where she worked (and which had as a central feature the celebrated Toulouse-Lautrec poster of music-hall star Aristide Bruant, 25 years before this was painted!).

'The gambling is as crooked as the gals,' one of the locals says as Panama heads for the joint, where fighting and whoring are in full swing. Roxy's employer, Pierre (Henry Brandon), pays her to fleece the customers, and this particular one has a lot of money to be parted from, having recently arrived in town with a valuable coffee cargo. Her trick is to match her victims, drink for drink – though her 'whisky' is nothing but weak tea – and, once they are drunk, lift their wallets and hand them over to Pierre. While she is trying to con Panama, the sheriff turns up to arrest her for a previous misdeed: having sussed her out, Panama instigates a brawl, during which they make their escape.

Panama has fallen for this decidedly rough diamond, though initially he is reluctant to admit this. 'There's a certain thing called class, and you just haven't got it,' he says. Nevertheless he hides her at his hotel, where coincidentally one of the guests is ailing young mother Linda Caldwell, whose husband Bob was killed in the Civil

War just three days after their wedding. Bob's super-rich family have never seen Linda or Bob's posthumous son, and when Linda unexpectedly dies, Roxy takes care of the funeral, assumes her identity and, stealing Panama's money, sets off for the Caldwell mansion in San Francisco, where she hopes she will find untold wealth.

The Caldwells take Roxy in and attempt to rid her of her vulgarity by organising lessons in etiquette and deportment. But while Bob's parents warm to her, Cousin Susan (Amanda Blake, who later appeared in television's *Gunsmoke*, 1955–74) thinks she is an impostor and hires a private detective. Meanwhile, Susan's brother Malcolm (Richard Denning), announces that he will one day marry her because he has set his sights on inheriting the Caldwell fortune. Then Panama turns up at her coming-out ball – he has tracked her down, knows her game, but being a reputable gentleman only wants back the money she stole from him. The good manners it has taken her months to acquire slip in an instant when she loses her cool. 'Once a saloon girl, always a saloon girl,' he quips. Later, Roxy visits him on board the *Atlantic Star* and is about to give him his money when Susan turns up. Panama shuts Roxy in the cupboard and she overhears Susan offering him $50,000 providing he can expose Roxy as a fraud. This he cannot do, though he warns Roxy that unless she comes clean to the Caldwells before he returns from his next sea journey, he will tell them himself. She agrees to this, and joins Panama and his crew for a dockside leaving party – where in the film's most hilarious scene she soon proves that she can out-brawl the best of them, taking on the men when someone pokes fun at her for being snobbish, and virtually demolishing the place. Sitting on the bar, Rock has never looked more endearing as he goofs his teeth and rocks back and forth with laughter – until the police arrive and they are forced to make a getaway. And, hiding in the shadows, they enjoy their first embrace, and Roxy realises how she has conned herself by aiming for the wrong goal. 'I just kissed you hello,' she murmurs. 'And a few million dollars goodbye.'

Roxy, however, has taken to her 'son' and wants to provide for his future and ensure that *he* inherits the Caldwell fortune, not the greedy Susan or Malcolm. When told by their private detective that

Roxy has no proof that the child is Bob's, in spite of her love for Panama, she agrees to marry Malcolm, provided he adopts the child as his own. She writes to Panama telling him that their romance is over, and the wedding is about to take place when she discovers that the boy can *only* be Bob's because he has an identical strawberry birthmark. She rushes out of the Caldwell mansion, having jilted the groom, and meets up with Panama in the dockside dive she helped wreck before. She even gets to repay him the money she owes . . . and when the Caldwell's detective turns up and looks like he may be about to cause trouble, Roxy and her lover–partner start yet another scrap as the credits roll.

Scarlet Angel was a corker of a film and, though the American critics were far from enthusiastic, in Britain the *Daily Mirror*'s Donald Zec pronounced it the most exciting production he had seen in months. Zec was so impressed that he dubbed Rock 'Mr Beefcake', a nickname he kept for most of his life. The two men eventually met and became friends. During the summer of 1952, the columnist wrote:

> Today's Hollywood looks at the man first, the muscle next, the mind last. Beefcake! That bulging expanse above the masculine waist is being howled for by the she-wolves, so it's being rounded up all over the place! The bobby-soxers wolf-whistled at Tony Curtis. They were ecstatic over Burt Lancaster. But now there's a boy they've stripped to conquer all. The studio says he's going to make a fine actor, but at the moment most of his talent is in his torso.

Rock's closest friends at this time – and they were still so at the end of his life – were Mark Miller and George Nader. Aged twenty-five and thirty respectively, the pair had become lovers in 1947 when Nader (Giorgio Nardelli) had been a struggling actor and Miller an operatic tenor in a Broadway chorus line. Nader had appeared in several minor films before hitting the big time in 1952 with *Monsoon*. Muscular, hirsute and every bit as good-looking as Rock, though lacking his innate charisma and raw sex appeal, he nevertheless enjoyed considerable success on the big screen over the coming decade, reaching mass audiences in the *Ellery Queen* television series (1975), which resulted in Miller giving up his own career to manage that of his partner.

The couple had taken to Rock at once, though initially, like Bob Preble, they had been dismissive of some of his personal habits – for some time he had owned just the one suit bought for him by Ken Hodge, and this was only brought out of mothballs for important occasions, much of the time Rock turned up at his pals' house in Studio City wearing old, frequently soiled clothes they would not have been seen dead in. Nader also complained about Rock's tendency never to wear socks, and his body odour – when asked why he never used deodorants, the young man responded truthfully that his stepfather had brought him up to believe that such things were only for 'sissies'.

These problems were easily resolved and the trio began spending much of their spare time together. Rock would say of Miller, 'He's my man Friday. He makes me laugh. He's my best friend, drunk or sober. I couldn't exist without Mark Miller.' And of Nader he would enthuse, 'I can trust him to tell the truth. George is always right.'

Socialising in an extremely prejudiced Hollywood, where it was the norm for actors to have mistresses or sometimes even be involved with organised crime, yet they were denounced as deviants if they were gay, the three friends never aroused suspicion – not even from those hacks whose sole aim in life was tracking down the ones who stepped out of line, regardless of sexuality, for they were sufficiently naive to believe that three men having a good time out on the town could not be anything but pals. Even so, for the rest of his life, Rock would never be knowingly photographed alone with a man, and at home the man he was living with was never allowed to answer the door or telephone.

At weekends, the friends would drive to Lake Arrowhead in Rock's convertible, usually with Bob Preble or one of Rock's pick-ups making up a foursome, where they would stay in log cabins, safe from the prying eyes of the media. Alternatively they would visit the men-only beach in Malibu, where nude bathing was permitted – and where Rock was frequently mistaken for a gay-basher on account of his size and his being so overly butch.

Sexual freedom was, of course, severely restricted to such locations and relatively free from media intrusion. Though when working, secretly homosexual heart-throb actors who were afraid of coming out of the closet – then as today not just on account of genuine fear of the media and public backlash, but of the knock-on effect this would have on their and the studio's bank balance – were forced to meet studio bosses halfway and allow publicists to fix them up with arranged dates. Such protection was of paramount importance to permit big earners such as Rock, Cary Grant and any number of others to live virtually open lives with their male lovers – 'buddies' who, upon the slightest whiff of suspicion, would invite the press into their homes so that the news could be relayed to fans how these red-blooded, eligible bachelors really lived – perpetually surrounded by beautiful starlets, always holding pool or barbecue parties.

Only very rarely did anyone slip up. One such occasion was when Rock was asked to contribute to Ivy Crane Wilson's Hollywood Album: *The Wonderful City & Its Famous Inhabitants*, a popular and nowadays immensely collectable fifties film annual for which gross sycophancy was the order of the day. Bob Preble answered the door when Wilson's reporter turned up before the appointed time to pen Rock's 'autobiography'. Rock told the young woman that his friend's name was Tom Preble and that they were sharing the house – an admission that made it to the printed page, though fortunately Rock's description of his easy-going existence and his somewhat boastful aspirations for the future managed to allay even the suspicions of some of Wilson's less gullible readers:

My present routine: a drive to the beach, a visit with some friends, or staying at home listening to records or playing the old-fashioned Pianola some pals gave me for my birthday . . . My ambition is for pictures with a punch, such as *Red Dust, Too Hot to Handle, Honky Tonk*. The height of success to me would be the chance to play a Rhett Butler, to achieve the stature of a Gable . . . I'd be hypocritical if I denied that I'm looking forward to the security that goes with being a successful star. Some day I hope to be having a look at the South Seas from the deck of a luxurious liner – not through a Navy porthole. I'll rate that swimming pool and a specially built convertible, but no matter how swanky the house there'll be room for my prized Pianola. Best of all, maybe I'll have a wife to share the fun. Then all the dreams I had in Winnetka will become realities.

For several months, Rock's regular studio-date was MGM dancer Vera-Ellen, a pert, effervescent blonde who had recently scored a big success in *On the Town* (1949) and whose publicity read that she was considerably older than Rock (at thirty she was just five years his senior) – Henry Willson's idea, in that if the scandal was created that Rock was having an affair with an older woman, this would take the heat off questions being asked in some quarters as to why Rock was living in a one-bedroom house with another man.

He was almost caught out when a journalist saw him driving away from the gay beach in Malibu in the middle of the night, and Willson offered a compromise – if Rock really wanted a break from Bob Preble, then instead of prowling the night in search of sex he would provide him with the pick of his stable-studs. Rock refused to have anything to do with the idea. Procuring bedmates, he told Willson, was an art form he had perfected and the thrill was in the chase – though in Rock's case he did not have to try too hard to have conquests flinging themselves into his arms. He even declared that he would be taking a man as his date to the 1950 Hollywood Press Photographers' Ball – having learned that Rudolph Valentino had taken his 'husband' André Daven to a similar event back in 1926. Fortunately, Henry Willson persuaded him to change his mind and he took Vera-Ellen instead.

The 'couple' made a spectacular entrance as Mr and Mrs Oscar – dressed in skimpy bathing suits and painted gold from top to toe. Columnist Hedda Hopper's arch-rival, the equally fearsome Louella Parsons, had been asked to broadcast a live radio programme from the ball, and it did not take her long, once she had interviewed 'the happy couple', to spread the rumour that Hollywood would soon be hearing wedding bells.

Vera-Ellen may have been Rock's 'fiancée' for the evening, but someone else caught his eye at the ball – one of his idols, Tyrone Power, then 36 and in his dark, dashingly handsome prime. The two fell for each other at once, though they are not believed to have had an actual affair. Though insistent that his lovers should be blue-eyed blonds, Rock might have made an exception, but Power was very apprehensive about starting anything with an actor who, as a relative unknown, could easily have fallen by the wayside, needed the money and sold him down the river – he certainly would not be the first. Later, when Rock was famous, he would see Power in the stage production of *John Brown's Body* in the early fifties and the two would spend a little time together, but with Bob Preble hovering in the background their friendship never progressed beyond mild flirtation. Not having Tyrone Power wake up next to him in the morning is said to have been one of Rock's biggest regrets.

Rock's next few films were not particularly memorable, though the parts were getting better, and an increase in salary enabled him to move home – three times in as many years while he was with Bob Preble – and acquire, courtesy of Universal, some of the luxuries expected to be afforded the movie star, so long as he toed the line, of course. Some years later, in a rare in-depth interview with the film-critic David Castell, he would say:

What Katharine Hepburn said about MGM in the thirties was still true of Universal in the fifties. Nothing was allowed to get in the way of the performance. If you wanted a new driver, a new house – anything – they would take care of it. Also, you were paid 52 weeks a year whether or not you worked. Mind you, the studio wanted their pound of flesh. Chances were that if you were under contract, you would work.

The critics generally agreed that Rock's best performance at this time was as Dan Stebbins in Douglas Sirk's *Has Anybody Seen My Gal?* (1952) based on the celebrated story by Eleanor H Porter. Its star was 75-year-old Charles Coburn, aptly described by film critic David Quinlan as, 'An actor whose paunch, monocle, cigar and thick lips lent superb character to a series of lovable but perceptive

upper-class gentlemen with hoarse voices and hearts of pure gold.'
Coburn was cast as Sam Fulton, an engaging skinflint who becomes
attached to the Blaisdells, a family who run a drugstore in 1920s
New York, and who are inadvertently responsible for his becoming
a millionaire. Years before the story begins, Sam's old flame
Millicent Blaisdell, subsequently deceased, dumped him, and in a fit
of pique he went off to the Yukon and struck gold. Thinking that he
is close to death, Sam wishes to bequeath his fortune to the
Blaisdells, but first he must discover for himself if they are worthy
of the honour. He infiltrates their household as Mr Smith, their
lodger, and for a while feigns poverty by working in their drugstore
as a soda jerk. He is trained by Dan, who wants to marry the
Blaisdells' daughter, Millie – played by Piper Laurie, who also
doubled as Rock's studio-date while the film was in production.

Sam watches the Blaisdells change from homely people into
avaricious snobs when a mysterious benefactor – himself – sends
them a cheque for $100,000. Now that they have suddenly moved up
in the world Dan is no longer good enough for their daughter and
Millie is affianced to the son of another wealthy family. Then, a
disastrous drop in share prices leaves them broke: they return to the
drugstore happier than ever now that their lives are back to normal.
Dan takes up with Millie again . . . and Sam Fulton wanders off, with
no one any the wiser to his true identity.

Has Anybody Seen My Gal? is an entertaining slice of whimsy, not
really a Rock Hudson vehicle, though he handles himself well and
when not upstaged by Charles Coburn looks astonishingly sexy in
his pushed-back fedora. Today, however, the film is remembered
chiefly for one lengthy, convoluted line – which caused the director
almost as much of a headache as the one Rock had fluffed in *Fighter
Squadron*. Sam Fulton has just learned the ropes from Dan in the
drugstore, when the studious-looking youth at the end of the counter
pronounces, 'Hey, Gramps, I'll have a choc malt, heavy on the choc,
plenty of milk, four spoons of malt, two scoops of vanilla ice – one
mixed with the rest and the other floating!' To which Sam responds,
'Would you like to come in Wednesday for a fitting?' The young
man, listed simply on the production sheet as 'Actor 1685', making

his third bit-part screen appearance but actually speaking for the first time, was 21-year-old James Dean.

Has Anybody Seen My Gal? also had its moment of irony, so far as Rock was concerned. In the scene where Sam Fulton takes Dan to the cinema to be reunited with his sweetheart, the actor on the silent-screen is William Haines, one of Hollywood's top stars of the pre-talkie era whose career successfully survived the transition to sound – only to be brought to an abrupt end in 1933 when a vice-squad raid discovered him in bed with a sailor in a San Diego YMCA hostel. It always amused Rock that Haines' final film had been entitled *The Marines Are Coming* (1934).

_____

2

Magnificent Obsession

'Thus the pattern was established from the outset: Henry Willson as the mastermind, calling all the shots, Rock as his consenting Galatea.'

Phyllis Gates, wife

Rock's next film, his eighteenth in less than four years, was *Horizons West* (1952), a tale of sibling rivalry directed by Chicago-born Budd Boetticher, who would achieve great acclaim a few years later for his productions with Randolph Scott. Boetticher offered Rock third-billing below Julia Adams, who aside from looking glamorous was given little else to do, and Robert Ryan in one of his typically thuggish, wholly uncharismatic roles as big-time bigot Dan Hammond, who, with his younger brother Neal (Rock), has returned to the family ranch in Texas after a four-year absence fighting in the Civil War.

While Neal is only interested in helping his father run the ranch, Dan is preoccupied with trying to seduce the wife of the equally horrible town big-shot, Cord Hardin (Raymond Burr), and rustling cattle from local landowners, which he and his gang of renegades and army deserters then sell to Mexican rebels in the Free Zone. For a while, no one suspects him, until Hardin alerts the town to the fact that the Hammonds are the only ones in the region not to have been robbed . . . and then Dan kills the marshall, though not before Neal has been appointed his deputy to track down the criminals and end their reign of terror.

Horizons West was swiftly followed by *The Lawless Breed* (1953), also with Julia Adams, but a cut above average and directed by Rock's old friend Raoul Walsh. Rock played a victim of circumstance, an alleged kinsman of the Raymond Burr character in the previous film. 'John Wesley Hardin has made the name of Texas stink in the nostrils of justice,' growls one of his detractors in this saga of gambling, shoot-outs and trial by public opinion.

Much of the action takes place in flashback. Wes, aged 18, is horse-whipped by his preacher father for gambling and fooling around with a gun. He is sweet on Jane (Mary Castle), the orphan-girl he has been raised with: they are to be married, but only after he has netted his fortune at the card table. Then, he says, he will buy a farm and breed the best horses in Texas. Wes's plans go awry, however, when he kills a cardsharp in self-defence. The man is one of the much-feared Hanleys, and his brothers pursue Wes as he flees town on a cattle-drive to Abilene. Here he dispatches another Hanley in a shoot-out and kills the sheriff, again in self-defence. Apprehended by Wild Bill Hickock, no less, and given one hour to get out of town, Wes is befriended by saloon-singer Rosie (Adams), who helps him escape and with whom he goes on the run after his fiancée is murdered.

For six years the couple evade the law, masquerading as brother and sister under an assumed name. They end up in Alabama, where Wes realises his dream and buys a farm. They are married, but soon after the birth of their son, Wes is caught and sent to prison. Sixteen years elapse and he returns home – with a few wrinkles and a grey wig courtesy of Errol Flynn's favourite make-up artist, Perc Westmore – to be reunited with his wife and now grown-up son . . . whom he discovers, as his father found him, showing off with a gun. Wes sees himself twenty years ago: in a fit of rage he hits the boy, who rushes off to prove his manhood by picking a fight in a local saloon. All ends well, however, when Wes saves him from making a fool of himself, getting shot in the process, though not badly wounded, offering the film a happy conclusion.

*

Rock had begun to tire of Bob Preble by this time, probably for no other reason than there were so many good-looking young men around who were more than willing to go to bed with him, and during the last two films he had several discreet flings with extras, though nothing apparently too serious.

Then, during the spring of 1953, he encountered the man he often spoke of to friends as his perfect lover.

Meeting all the usual physical requirements, 22-year-old Jack Navaar had recently returned from military service in Korea, was recruited by Henry Willson, and practically pushed into Rock's arms by Mark Miller and George Nader, who for some reason had never approved of Bob Preble. It was love at first sight and the pair began dating, mindless of the fact that Rock and Preble were still living together, though Navaar did make it clear from the outset that he was also sexually interested in women.

At around this time, Rock's mother moved to California. Kay had recently married for the fourth time, to a man named Joseph Olsen, and she seemed to have had no qualms accepting her son's relationship with another man. Rock and Navaar spent most Sundays at the Olsens' home in Arcadia, and every now and then they would come over and stay at Rock's place on Avenida del Sol.

When Bob Preble finally moved out in May 1953 to marry the actress Yvonne Rivero, Navaar was asked to move in, but refused to set foot inside the same building – let alone sleep in the same bed – that had been occupied by his predecessor. Navaar, like many of Rock's lovers, also seems to have been averse to, or certainly wary of, his friendship with Miller and Nader, despite the fact they always maintained that they had never been sexually involved with Rock, though Nader is widely reputed to have been intimate with him on numerous occasions when they first met. Rock would say in 1983, 'Every new person that's come along, the first thing he does is try to get rid of Mark and George – and it's never worked!'

Rock did, however, oblige Navaar by renting a larger, two-storey property in Grandview, and he spoiled his new man rotten with expensive gifts, the first of which was an eye-catching cashmere sweater to match the buttercup-yellow convertible he had bought for himself. Taking a leaf out of Raoul Walsh's book, he even paid for him to have drama lessons – not that these did much good, for Navaar, aka Rand Saxon, never made the grade as an actor and, according to Mark Miller, the only success he ever enjoyed was in his private role as a 'movie wife'.

The change of address coincided with an increase in salary. Universal were now paying Rock $200 a week, enough for him to be assigned his first publicist, whose first task was to ensure that those all-important movie magazines were told the 'absolute truth' about Rock's hectic love life – the scores of marriage proposals he was getting every week, which he was naturally rejecting because Rock was far too busy forging his career and too preoccupied with being out on the town with a different girl almost every night, to think of settling down. Henry Willson supported the fabrication by organising some of these dates, though even he slipped up from time to time by fixing Rock up with renowned, self-confessed 'fag-hags' such as Tallulah Bankhead and Joan Crawford.

Tallulah, never one to mince words, probably helped the Hudson 'heterosexual cause' by broadcasting to all and sundry, 'This divine young man is hung even better than Gary Cooper – and believe me, darlings, he sure knows how to handle that two-hander of his!'

The comparison with Cooper was also made by the ferociously predatory Crawford, who circulated the story – repeated in Shaun Considine's excellent *Bette and Joan: The Divine Feud* – of how she had defined Rock as a cross between Cooper and Robert Taylor after seeing him in *Captain Lightfoot* (1955). Subsequently, he had been invited to her Brentwood home for dinner, and afterwards she had persuaded him to strip off and swim in her pool. Considine writes, 'The story told, true or fabled, is that Rock was back in the pool house taking a shower, when the lights went out. Suddenly he felt the warm, naked body of Joan Crawford beside him. "Sssh, baby," she whispered. "Close your eyes and pretend I'm Clark Gable."'

Word of Rock's fondness for exhibitionism got around and he was inevitably asked to remove his shirt and flex his muscles for magazine picture spreads. On one such occasion when *Photoplay* sent along a hunky snapper–journalist, Rock took this routine one step further and stripped naked in the bedroom – purposely leaving the door open so that the other man could get an eyeful – then pulling on a pair of skimpy shorts so that he could be photographed in his den, poring over his extensive record collection. By all accounts the ruse worked: after the shoot the pair retired to Rock's boudoir where the young man was able to find out first-hand if there had been any truth in Tallulah's admission – and something else that seemingly every Hudson fan yearned to know, as he himself explained:

> I couldn't understand who could give a damn about my sleeping habits . . . As a matter of fact, I went through a great deal in learning to sleep in the nude. From my childhood I remember my mother saying, 'Well, what if there's a fire?' And I thought, 'Indeed what if there's a fire! I'd have to run out naked and people would see my pee-pee!' Then when I was 21 I thought, 'Hell, if there's a fire you can just wrap a blanket around you!' And I've slept in the nude every since. But who the hell cares!

Universal were certainly intent on getting value for money now that Rock's star was in its ascendancy, for in 1953 alone he appeared in five more films. The first was *Seminole* – which he referred to as Semolina – directed by Budd Boetticher and co-starring Anthony Quinn and Barbara Hale. The *Daily Mirror*'s Donald Zec visited the set and Rock contravened his own rules by allowing himself to be photographed alone with James Best, an extremely good-looking actor who had a small part in the film. Henry Willson's attempt to prevent this from being published failed, and it appeared with the caption, 'The beefcake and his buddy perform in front of the crew'. Rock is seated, supposedly singing a folk song and laughing his head off, while Best is posed on a stool next to him, pretending to play the guitar and looking seductively into his eyes. Neither were they entertaining the film crew, but jamming in Rock's dressing room. So far as the conservative British press were concerned, the picture was innocuous enough, but it would soon prove dangerous fodder for the Hollywood scandal rags.

Seminole, a superior 'Western with a conscience' set in the Florida of 1835, purports to be the true story of Lance Caldwell, a young army lieutenant who, when the film opens, is facing a court-martial for insubordination and murder.

The story is told in flashback by Caldwell to the court in an attempt to save himself from the firing squad. Fresh out of the military academy, the young man arrives at Fort King to find the otherwise peace-loving Seminole wreaking terror in the neighbourhood. He learns that they are being persecuted by his odious superior, Major Degan (Richard Carlson), who is intent on driving them off their territory for the sheer hell of it. Caldwell is at once sympathetic – the girl he loves, Revere Muldoon (Hale), is an ally of the Seminole chief, Osceola (Quinn). What Caldwell does not know is that Osceola is actually John, his best friend who disappeared many years ago, having eschewed army life to lead his people. Neither does he know that Osceola and Revere are also lovers.

Caldwell tries to dissuade Degan from attacking the Seminole settlement in the heart of the Everglades swamps, claiming that his men are unfamiliar with the alligator-infested terrain. Degan refuses to listen, and the platoon is almost wiped out. Caldwell is wounded, but instead of being left to die is rescued by the Seminole, reunited with his old friend, and nursed back to full health – an elongated scene that allowed Rock's fans to drool over his magnificent pectorals. Caldwell also learns that the Indians have a traitor in their midst – Kajek (Hugh O'Brian), who has been organising the recent raids and who is secretly plotting to depose Osceola.

Degan, meanwhile, is incensed at the failure of his mission: he doubles the rest of the platoon's drill time, threatens Revere with imprisonment for assisting the enemy, and orders her and Caldwell to return to the Seminole and escort Osceola back to Fort King under a flag of truce. This is a setup. The chief is beaten up and thrown into the prison pit, and when Caldwell tries to rescue him he catches Kajek trying to kill the chief. A fight ensues: Osceola dies and Caldwell is accused of the crime, bringing us back to where the film began.

Audiences watching *Seminole* were kept on the edges of their seats until the very last moment – believing that Rock really was going to die in this one. Stripped of his stripes, the execution rifles are actually pointing at him, triggers cocked, when the Seminole – headed by Kajek and Revere – arrive to collect Osceola's body. Kajek confesses all, the charges against Caldwell are dropped, and he and Revere walk off arm in arm.

Hot on the heels of *Seminole* was *Back to God's Country* (1953), a thought-provoking production with the little-known but dependable Marcia Henderson. Billed as 'A tale of the courage of two men, a woman and a dog', this was set in Alaska in the wake of the 1872 Gold Rush. Rock played Peter Keith, the skipper of the schooner *Flying Moon*, who is prevented from taking his valuable fur catch back to Seattle by local baddie, Paul Blake – a superbly glowering Steve Cochran in a role that can only be described as psycho-homoerotic, particularly in Blake's attitude to his simpering sidekick, Hudson (Hugh O'Brian as the villain once more). Blake had done this sort of thing before, disposing of a young couple so that he could purloin their boat, and he had also murdered an Eskimo to acquire a map that supposedly marked the spot of a gold mine. This scene opens the film: the Eskimo is kneeling at a holy shrine and, after killing him, Blake takes his dog, beating it into submission.

When two of his crew jump ship to go off in search of the bogus gold – all part of Blake's plan – Peter goes after them, leaving his wife, Dolores (Henderson), behind. Blake makes his move on her, but when he attempts to rape her, she is saved by the dog (who pulls him off). When Peter returns he is beaten up by the two thugs – leaving him so severely wounded that he must travel hundreds of miles across the snowy wasteland by dog-sled to the nearest town, where there is a doctor who might save him. Dolores and the dog accompany him – and Blake, after shooting Hudson dead during an argument, sets off in pursuit. The trio brave wolves, the treacherous cold and a spectacularly shot avalanche before Blake finally gets his comeuppance when he catches up with the Keiths, within sight of their journey's end at the Eskimo shrine – the dog, its memory jogged by the locale, recognises Blake as the killer of his original master and savages him to death.

Although Rock loved working with director Joseph Pevney again, he later said that he had achieved the greatest personal satisfaction from two other films he made that year with Raoul Walsh. The first, *Gun Fury* (1953), was a routine Western set immediately after the Civil War; Rock played soldier-turned-pacifist Ben Warren, who only takes up his gun again and re-employs his fists when his fiancée (Donna Reed) is kidnapped by a gang of roughnecks.

Much better was *Sea Devils* (1953). Originally entitled *Toilers of the Sea*, the story was to have been based on Victor Hugo's 1866 novel, *Les Travaileurs de la Mer,* and the exteriors were filmed on the Channel Islands where Hugo had been exiled by Napoleon III. However, the final script was actually based on a screenplay by Borden Chase. Even so, it is a ripping yarn of espionage and smuggling, with a superb orchestral score by Richard Addinsell.

Set on the eve of the Napoleonic Wars, *Sea Devils* tells of a voluptuous English spy (de Carlo) who, to-ing and fro-ing across the Channel on a mission of national importance, encounters the handsome but irascible Captain Gilliatt (Rock). With a wealth of beefcake scenes where Rock gets to shed his shirt and sport some very sexy-looking designer stubble, a love story unravels that is more convincing and realistically played than in any of Rock's previous films.

Initially, Gilliatt distrusts the lady when she tells him the woeful tale of how her parents have died on the guillotine, and that she now has to rescue her doomed brother, only to subsequently observe her at a French chateau and be told that she is actually the Comtesse Ramuset. Therefore, assuming that she must be a French spy, Gilliatt kidnaps her and returns her to the English – unaware that she is only impersonating the Comtesse so as to discover the location of Napoleon's fleet. Later, when he learns the truth, Gilliatt rescues her from her enemies and the film ends with the sweethearts sailing off into the sunset.

Among the privileged few allowed on to the closed set was Donald Zec, this time reporting for the *Daily Mail*. 'I was engaged once,' volunteered Rock, without even being questioned about his love life, 'but that's all over, now. No, it wasn't Miss de Carlo. We're just good friends!' Another journalist who talked to him then was *Picturegoer*'s John Neton, who informed his readers of how he had been dreading their meeting because he had been acutely embarrassed by the Hudson biography sent out by Universal's publicity department:

> I learned that he was just a 'big kick-the-dirt boy' with his own 'wind-blown hair-do', and that his biggest asset was 'simply stamina'. After reading it I didn't know who to feel more sorry for, Mr Hudson or the picture-going public. I'm happy to be able to report, therefore, that far from being just a hunk of beefcake, Rock Hudson looks, talks and acts like a normal human being.

During a break in shooting, Rock made a lightning visit to London, where he told reporters of his fondness for muffins and tea, but could not understand why the British were so fanatical about cricket, which he considered the most boring sport in the world. He added that as soon as the film was wound up, he would be spending a few days in Paris and Rome 'looking for fun', as he put it. Such plans were scuppered, however, when he was summoned back to Hollywood to appear in *The Golden Blade* (1953) opposite Piper Laurie – a role that had already been rejected by Tony Curtis.

Camp does not begin to describe this otherwise entertaining *Arabian Nights*-style romp, packed with enough double entendres (in the uncut version) to have Rock's gay fans howling when the film was re-released during the more liberal mid-seventies. Rock played Harun, a young Basran aristocrat who takes on the wrath of Baghdad after his father is killed in a dispute over land. 'By Allah, will I depart, my son,' the old man gasps before expiring, having given Harun the medallion snatched from the neck of the enemy who has delivered the fatal blow.

In the city, Harun purchases a sword from a second-hand shop, one that proves to have magical and healing powers, but only when he is using it. He meets the Princess Khairuzan (Laurie), something of a political activist, falls for her, and immediately falls foul of the bad guys – Jafar (George Macready), who wants to see his son Hadi (Gene Evans) married to Khairuzan so that they can depose her and her caliph father (Edgar Barrier) and usurp the throne.

Confined to the harem on account of her soap-box ranting, Khairuzan escapes dressed as a boy and steals a horse, which just so happens to belong to Harun. He apprehends her, realises at once who she is, but goes along with her gender-bending game. She would like to be his servant, so he gives her a friendly grope and quips, 'You should exercise more. You're as soft as a woman.' Then he gives her money and says, 'Here, attach yourself to some other man – one with less important things to do!' The 'lad' is, however, persistent, so Harun suggests that they should dine, then go a-wenching. Khairuzan is horrified – 'he' is far too young for such things, bringing the response (which had to be shot several times because Rock kept having fits of the giggles) 'When I was your age I'd already tasted the nectar that lies in the kiss of a pretty damsel!'

Khairuzan sheds her disguise, though the palace guards fail to recognise her, and she and Harun are arrested as spies. They are incarcerated long enough to share their first kiss, then released. The preparations for Khairuzan's marriage to Hadi are almost completed. She hates him, naturally, and persuades the caliph to arrange a joust – with her hand going to the victor because she is convinced this will be Harun. 'I have learned that he carries a magic weapon,' she purrs, a line which Tallulah Bankhead would repeat to a reporter a few years later, when asked why she had been invited along as Rock's date for an Academy Awards ceremony.

To show that he has no hard feelings, on the eve of the joust Hadi invites Harun to a magic party. Here, Harun is drugged by Khairuzan's handmaiden – Hadi's mistress – and his sword stolen. Needless to say, the thug wins the contest – not on account of the purloined sword, but because Harun's saddle was sabotaged. The wedding ceremony begins, as of course does the long anticipated fight to the death, with Rock swashbuckling almost as well as a Flynn or a Fairbanks and doing his own stunts: kicking down doors, hauling furniture around, swinging from chandeliers, fencing up and down staircases. The caliph is killed, and the scenario switches to Arthurian legend when Harun's 'magic weapon' ends up embedded in a stone pillar where it will remain, according to the inscription etched on to its blade, until unsheathed by the one who is rightful claimant to the Baghdad throne. All and sundry try – by hand, winch and battering ram – but it is Harun who frees the sword on behalf of his love, causing the pillar to crumble and the roof to collapse on top of the traitors, bringing to a close their reign of terror. And needless to say, in keeping with tradition, all live happily ever after.

For obvious reasons, Jack Navaar was not allowed on to the set of *The Golden Blade*, and because Rock frequently needed 'quick-fix' sex during his working day, he latched on to one of the palace guard extras. News of this was relayed to Henry Willson, who immediately called a press conference. Progress on the film was discussed, along with Rock's future projects. Then the usual questions were asked about Rock's love life, which of course was why Willson had summoned the meeting in the first place. His star, he reluctantly confessed, was starting to get out of hand – though what could he do? In the past, he added, Rock had never been short of female company, but it had always been one girl at a time. Now, this irrepressible red-blooded young man was dating three lovelies from the film: Piper Laurie; Kathleen Hughes, who was playing her treacherous handmaiden; and bit-part Anita Ekberg, a busty Swede who would go on to much bigger things during the next decade.

A few days later, Universal released what they claimed was a still from the film – in effect, a staged pose of Rock, lying on a trestle of fruit and vegetables, with a laughing leading lady dangling a bunch of grapes above his face. The caption read, 'The Hollywood grapevine reports that, while making *The Golden Blade* opposite Piper Laurie, Rock began to find that his love-making wasn't all play-acting!'

As usual, the serious journalists amongst the gathering swallowed every word, but the less gullible tabloid harpies who had seen through Willson's charade were already sharpening their talons, getting ready to pounce.

In February 1953, with *Sea Devils* yet to be edited, Henry Willson pulled the strings for Rock to be tested for the part of Bob Merrick in a remake of *The Magnificent Obsession* (1954), a big hit for Robert Taylor and Irene Dunne in 1936. The producer, Ross Hunter, had been impressed with Rock's portrayal of Speed O'Keefe in *Iron Man* – more than this, he had fallen in love with him, though the close bond they later formed would remain strictly platonic. Setting aside personal feelings, however, Hunter also followed the studio's instructions and tested Jeff Chandler . . . who dismissed the script as 'soppy' and declared that he was happy the way he was, typecast in action roles. By the end of the month Rock had signed the contract. His love interest in the film, who had approved him after seeing him in *The Lawless Breed*, was to be Jane Wyman. Yet many critics unfairly predicted that even with big names such as Wyman, Agnes Moorehead and Otto Kruger, Rock's very presence would ensure the film's failure at the box office. *Picturegoer*'s influential Elizabeth Forrest, on the other hand, accused the studios of pointing Rock in the direction of disaster by persistently putting him into the wrong vehicles. 'A star is only judged by his last performance,' she observed, 'and so far, the Hudson past performance doesn't measure up to his big star potential.'

Meanwhile, in May 1953, Rock filmed *Taza, Son of Cochise* (1954) with Barbara Rush. There was a cameo from gay heart-throb Lance Fuller, who unusually gets to keep his clothes on in this one, and a sixty-second appearance by an uncredited Jeff Chandler, playing Cochise for the second time. There is much of Hollywood's usual disregard for historical accuracy and today the film views like any routine 'Cowboys and Injuns' B-movie. Back in 1954, however, when it was released, it provided *the* homoerotic experience for closeted gay men across the United States, with its lashings of oiled pecs, bulging biceps and sucked-in stomachs.

It is 1875, three years after the peace treaty signed between Cochise and the US Army, and the great Apache chief now lies dying (one year *after* the actual event). He looks supremely fit and expires nicely on cue after trying to persuade his sons to continue with the peace process he brought about. Taza (Rock), the elder of the two and now the new chief, swears allegiance while Naiche (Bart Roberts) is the unsmiling villain who conspires with tribal elder Grey Eagle (Morris Ankrum) and the infamous Chiricahua warlord Geronimo (Ian MacDonald) to bring about his downfall. Complications arise when both brothers fall for Grey Eagle's pretty daughter, Oona (Rush), who of course loves only Taza. The pair fight over her. Taza overpowers Naiche, but ignoring Oona's pleas to finish him off and save future bloodshed, Taza merely places him under house arrest: he is rescued by Geronimo's men and, ten years in advance, the Apache insurrection gets underway.

Enter the US cavalry led by the superficially gung-ho Captain Burnett (Gregg Palmer). Initially, he is unsure how Taza will shape up and assumes the worst of him. Burnett runs the San Carlos reservation and is here to investigate the murders of three white settlers. Geronimo is the obvious suspect, but Taza confesses that his people, Naiche and his renegades, were responsible, that they are already being punished by Apache law so there is no point in Burnett arresting them. The captain accuses him of personally breaking the peace treaty. Under government rules, the entire tribe must therefore be relocated to the reservation. Taza convinces him otherwise. There are a few unintentional amorous glances, which gay critics later picked up on, particularly when Rock makes his first appearance *torse-nu* in war paint! By way of compromise they are taken to Fort Apache, where the tables are quickly turned. Taza threatens to torch the place and fight alongside Geronimo unless his demands for internal justice are met. The arrival of General Crook (Robert Burton) consolidates his position. He is permitted to appoint his own 'police' to keep would-be Apache rebels in check and further designates Captain Burnett as his *nantan*, a 'special friend' he will protect with his life, if need be.

The Apaches under Taza's command move to the reservation and, while Burnett watches, he strips and dons his US uniform that, he drawls, fits his body more easily than his mind. Geronimo meanwhile surrenders to General Crook (again, ten years before this really happened), but with his network of spies relaying messages to his vast army of supporters, his power shows no sign of diminishing. Taza asks Grey Eagle for Oona's hand in marriage. Traditionally, he must bring his future father-in-law gifts, but manages only a few trinkets while his brother offers the money he stole from the 'white eyes' he murdered. These will buy guns and bullets for Geronimo. Taza *may* still have Oona, Grey Eagle tells him, but only if he gets Geronimo the contents of the San Carlos armoury. He therefore has to choose between betraying his people or losing the woman he loves. As if sensing that good always triumphs over evil (in Hollywood, at a time when matinee idols had to be seen to be never less than perfect), Taza opts for the latter.

There is a hitch when Taza and his 'police' are confined to base prior to the inevitable showdown. In a fit of pique he swaps his uniform for a native one, leaving off his war paint so that no one knows which side he is on until the cavalry have been near annihilated. Geronimo surrenders (again!) but Grey Eagle and Naiche refuse to capitulate and are killed. And, of course, Taza gets his girl, telling her as the credits are about to roll, 'My brother's shadow has walked away. Oona will be Taza's wife!'

Shot in primitive 3-D, *Taza, Son of Conchise* may have titillated a certain section of Rock's fan base, but it did him few favours so far as certain critics were concerned. They beefed that he was not yet ready to tackle a major role opposite an established non B-movie star like Jane Wyman. Rock always regretted making it, as he explained to Gordon Gow in a *Films & Filming* magazine interview:

I know I didn't look right in it. Indians, Mexicans, the Eskimo, they're all really the same race, with a similar semi-Oriental appearance. Furthermore, I'm too tall. The fact that you make up darker and wear a wig does not help you to resemble an Indian. I couldn't even keep my wig on. It kept blowing off in the wind when I rode horseback. An actor takes a role, and an audience either accepts it or rejects it. If they don't see him in the role, it's because he played another role better in a previous film and therefore the audience is married to that image. In the opera-house people would accept Leontyne Price as Madam Butterfly – she's black and she's playing a Japanese. But in a film, could you see Mickey Rooney playing Hamlet?

In August 1953, less than two weeks before shooting was scheduled to begin on *Magnificent Obsession* (as it had now been retitled), Rock and Jack Navaar went off for the weekend to Laguna, where they spent much of their time wave-riding – a potentially dangerous pastime where inflated car inner-tubes were used instead of surfboards. Rock was caught by a freak wave and dashed against the rocks, fracturing his collarbone.

The fact that the accident had happened on a men-only section of the beach, and that Navaar had ridden in the back of the ambulance that had conveyed Rock to the hospital, did not go down too well with Ross Hunter. When advised by Universal's doctors that Rock's shoulder would have to be set in a splint and that filming would have to be delayed for six weeks until he was fit again, the producer, under explicit orders from studio bosses and therefore unable to take his personal feelings into consideration, ordered Douglas Sirk, the German-born director of *Taza, Son of Cochise* and *Has Anybody Seen My Gal?*(1952) to find a replacement.

Fortunately, the situation was saved by the wily Henry Willson. Apparently, not so long before, Rock had been offered 'lip-service' by a top Universal executive. According to Sara Davidson (who later collaborated with Rock on his autobiography), 'Rock told his friends stories of how the executive would lock his office door, have his secretary hold the calls and come after Rock on his knees. Rock did not see him frequently, but it was enough to keep the executive hooked and eager to help Rock's cause.'

Almost certainly this man was Sirk himself – the director is known to have been similarly involved with several of his male stars, who regarded him as a kindly, benevolent sugar daddy. As indeed did Rock. 'He was like Ole Dad to me, and I was like a son to him, I think,' he told Ron Davis. 'When you're scared and new and trying to figure out this thing, suddenly an older man will reach out and say, "There, there it's okay!" That was Douglas Sirk.' Rock also praised Sirk's skills as a teacher, telling John Kobal:

When you're in a drama class, you're urged to get everything out of that scene that you can. Sirk was the first one to make me realise that you don't push, you hold back and let it come out. Don't hammer! React instead of act! He was the first good director I worked with, and I had by then worked with a lot of bad directors, which is, by the way, invaluable experience because you learn what not to do.

Henry Willson warned both Sirk and Ross Hunter what would happen should news of their private lives be leaked to the press, adding that such a risk would naturally be minimised should Rock be allowed to continue with the film. Needless to say, the requisite strings were pulled and Rock got to keep the part, but rather than hold up the production he himself suggested a compromise – he would have his injured shoulder strapped up during shooting, mindless of the agony this would cause him.

Magnificent Obsession, shot on location around Lake Arrowhead, remains the quintessential tugger of heartstrings, an undisputed classic of its genre. In his debut romantic lead Rock plays Bob Merrick, a failed medical student who, since inheriting his father's $4 million fortune, has become a selfish, hard-bitten playboy, having decided that since his father died young, he has every intention of enjoying life while he can.

When Merrick crashes his speedboat, despite being advised not to go out on to the water on account of adverse weather conditions, the police fetch the town's only resuscitator from the home of Dr Phillips. And while Merrick's life is saved, Phillips, an eminent and much-loved surgeon who owns the local hospital, dies of a heart attack, which might have been avoided had the equipment stayed put.

Merrick learns from Phillips' feisty nurse, Nancy (Agnes Moorehead), that the whole town holds him responsible for the great man's death. He discharges himself from the hospital and is picked up by Phillips' widow, Helen (Wyman), after collapsing at the side of the road. He cannot resist making a pass at her until she tells him who she is, that her husband has left her financially insecure and that the future of the hospital is in jeopardy because the ever-caring medic gave away most of his fortune to deserving causes. But when Merrick offers Helen a large pay-off she hits the roof.

Feeling culpable, Merrick gets drunk and crashes his car outside the home of Edward Randolph (Otto Kruger), an eccentric painter who benefited from Phillips' benevolence and subsequently became his closest friend. 'As far as I'm concerned, art's just a guy's name,' Merrick arrogantly admonishes, though by the time he leaves Randolph's place his entire outlook on life has been changed forever. The secret of his own success, Randolph confides, is that Phillips taught him how to be connected to the infinite source of power. 'This does not come cheap,' he adds, to a background accompaniment of angelic voices. 'Once you go into it you're bound, you'll never be able to give it up. You'll find this furnishes your motive: power. It will obsess you. Believe me, it'll be a magnificent obsession!' And all of a sudden Merrick has a burning desire to right the wrongs he has inflicted: he begins helping people and taking a leaf out of Phillips' book, but insists on anonymity.

When Merrick bursts in on Helen, who is sitting in the back of a taxi, to inform her what he is doing, she angrily accuses him of twisting her husband's beliefs into something cheap and tawdry and jumps out into the street into the path of a passing car, acquiring injuries that include an inoperable optic lesion, which leaves her blind. This only adds to Merrick's guilt and, monitoring her progress through allies at the hospital, he clandestinely pays her hospital bills and renders the hospital solvent once more. He also pays a large amount of money into Helen's bank account, which she is led to believe has come from a hitherto undisclosed insurance policy her husband took out shortly before his death.

Merrick and Helen next have a chance encounter on the beach: he introduces himself as someone else, and because he has been magically transformed into a compassionate, genuinely sincere person, Helen falls in love with him – the scenes in this section of the film, played against a beautiful Chopin and Beethoven score with more angelic voices, are arguably the most moving of Rock's career and affected him so much he actually burst into tears while watching the rushes.

Henceforth, Merrick's kindness is limitless. He becomes the mysterious buyer of Helen's house, the proceeds from which enable her to travel to Switzerland to be treated by doctors who will hopefully restore her sight. However they can do nothing and when Merrick joins her and tells her the truth about himself – something she has apparently known for some time – she accepts his marriage proposal, only to disappear without trace soon afterwards because she does not wish to become a burden.

Distraught, Merrick returns to America. He takes up medicine again, graduates and becomes a neurosurgeon and, in memory of his lost love, gives away most of his high earnings. Helen is finally discovered at a hospital in New Mexico, gravely ill with a brain tumour. Merrick, despite the fact that he has not carried out such a procedure before, is compelled to operate – offering fans the only glimpse they are going to get in this film of the superb Hudson torso, when he strips to scrub up for theatre – and not only does he save Helen's life, he restores her sight.

An improbable story without any doubt, but a masterpiece all the same and hugely successful. *Magnificent Obsession* cost a modest $850,000 to make, but grossed over $10 million at the box office. Rock's performance was also singled out by Bosley Crowther, the infamously acerbic film critic with the *NewYork Times*. Though he was not overtly fond of the production as a whole, he wrote of its star, 'The strapping, manly Rock Hudson gives a fine, direct account of himself – in the film's only real surprise.'

In April 1954, Ross Hunter – now a privileged member of Rock's inner circle – learned that Warner Brothers, who three years previously had purchased the rights to *Giant* (1956), Edna Ferber's epic novel centred around the all-American dream, were due to start casting. Testing was about to begin for the leads and director George Stevens was very close to signing William Holden for the role of Texan millionaire Bick Benedict, having already considered and rejected Alan Ladd and Clark Gable. Whoever got the part would star opposite either Grace Kelly or Elizabeth Taylor, both of whom were then contracted to MGM. Taylor's close friend, Montgomery Clift, was pencilled in for the film's third lead, the rebellious outsider Jett Rink.

Ross Hunter at once called Henry Willson, declaring that he had read Fred Guiol's and Ivan Moffat's screenplay and that the part of Bick was tailor-made for Rock. Within the hour Ferber, Stevens and the producer, Henry Ginsberg, were invited to Willson's Stoke Canyon home for private screenings of *Magnificent Obsession* and *The Lawless Breed* – in the latter, Rock had 'aged' more than two decades for the final scene, something he would be expected to do in *Giant*. Because Stevens was an independent director lacking the financial backing of a major studio, he had formed a corporation with

Ferber and Ginsberg to get his project off the ground. However, since then, Jack Warner had come forward with a substantial cash injection, and he believed that the film would be more credible if younger actors aged as the story unfolded, rather than the other way round – which was why he had dismissed the 53-year-old, over-the-hill Gable.

Stevens was impressed with the films, but he kept Rock hanging on for a week before offering him a contract. Rock's still persistent lack of confidence in his abilities niggled him, but Stevens attempted to boost this by asking him which leading lady he would prefer, should he be given the part. Rock chose Elizabeth Taylor, which was just as well as she had already signed her contract days before. Then, when the part was definitely his and the temporary release document had been signed between Warner Brothers and Universal, Rock was asked to choose the colours for the interior of the Benedict mansion, which was being constructed on a studio backlot.

George Stevens' track-record was impeccable, and as such he was the undisputed king of the epic movie. After working as assistant cameraman on some of the Laurel and Hardy shorts, Katharine Hepburn chose him to direct her in *Alice Adams* (1935), since then he had worked with Fred Astaire and Ginger Rogers, Carole Lombard, Barbara Stanwyck, Cary Grant and Spencer Tracy. He had already won an Oscar for directing Elizabeth Taylor and Montgomery Clift in *A Place in the Sun* (1951), and only recently had been nominated for *Shane* (1953), with Alan Ladd.

In the meantime, *Magnificent Obsession* was premiered at the Westwood Theater, and for the occasion Rock and Jack Navaar – who had thus far thwarted all of Universal's attempts to split them up – travelled to the venue in separate studio limousines. Both had been supplied with studio-dates – Rock with Betty Abbott, a close friend and the niece of comic Budd – Navaar with a starlet named Claudia Boyer. Henry Willson's eagle-eyed aides also ensured that the two men were kept apart all evening in what would, in retrospect, herald the end of their affair. Hundreds of girls screamed as Rock strode along the red carpet into the foyer, directly behind Jane Wyman and her husband Ronald Reagan, but one voice rose high above the cacophony – that of a young man who bellowed, 'Faggot!'

Rock tried to laugh off the incident, and the large contingency of reporters who witnessed the event certainly made nothing of it at the time, their preoccupation was in giving Rock the praise he deserved for his stupendous on-screen performance. Within weeks the so-called 'Midwest hick' would be elevated to the position of third most popular movie actor in America. Universal would reward him with a substantial increase in salary, his own monogrammed dressing room, and an exhaustive wardrobe tailored by the best designers in Hollywood.

According to some of those close to him, success went straight to Rock's head. Some years later, Mark Miller told Sara Davidson, 'Before, Rock would answer the phone, "Hiya!" Now it was a deep, "Hello? Hello? This is Rock Hudson speaking." He became an instant authority on everything. He could walk on water.'

And, of course, as he was pocketing a hefty percentage of Rock's salary, the more his protégé earned, the more Henry Willson grew concerned about Rock's sexual activities, particularly when he learned that reporters from the scandal rag *Confidential* had been snooping around the set of Rock's latest film, *Bengal Brigade* (1954), having been told that he was having an affair with one of his male co-stars.

For years the studios had been feeding the press with mostly fictitious stories about their stars, but as the power of the moguls and the credibility of their press offices slowly declined, a new form of exposé was launched on a public greedy for scandal and titillation: cheaply produced periodicals where readers could find pictures of their favourite movie idols accompanying lurid, no-holds-barred accounts of their indiscretions, wedged between advertisements for impotency pills, personal horoscopes, slimming aids and other usually useless paraphernalia. With titles such as *Inside Story*, *Whisper* and *Tip-Off* and with self-explanatory headlines – 'The Wild Party That Helped Sinatra Forget Ava Gardner', 'John Carradine's Other John', etc. – they could be found stacked on newsstands everywhere: in supermarkets, laundromats, gas stations and mostly outside cinemas where they were showing the films of whichever unfortunate happened to be on the cover of that week's issue.

Confidential was the most horrendous and feared publication of them all and its motto 'Tells the Facts and Names the Names' appeared on the cover beneath the title. The magazine was launched in 1952 by Robert Harrison, who got the idea because of his infatuation with the top-rated televised crime investigations hosted by Senator Kefauver. According to Kefauver, America was gripped in a wave of vice, corruption, gambling scams and organised crime that was rapidly transforming it into a mafioso state. Harrison therefore decided that he would explore the nucleus of this so-called den of iniquity – Tinsel Town – and thus far he had managed to stay one step ahead of orthodox scandalmongers Hopper, Parsons and the overbearing Elsa Maxwell by not always checking the authenticity of his stories before printing them – usually alongside the most unflattering or suggestive photographs, many of which had nothing to do with the accompanying feature. By the time he became interested in Rock, such was the demand for this sensationalist trash that Harrison's magazine was selling upwards of four million copies per issue.

What everyone in Hollywood detested most about Robert Harrison, according to Marlene Dietrich, were the devious methods he employed to obtain some of his exclusives; whores of both sexes were paid huge sums of money to coerce stars into compromising situations, while a tiny machine concealed in the bedroom whirred away, capturing not just the sex act itself but the all-important post-coital small talk. Jealous or thwarted stars were encouraged to rubbish rivals so that they could step into their shoes when important parts were up for grabs. For 'special' cases such as Rock and Elvis Presley (homosexuality, real or alleged), Errol Flynn (two-way mirrors) and Lana Turner (sharing lovers), Harrison supplied his 'detectives' with tiny, sophisticated infra-red cameras. 'We all read it,' Marlene told me, 'not because it was any good – it was rubbish and worse even than some of the garbage you get on newsstands nowadays – but to find out if we were in it. Sometimes you never got an inkling until it was too late.'

Harrison decided to pounce on Rock as soon as *Bengal Brigade* was finished shooting, offering former lover Bob Preble a reputed $5,000 for his story, which Harrison said would be published in the magazine's September 1954 issue along with two previously published photographs – the shot with the alarm clock and the one of Rock in his undershorts poring over his record collection prior to bedding his interviewer.

Whether Preble actually agreed to sell his ex-lover down the river is not clear, though unlikely judging by the restraint he has exercised since Rock's death. Henry Willson, however, was taking no chances. While Cary Grant, arrested after being caught in a department store men's room with a marine, had managed to 'buy back' his story, Willson, in an act of pure spite, traded the Hudson exclusive for a feature on another of his discoveries, the less-marketable and therefore, in his eyes, dispensable Rory Calhoun. 'But for the Grace of God Still a Convict', the headline ran, alongside mug-shots from the Salt Lake City Police files of the younger Calhoun who, it emerged, had once served a prison sentence for burglary. For the time being, Rock's reputation was allowed to remain as solid as his name implied.

In fact, the double-dealing Harrison had no intention whatsoever of running an exposé on Rock, or any other known homosexual star, and Bob Preble had only been offered a large amount of cash in the first place to entice Henry Willson or Universal into paying Harrison considerably more not to publish. It was all very well, the editor knew, to publish stories about alleged thieves, gangsters, bluebeards and loose women who were wildly promiscuous with the opposite sex, but Rock and his friends belonged to a completely alien group of individuals whose extra-curricular activities were taboo. Less than five years after the infamous Kinsey report, few of even *Confidential*'s liberated buyers would have wanted to acknowledge their existence by reading about them.

Alfred Kinsey (1894–1956), the zoologist–sexologist, had published the results of his studies into the sexual behaviour of the American male, the first serious research into the topic, in 1948; the one dealing with female sexuality would appear five years later. For his paper Kinsey had interviewed, via questionnaire, some 12,000 men of all ages and walks of life, and the American public at large were shocked to discover that there were variations of sexual practice other than the conventional one. Until the Kinsey report, most Americans outside the acting profession had not even heard of homosexuality and now they were being told by no less an authority than the Director of the Institute for Sex Research that one in ten American males actually liked having sex with other men, and that in doing so they were not necessarily abnormal.

Henry Willson, though perhaps not his protégé, would have been well aware that Robert Harrison would not have been permitted to publish words such as 'faggot' or 'sodomy', but the threat of his describing Rock as 'an actor who prefers unconventional behaviour as defined by Dr Kinsey' would have finished his career in one fell swoop. He therefore encouraged Universal to pay Harrison to keep quiet. As for Harrison, he was such a detested figure and he received so many death-threats, that towards the end of *Confidential*'s run he had to have round-the-clock protection.

Rock is reputed to have told Jack Navaar that, should he be outed by the press, he would sooner give up Hollywood than his lover. One finds this hard to believe, though the pair were still very much an item during the summer of 1954, when Rock left for Ireland to film the locations for *Captain Lightfoot*. The reason for these being shot overseas and not in California was that Henry Willson had assured the Universal executives that, should they bear the expense of Rock's trip, he would make it worth their while by ridding them of Jack Navaar – who of late had been taking his role of 'movie-wife' too seriously, calling Douglas Sirk's secretary most evenings to enquire when Rock would be home so that he could 'get the dinner going'.

With several weeks to go before shooting began on the new film, Rock flew to Paris with Betty Abbott and his co-star Barbara Rush, who had separated from her husband, Jeff Chandler. They stayed there for a few days before hiring a car to tour Southern France and Italy. In Europe, Rock was able to shrug off all those inhibitions imposed on him of late by Hollywood stardom. He dated men openly in Paris, Rome, Florence and in Venice where he began a passionate affair with Massimo, a 21-year-old actor, which would endure, off and on, for more than twenty years.

While Rock was in Europe, Jack Navaar stayed put at the Grandview house – as much his as it was Rock's, though the

Universal chiefs took exception to 'Mrs Hudson' opening the door to callers and driving around town in his lover's blatantly recognisable yellow convertible. Initially, Henry Willson attempted to resolve the situation by pairing Navaar with a young employee, Phyllis Gates, an attractive brunette who very soon would add even more confusion to the already complex Hudson–Willson equation.

Just three weeks Rock's junior, Phyllis Lucille Gates had been born and raised on a farm near Montevideo, a small Minnesota town, to an Anglo-German father and a Norwegian mother. Following brief spells and varying occupations in Minneapolis, Kansas City, Miami and New York, Phyllis had moved to California at the end of 1953, and shortly afterwards had been engaged as Henry Willson's private secretary, though initially she does not appear to have liked him very much, recording in her 1987 memoir, *My Husband, Rock Hudson*, 'His exquisite grooming could not compensate for his basic unattractiveness. His face was a misshapen mask: the weak chin, the fleshy lips, the bulbous nose, the wide-apart lifeless eyes, heavy eyebrows and receding black hair. You could understand why he made a career of discovering and exploiting beauty.'

In her book, Phyllis Gates refers to Jack Navaar, as 'Bill McGiver', and tells of how, when she asked Henry Willson for time off so that she could visit her parents in Minnesota, Willson had come up with a suggestion that would save her the air fare – one of his clients, a failed actor, was driving out to the Midwest to spend some time with his family – he would be able to drop her off in Montevideo then pick her up one week later and bring her back to California.

According to Phyllis – who must have been aware of Willson's recruitment techniques and the fact that most, if not all, of his male stars were gay or bisexual – Navaar did not tell her that he was living with Rock until they were several days into their journey . . . and even then she does not appear to have worked out the obvious, doubtless because Navaar seems to have treated her as though they genuinely had been going steady. He later confided in Sara Davidson that he had soon developed a tremendous crush on her, adding, 'I could understand why Rock thought he could fall in love with her, because I could have. She knew how to make a guy feel fabulous.

She had a marvellous laugh and an incredible personality – you'd meet her and in ten minutes you'd feel you were the most important person in her life.'

Navaar also said that throughout the trip he and Phyllis had checked into hotels and motels as husband and wife, but though they had slept in the same room purely to save on expenses, they had never shared a bed. By the time they reached Montevideo they had become so close that Phyllis asked Navaar to stay with her before they moved on to Kansas, where they attended both gay and lesbian parties. The fun continued, as discreetly as was possible, when the pair returned to Los Angeles. They were seen regularly at Camille's, a women's venue near Laguna Beach – where Navaar claimed Phyllis had gone off with a woman and not been seen for two days – and in Santa Monica's Tropical Village, one of Rock's favourite watering holes.

When Willson realised that his plan had backfired, he called Rock in Ireland and ordered him to end his relationship with Jack Navaar before it was too late and he was outed by the press. Without even asking Rock's permission, Willson cancelled Navaar's weekly allowance, which Rock had been paying since setting up home with him, and forbade Phyllis Gates from ever seeing him again. Rock's behaviour towards the man for whom he had once declared that he would have given up everything was equally heartless. He insulted Navaar over the telephone – audaciously calling him a 'dirty faggot' – and threatened him with physical violence should he still be hanging around when he arrived home.

Within 24 hours one of Willson's cronies had relieved Navaar of his lover's car, confiscated his keys to the Grandview house and removed all evidence that he had ever been near the place. Willson's actions, though, were quickly relayed to *Confidential*'s Robert Harrison – if not by Navaar himself then by friends who had quite rightly decided that Rock and his manager deserved all that was coming to them. The story, like its predecessor, never made it to the printed page because Willson once more traded Rock for someone else – really rubbing the salt into the wounds, for this time the scapegoat was George Nader, who had just completed *Robot Monster* (1953), listed in 'The Golden Turkey' awards as one of the worst films of all time. Nader, who spends much of his on-screen time flexing his not inconsiderable muscles and looking lost had, according to Harrison's ever-dubious source, been involved with one of the other actors.

Again, the exclusive was spiked following a large pay-off from the studio, and when Harrison threatened to tell Universal who had set Nader up in the first place, Willson sent two heavies to Harrison's office to threaten him with a fate worse than death should he ever let on what had happened. Suffice to say, once Rock realised that even one of his closest friends – a supposed model of discretion – was not safe from the gutter press, he swore that he would never risk living with another man, a promise he would stick to for another twenty years.

3

Why Aren't You Married, Bick?

'If you're cast in crap like Taza, *it doesn't matter if you experiment with a scene and it goes wrong. Who's gonna notice? But if it works, you can use it in a better film. Like* Giant, *perhaps.'*

Rock Hudson

In August 1954, Rock returned to Hollywood, thinking himself free from Robert Harrison's threats, but he found himself instead recoiling at the horrendous headline penned by Louella Parsons, 'Rock Hudson: Will He Put His Career Ahead of Matrimony?'

Parsons might just as well have told her readers the truth – there was enough innuendo in her column to finish him once and for all. Worse still was a follow-up article in *Movie-TV Secrets,* which posed, 'Rock Hudson. He is handsome, personable, intelligent, and a top-salaried actor. So what's wrong with Rock where the fair sex is concerned, we ask?'

Henry Willson realised that if he were to save his and the studio's most prodigious investment, he would have to act fast and actually supply Rock with a wife. His one stumbling block in this respect, however, was finding a suitable candidate – one who would not be recognised by Rock's peers, particularly the ones he had 'serviced' – as a 'lavender' bride, who had been foisted on to him to curb the gossips. In other words, as the archetypal ultra-macho, wholesome boy-next-door type, Rock Hudson would be expected to fall in love, become engaged and marry a woman from a background similar to his own – certainly not some glamour-puss or bejewelled movie-queen. And, of course, to prevent a repeat of the Parsons piece it would have to be a whirlwind romance.

Once again, Henry Willson provided the ideal candidate; for the second time, Phyllis Gates claimed she was coerced into playing the stooge, though whether she realised she was being set up has been a matter for conjecture for almost half a century. Rock certainly was party to Willson's devious plan, and as such complied implicitly with his every instruction.

The Hudson–Gates 'affair' began innocuously enough in June 1954 when, having met her several times in her capacity as Willson's secretary, Rock asked her out on a series of dinner dates, which were all subsequently cancelled, usually because he had already made arrangements to be interviewed by movie magazines: this meant that he would be able to fuel the gossip columns by explaining that his fans were so important that he had had to let his girlfriend down. Phyllis, however, saw things differently, and recalled telling Willson, 'I don't enjoy having people make dates with me and then cancel them. Tell your number one client to stop bothering me.'

Willson did no such thing, and a few days later Rock 'just happened' to bump into Phyllis while she was out shopping for Christmas decorations. Rock was with a lover he introduced as 'Craig', thought to have been the actor William Reynolds, who had been contracted to appear in his next film, *All That Heaven Allows* (1956). Indeed, this very scenario would be incorporated into its plot, though of course with Rock's character being with a female companion. This time, Rock kept his dinner appointment, though he did bring along Henry Willson and another male friend, doubtless so that the all-powerful Svengali could witness first-hand the progress his protégé was making. Willson must have been pleased with the way things were developing, suitably aware that Phyllis had fallen for their ruse.

The two began dating regularly – and according to Phyllis, also sleeping together – though in her memoirs she recalls, 'His big hands were amazingly gentle as he began to explore and I fell completely under his spell. The love act itself was sublime, passionate, though it ended sooner than I would have liked. I figured Rock had been overly excited.'

Like any dutiful son, Rock took his new 'girlfriend' to meet his folks – though Kay, aware of his sexuality and said to have been saddened at his break-up with Jack Navaar, must have seen through the charade. And of course the press were alerted to the fact by Henry Willson that his client's relationship with his curvy young secretary was indeed 'hot'. The moralists, Willson knew, would attack Rock for his so-called 'out of wedlock practices', but at least he would be at the centre of a scandal that involved a woman, and hopefully be free from attack from the likes of *Confidential*'s Robert Harrison – and with the latter still pestering Jack Navaar, Rock must have been relieved when the story about him and Phyllis broke in the *Hollywood Reporter* early in 1955.

At around this time, Universal were approached by MGM and offered $1 million for a six-month loan of their biggest draw, which would commence immediately *Giant* had been completed, and involve Rock appearing in two films. The offer was refused because shooting was about to begin on *All That Heaven Allows*, Rock's second coupling with Jane Wyman and Agnes Moorehead. To make up for his disappointment and resentment, Universal raised Rock's salary to $1,250 a week and loaned him the $38,000 for a house that had recently taken his fancy. On top of this he was given $10,000 to furnish it to his requirements – a task which he assigned to Phyllis, seeing as she was going to be expected to share this 'love nest' with him.

Though not as good or as successful as *Magnificent Obsession* – some thought that the on-screen age difference between Rock and his co-star was not overtly obvious because he looked older than 29 and she younger than 41 – *All That Heaven Allows* remains a moving tale of small town bigotry, prejudice and narrow-mindedness, highlighted by Frank Skinner's haunting, Chopinesque score, beautifully photographed wintry landscapes and lots of stylised, very searching reflections.

Ron Kirby (Rock) is the faceless freelance maintenance gardener, the lower-class 'nobody' relegated to anonymity by his snooty clients, until he inadvertently and innocently charms his way into the affections of wealthy widow Cary Scott (Wyman). At first they exchange small talk about his life's passion – tree conservation – and when he presents her with a sprig of golden-rain from her garden and confides that this only flourishes in a home where there is love, she keeps it almost like a sacred relic and quickly falls in love with him. Soon, she announces that they are to marry and that they will live not in the family home, but in the old mill-house Ron is renovating.

The relationship is condemned by Cary's grown-up children – Ned (William Reynolds), who accuses her of besmirching her late husband's memory, and Kay (Gloria Talbott), who endlessly quotes Freud and wants to see her mother eventually settled with her much older family friend, Harvey (Conrad Nagel). Even Cary's best friend, Sara (Moorehead), initially disapproves, though in her blinkered way of psychoanalysing the situation she believes that she has the perfect antidote to what she sees as a classic case of middle-class domestic boredom. 'Look, Cary,' she advises, 'you can't sit around here with nothing to do. You should at least get a television set.' And when Cary says that she does not want this, the other cannot resist the crack, 'Why – because it's supposed to be the last refuge for lonely women?'

Worse still are Cary's neighbours and social set, headed by odious gossip Mona Plash (Jacqueline de Wit), who very soon spreads the rumour that, as Ron was tending Cary's garden while Mr Scott was alive, the pair must have been having an adulterous affair then. 'He's fascinating,' she haughtily opines. 'And that tan, I suppose from working outdoors. 'Course, I'm sure he's handy indoors, too?'

While Cary takes such insults to heart, Ron is quietly philosophical. He introduces her to *his* friends – genuine, no-nonsense, fun-loving people like himself, for whom material possessions mean nothing. Yet still she cannot summon the strength to face up to the bigotry that surrounds her back home, and the last straw comes when Ned tells her, 'I think all you see is a good-looking set of muscles.' Cary tells Ron that it is over between them, and the pair sink into a pit of self-inflicted misery: Ron sulks alone in a snowy wasteland, and the much-heralded television set arrives at the Scott household, an unwelcome Christmas gift courtesy of Ned and Kay.

The film's most moving and thought-provoking image occurs when the salesman explains, as the camera captures her in jaundiced close-up, her forlorn expression reflected in the screen, 'All you have to do is turn that dial, and you have all the company you want right there on the screen – drama, comedy, life's parade at your fingertips.'

Finally, Cary decides that she must be the one to make the first move and she drives out to Ron's place. He is out shooting and calls her name from far off, but she neither sees nor hears him, and as she leaves he plummets from the snow-covered cliff-top and suffers severe concussion. The film ends with her sitting by his bedside. At first it is touch and go and the doctor warns her that his recovery will be slow. Cary does not mind this now, for her belated courage has enabled her to stand up to her oppressors and she has no intention of ever leaving him again. 'Yes, darling,' she breathes as he regains consciousness, 'I've come home!'

The two-bedroom property that Rock had recently bought was at 9151 Warbler Place, off Sunset Boulevard. Surrounded by tall trees and with a several-hundred-foot ivy-clad rock face as its backdrop, the building resembled a hunting lodge, though the features that most impressed Rock were the automatic gates that would keep out fans and, more importantly, snoopers, and the wealth of interior woodwork, heavy rustic beams and the huge floor-to-ceiling barbecue.

Rock took Phyllis to inspect the house before signing the deeds and promptly asked her to move in with him, unthinkable in those days in Hollywood, though the brouhaha evoked by Rock 'living in sin' with a woman, Henry Willson truthfully argued, would be infinitely preferable to the public finding out that he had been 'screwing his room-mates' for years. Phyllis did not even deliberate.

'I was thunderstruck,' she recalled. 'I had never contemplated the possibility of living with a man to whom I wasn't married. And I certainly couldn't consider it now, even though I felt a growing affection – call it love – for Rock.'

It would seem inconceivable that Phyllis did not know by now that Rock was gay, though not impossible for her to genuinely believe that falling in love with her had 'turned him straight'. Such was his charm and irascibility that, throughout his life, Rock would have an infallible propensity for seducing even the most die-hard heterosexual males – as had happened during his recent trip to Europe – men who, after having sex with him, would return to their girlfriends and wives and probably never think of having sex with another man again. He certainly lavished Phyllis with affection over the coming weeks, giving her the impression that he really had amended his ways.

Phyllis was his legitimate date for the premiere of *Captain Lightfoot* in February 1955, and she regularly visited the sets of his next two films, *Never Say Goodbye* (1956) and *Four Girls in Town* (1956) – the latter also co-starring George Nader.

The interiors of *Giant*, regarded by many critics as Rock's finest hour, began shooting in Los Angeles in the May of 1955, once George Stevens had assembled what was, in retrospect, the most perfectly matched cast for a big budget saga since *Gone with the Wind* (1939). Twenty-four-year-old Carroll Baker had recently made her debut in *Easy to Love* (1953) and within the year would achieve notoriety with *Baby Doll* (1956). Mercedes McCambridge had scored a triumph opposite Joan Crawford in the Western *Johnny Guitar* (1954). Sal Mineo and Dennis Hopper were lifted straight out of the yet-to-be-released *Rebel Without a Cause* (1955), as was Stevens' biggest scoop, James Dean, who played Jett Rink.

Montgomery Clift, perennially on the skids with his sexuality-linked drugs and drink dependency, had been pencilled in for the role of Jett Rink, only to be deemed too much of a risk by the studio's insurance company. Dean was no less of an enigma, and his own reputation left much to be desired. Though only one of his films had been released (*East of Eden*, 1955) and the public at large were yet to be captivated by his spellbinding talent, Jimmy was already being variously hailed as a lost cause, a cock-hungry schizophrenic, a pre-Brat Pack prima donna, whose only truly happy, but not entirely sane, moments occurred when he was creating merry hell. He was nevertheless the archetypal control freak, whose every photogenic gesture had to be meticulously rehearsed and perfected.

Jimmy was a self-confessed neurotic, impossible to work with unless he was getting his own way, exacting his revenge on what he termed 'third-rate lumps' – such as he considered Rock – by improvising carefully plotted scenes with alien gestures, and above all not easy to socialise with if one was not positioned on his decidedly precarious side of the fence. Jimmy had also, unlike Rock and his closeted gay contemporaries, never given a damn about his public image.

When the MGM moguls had tried to prevent him from cruising for, frequently very rough, gay trade by fixing him up with studio-dates, Jimmy had begun finding his own heterosexual conquests, such as Maila Nurmi, popular with television audiences as Vampira, and according to his lover, Jonathan Gilmore (*James Dean*, Robson, 1995), a one-legged woman with whom Jimmy had liked to watch him having sex, but only after he had drawn a face on her stump.

And yet James Dean's single-handed, inadvertent championing of the rebellious youth of America at a time when the country was trying to live down the ravages of McCarthyism – with many parents failing to furnish their offspring with a good example, and most youngsters in any case interested only in teenage independence – made him an icon to an entire generation. There was little doubting from Jimmy's peers and critics alike, once *Giant* got under way, regardless of the fact that his total screen time would comprise less than twenty minutes of a three-hours-plus production, that this would be *his* film, never Rock's or even Elizabeth Taylor's.

As with Douglas Sirk, despite the fact that he worked with him just the once, Rock placed director George Stevens on a pedestal. He told Ron Davis:

George Stevens, he's another one I fell in love with. He was like a god to me. I followed him around like a puppy. Stevens had a richness to him. He read everything, digested everything. He so inundated himself in Texas and Texanism that whatever decision he made was absolutely right. He did all the directing with me *before* the picture began, and hardly a word during shooting. He had me so right and bigoted. I *was* Bick Benedict before we even shot Frame One. And you didn't dare lie to the man because he could just see right to your core . . . He gave me such *power* that I felt I could run the studio!

Rock got on like a house on fire with Elizabeth Taylor, then as now the undisputed champion of the oppressed, troubled homosexual. Over the ensuing years, and with undying loyalty, she would befriend, comfort and defend Rock, James Dean and Montgomery Clift, wayward souls who would look upon her as an indefatigable ally and surrogate mother figure, even though she was younger than all three. Rock and Phyllis Gates spent many contented hours with Elizabeth and her second husband, Michael Wilding, at their Hollywood home. Her theory was that she should inject a little Method into their on-screen personae, in other words, in order to find out how they would get on as Mr and Mrs Benedict, they would have to be together as much as possible, through thick and thin. This involved 'Bessie' and 'Rockabye' – their pet names for each other – living life to the full, getting drunk a lot and throwing up a lot on the set. It also involved Rock being third-party to the rows between the fiery actress and Wilding, now reaching the end of their marriage – arguments that were exacerbated when *Confidential* published a shattering expose on Wilding, who, it was claimed, had organised a noisy poolside party complete with strippers while his wife had been away filming.

On the other hand, Rock gave every impression of intense loathing where James Dean was concerned. Though if a later comment made by Elizabeth Taylor has any credence, and there is no reason to think otherwise, the much-publicised dark looks and on-set dissension between the two actors was almost certainly little more than a charade to camouflage their true feelings for one another. Speaking to *Star* magazine in 1987, she said, 'After I found out the truth about Rock, I began to feel a strong affection for Jimmy. But my feminine intuition told me that a mysterious understanding was being born between the two actors and at times I felt like an uncomfortable third party.'

The shooting schedule for *Giant* was well under way by the time James Dean met up with the rest of the unit early in June – catching the train out of Hollywood just thirty minutes after completing the post-recording on *Rebel Without a Cause*. By this time the production had transferred to Marfa, Texas, for the location work, taking with it the huge $200,000 Gothic Benedict mansion. This was re-erected to rise spookily out of the blistering desert sands and once the film was finished it was sallowed to decay and crumble back into them.

Henceforth, shooting would be hampered by frayed tempers aggravated by the scorching heat, and a severe water shortage, which led to an over-consumption of alcohol. Worst of all were the personality clashes instigated by George Stevens and stage-managed by James Dean, whose Method training had taught him that if two characters were supposed to hate each other on screen, then they must also hate each other away from the set or during rehearsals to make their scenes truly authentic. Professionally, Rock and Jimmy were worlds apart. Jimmy had been schooled by the same team that had produced Brando, Clift, Lee J Cobb, and a handful of other distinguished thespians who had also scored fantastic hits on the stage. And for most of these actors, hard work and often self-sacrifice had preceded triumph. In Rock's case, in common with most of the other graduates from the so-called Henry Willson Academy of Glamour, sex had been the motivating factor towards fame, and acting ability had been picked up along the way – or in cases such as Guy Madison, Tab Hunter and several others, not at all.

Jimmy, by far the better actor, resented this. On the other hand, with his complex psyche, he was obviously attracted to Rock Hudson the superbly packaged slab of beefcake, yet he would have easily been capable of separating sexual desire from professional opinion: it was not difficult for Jimmy to walk out of a room ten minutes after having sex with a co-star and immediately begin attacking him, verbally and physically. Compared to Rock, he was diminutive, but he was wiry, immensely strong and agile, wholly capable of challenging any man to a fight, even if he came off the loser. Again this mirrored his Method training: to stay in character between takes, even with the man he was currently involved with.

It must, however, have been extremely unnerving for someone of Rock's laid-back, still shy approach to witness James Dean 'psyching up' for a take as was witnessed several times by visitors to the set of *Giant*: sitting on a chair he would slowly draw his knees up to his chin, then bring them down with a thud, stamping his feet on the ground dozens of times before leaping high into the air and finally tearing around the set, screeching like a banshee!

Jimmy also loathed the way George Stevens expected everyone to be on the lot, in full costume, at the crack of dawn even if they were not going to be called to do a scene until much later in the day. On one occasion when the director kept Jimmy sitting around a whole day for nothing, Jimmy did not show up at all the next morning, and when Stevens finally caught up with him and bawled him out in front of the entire set, Jimmy got his own back by summoning his friend Hedda Hopper and getting her to denounce Stevens in her column for his 'lack of professional ethics'. Like everyone else involved with the film he also complained to the studio about Stevens' infuriating habit of shooting some scenes dozens or, frequently, hundreds of times, from every conceivable angle, often utilising over a thousand feet of film for just a few seconds of screen time. In all, Stevens would use up 700,000 feet of film, of which only 25,000 feet would form the 198 minutes of the final print of *Giant*.

Edna Ferber had based her novel on the real-life rags-to-riches story of Texan oil magnate Glenn McCarthy. The film is also said to have inspired the flossy television soap *Dallas* (1978–91), and its resident tyrant J R Ewing – the latter taking his initials from those over Jett Rink's podium in the film's closing scene.

Complemented by Dimitri Tiomkin's superb score, the story opens in 1923 with Jordan 'Bick' Benedict II on the train to Maryland, where he is to purchase a fine black stallion that he sees being exercised by the lovely Lesley Lyntonn (Taylor). 'That sure is a beautiful animal,' he drawls, not referring to the horse. Later, Bick faces a barrage of questions at the dinner table, Lesley posing the one that got Henry Willson hot under the collar: 'Why *aren't* you married, Bick?' – an easily solved conundrum at least so far as Rock's character is concerned, for such is their mutual attraction that, a few days later when Bick leaves for Reata, his 595,000-acre ranch in Texas, Lesley accompanies him as his bride.

Here, in a big house stuck literally in the middle of nowhere, the new Mrs Benedict struggles to adapt to her new life in an environment where everything that has a Reata brand on it belongs to Bick, including his wife. First she has to come to terms with Luz (McCambridge), her butch, domineering sister-in-law, a woman who 'would rather herd cattle than make love'. Luz dislikes Lesley almost as much as she dotes on her wayward hired hand, Jett Rink, who she had taken in as a boy – McCambridge, another of Jimmy's surrogate mother figures, affectionately referred to him as 'the runt in a litter of thoroughbreds' – a man whose stubborn arrogance stems from Bick's jealousy of him, and Jett's hatred of the way Bick thinks he has a right to control everyone about him. 'Ain't nobody king in *this* country,' Jett mutters under his breath shortly after making his first appearance.

Almost at once, Lesley becomes involved with the plight of the ranch's Mexican neighbours. She is appalled by their abject poverty and lack of even half-decent medical facilities, but only incurs the wrath of her racist husband when she tends a sick baby and saves its life . . . an act which coincides with Luz's death following a fall from the very stallion that brought about Bick's and Lesley's introduction. Luz has bequeathed Jett Rink a token ten acres of land, which he refuses to sell to the grasping Bick for twice its value because it holds for him precious memories of the woman he worshipped. Laughing in the faces of the bigots who have shown him compassion for the first time in his life, but only because he has something they want, Jett leaves Reata and in the subsequent classic tableau we see him ambling across the terrain, 'striding out' his land before scrambling up an oil derrick to survey the horizon.

Jett names his acquisition Little Reata, and for a time he struggles to make ends meet. Lesley – who meanwhile has given birth to twins, a boy and a girl – visits him clandestinely. When she sees pictures of herself on the wall of his shack and realises that, as had happened with Luz Benedict, the young man has a crush on her, she asks, 'When are you going to get married, Jett?' – a repeat of her earlier, allegedly unscripted question to Bick. Jett responds only with his eyes, and in the film's most touching moment serves her tea and sneaks a large slug of whisky to give him courage – again unscripted.

Jimmy was so nervous about filming this first scene with Elizabeth Taylor – the highlight of which sees him standing in his famous mock-Crucifixion pose, with his rifle threaded between his outstretched arms, behind his lowered head, while Taylor emulates Mary Magdalene by crouching at his feet – that before the camera began rolling for the film's only single take he strolled out of its range to face the huge crowd of onlookers that George Stevens had allowed on to the lot. Smiling coyly he unzipped his 'shit-kicker' denims, urinated, then shook his penis at the sea of astonished onlookers. Later he told Dennis Hopper, 'I figured that if I could pee in front of four thousand people, then I could do anything on film.'

Soon afterwards, Lesley gives birth to another daughter whom Bick names Luz. Jett unexpectedly strikes oil, resulting in his becoming one of the wealthiest men in Texas – even richer than Bick Benedict, whose jealousy of his rival and loathing of Lesley's involvement with the Mexican community puts a strain on their marriage. Taking the children with her, Lesley returns to Maryland, but Bick follows and they make up. Then Jett turns up at the Benedict house, drunk and drenched in oil. 'I'm gonna have more money than you ever thought you could have, you stinking sons of Benedict,' he levels, before making a pass at Lesley. Bick hits him, but gets more than he bargained for when Jett lays into him – a scene within which the punches were reputedly for real.

Bick exacts his revenge by taking out a writ, prohibiting Jett from cashing in on the Reata logo – Jett changes it to Jetexas, and the action leaps forward almost two decades to find the Benedicts still squabbling, this time over the futures of their offspring, none of whom are interested in taking over the ranch and ending up like their father. Jordan III (Hopper) aspires towards medicine and marries a Mexican girl. Julie (Judith Evelyn) refuses to attend any of the finishing schools selected by her parents and weds a local boy with whom she sets up her own ranch. Luz, the flighty one (Baker), gives Lesley and Bick their biggest headache of all by developing an interest in the now middle-aged Jett Rink, who shows only contempt for those who sneered at him when he was penniless.

The United States then enters World War II, and in the wake of Pearl Harbor, Reata suffers its first casualty when Angel Obregon (Sal Mineo), the Mexican boy whose life was saved by Lesley, is killed in action and for the first time ever the increasingly bitter Bick shows sympathy for the people he once loathed. He even submits to Jett, selling him his land so that oil may be prospected to help with the war effort.

From this point in the story, unfortunately, while the protagonists become more vengeful and twisted, *Giant* starts to lose its power. The main source of irritation is the ageing of the characters. James Dean had some say in this, telling George Stevens how 'wrinkles come only with good acting'. With his ever-present shades, slightly greying temples and receding hairline *he* certainly looks authentic enough, whereas Rock and Elizabeth Taylor appear ridiculous, crude caricatures with absolutely no facial lines and *blue* hair.

Jett builds an airport and swish hotel complex (inasmuch as Glenn McCarthy had constructed Houston's famous Shamrock Hotel), to whose opening the whole of Texas society is invited. The so-called 'virile son of Texas', however, has been transformed into a lonely, hard-drinking, Howard Hughes-type figure. He proposes to Luz – who tells him she is flattered, but rejects him all the same. Jordan III confronts him when he insults his half-Mexican baby, and Jett flattens him before being challenged by Bick to the return bout, which has been on the cards these last twenty years – and which still does not take place. 'You're all through,' Bick snarls before wrecking the room. Jett then steps on to the podium where he is to deliver his speech of thanks to the distinguished gathering – only to pass out and slump across the table before he even begins.

The Benedicts resume arguing amongst themselves after the party breaks up, while in the massive, now-empty stateroom Jett comes to and slurs his drunken, emotive address, straying from the printed page to pour out his long-suppressed feelings for Lesley before collapsing again. And *Giant* concludes with Bick and the Benedict women driving across the Texan desert and singing 'South of the Border', stopping off at a diner where anti-Mexican prejudice runs high as it once did with the now-reformed Bick. When the proprietor makes ill-chosen remarks about Bick's Mexican daughter-in-law and tries to eject a Mexican family from his establishment, Bick defends them and starts a fight, which he loses. It is only when he comes to after being knocked out that Lesley, after more than two decades, finally accepts him as her hero – and the last, lasting image we see is that of the Benedicts' Mexican and American grand-children, whom they are now relying on to continue the family tradition with less bickering and bias than they have encountered or created themselves.

Exactly why Phyllis Gates was summoned to Texas halfway through the shooting of *Giant*, mindless of the conflicting reports, is not difficult to discern. One stated that Rock, distressed because James Dean was effortlessly stealing every scene they appeared in together, called Henry Willson and begged him to send Phyllis to comfort him. Another declared that she was so angry over the rumour that Rock was having an affair with Elizabeth Taylor that she wanted to sort out the pair of them. Michael Wilding, whose visit to the set accompanied by their two children preceded Phyllis' by a few days, seems to have been thinking along the same lines. Elizabeth later admitted that she *had* been attracted to Rock, but that she was well aware that, like Montgomery Clift before him, he would never be hers. After his death she recalled, 'I looked at Rock, so handsome and so apparently masculine. But I soon realised that *no* woman would succeed in igniting *his* enthusiasm.'

Phyllis herself adhered to the jealousy theory, maintaining that Rock had marched into her hotel room, quipped, 'Hi, Bunting, welcome to Texas!' then carried her to the bed where they had frantically made love. She wrote in her memoirs, 'He was over-whelming, as passionate as he had ever been,' and added how she had got along well with James Dean, who had taken her to breakfast on her first morning in Marfa and afterwards taught her how to spin a lariat – as he had the 68-year-old Edna Ferber during her visit to the set. She also recalled a caustic quip from former child-star Jane Withers, who played the curiously named Vashti Snythe, 'I can't understand what Rock is going to do with *her* here,' from which she

deduced there must have been something going on between Rock
and Elizabeth Taylor:

> He devoted so much attention to Elizabeth. They were almost
> childish with each other, talking a kind of baby talk and playing
> pranks like throwing water at each other . . . When I saw Rock
> and Elizabeth together, I understood the reason for Jane
> Withers' crack . . . Was I jealous? Not really. I realised that no
> normal male could resist the fabulous charms of Elizabeth
> Taylor. I had no claim on Rock, no reason to be possessive. If
> there had been an affair, I doubted that it would last. I was
> content that Rock had, with his passionate welcome to Texas,
> demonstrated his feelings to me.

The most likely explanation for Phyllis' sudden appearance, of
course, is that someone at Warner Brothers had been tipped off that
Rock and Jimmy – who were sharing a house in Marfa with fellow
actor Chill Wills – were well on their way towards evoking a scandal
that, if it reached the likes of *Confidential*, might easily have shut
down the production, particularly when Jimmy boasted not just to
friends but to studio executives, 'I've had my cock sucked by five of
the biggest names in Hollywood – all of them guys!'

Tempers settled somewhat towards the end of August 1955, when
George Stevens moved everyone back to Hollywood, though
according to Phyllis, Rock spent much of the long journey in a
foul mood, away from the rest of the company. 'We did manage
some lovemaking,' she remembered. 'My first on a train. It was
wonderful.'

Elizabeth Taylor rejoined her family, though the death-knell had
long since sounded on her marriage to Michael Wilding, and in the
meantime Rock was thrilled to be interviewed by *Life* magazine,
until he learned that James Dean had made the cover of America's
most prestigious magazine before him, and without the usual snide
remarks about *his* single status. Though he was pleased with his
stunning cover shot on the 3 October issue – he looks resplendent
and wholesome, with the sleeves of his twill shirt rolled up, wearing
a cravat, and with his thumbs hooked into the waistband of his

denims – he soon wished that he had never spoken to the magazine, for the implications of the piece were positively dynamite:

THE SIMPLE LIFE OF A BUSY BACHELOR: ROCK HUDSON GETS RICH ALONE.

Since 1949, movie fanclubs and fan magazines have parleyed a $75-a-week ex-truck driver named Rock Fitzgerald into a $3,000-a-week movie hero NAMED Rock Hudson . . . But they are now beginning to grumble. Their complaints, expressed in fan magazine articles, range from a shrill SCARED OF MARRIAGE? to a more understanding DON'T RUSH ROCK! Fans are urging 29-year-old Hudson to get married – or explain WHY NOT?

Until now, though Rock and Henry Willson had been dreading his name cropping up in the trash-mags, there had been some slight solace in the fact that by the end of 1955 *their* stories were becoming so convoluted and outrageous that most of their victims, with the aid of a good lawyer, rarely had much difficulty in proving that the editors had made them up. *Life*, however, with its eight-million-plus weekly circulation figures worldwide, was a highly respected institution that did not risk attracting libel suits unless absolutely sure of its facts. And its editor was certain of one thing: reading between the lines, it was obvious that there was much *more* he could have divulged to his readers, even if he had made a lame attempt at defending Rock's bachelor status by adding the coda, 'Hardly anyone has noticed that Rock has been so busy making movies that he has barely had time to get a haircut, let alone a wife.'

The *Life* feature, not unexpectedly, spurred *Confidential*'s Robert Harrison into immediate action, but when Harrison dug out the old Jack Navaar story, vowing to print it with a few recently acquired embellishments, including a 'topless' (in effect, taken on the beach) shot of Rock and George Nader, Henry Willson bought him off again by trading an exposé on Tab Hunter, then involved with the actor Anthony Perkins. Willson also put his foot down with Rock. Dating Phyllis Gates would no longer be deemed sufficient. From now on the pair would have to be seen to be 'co-habiting'.

Exactly how Rock went about persuading Phyllis to do this *and* go away with him most weekends, bearing in mind she had already turned him down not so long before, is not known – though there may be some truth in the sarcastic crack she made after his death, that Rock's finest performances had always been *off* the screen. However, unsure of his exact intentions she did hang on to her apartment and, effectively, her independence.

Phyllis moved into Rock's house on 30 September 1955, the day on which James Dean died. Although Jimmy's love life had always been in turmoil, the real love of his life over the last few months had been his Porsche Spyder – top speed 170 mph – which, on account of his recklessness on the road, his Warner Brothers contract had prohibited him from driving. Jimmy had been scheduled to race professionally at Salinas a few days after completing *Giant* – he had already won a number of trophies – and, ironically, his last celluloid appearance had been on television for a road-safety advertisement commissioned by the National Highway Committee. 'Take it easy driving,' he told Gig Young. 'The life you might save might be mine!'

Jimmy and a driver-mechanic friend, Rolf Wütherich, had set off for Salinas in the silver Spyder, whose colour and minuscule size had rendered it almost inconspicuous in the fading light. Close to the intersection of Highways 466 and 41 near Chalome, well over the speed limit and with his headlights not yet turned on, Jimmy had crashed into another car and died almost instantly . . . his death, three days before the *Rebel Without a Cause* premiere, opening the gates to the most intense, but in this case wholly unprecedented, wave of grief and idolatry since that of Valentino three decades previously.

Jimmy's death affected everyone who had known him professionally, even those who had not liked him much. Elizabeth Taylor was so overcome with shock that she had to be admitted to hospital and kept under sedation. Montgomery Clift, who had carried a torch for Jimmy but never got around to having an actual affair with him, is reported to have 'thrown up over his satin bedsheets'. Phyllis Gates claimed to have discovered Rock sobbing like a child because, he told her, he had felt guilty for wishing Jimmy dead throughout the shooting of *Giant*, peeved because Jimmy had been stealing his thunder. One finds such an admission somewhat hard to swallow, whether or not Rock and Jimmy had been lovers – his surviving friends have ceaselessly proclaimed that with his fun-loving, live-and-let-live outlook on life, Rock was never a malevolent man, not even to his real enemies. Therefore the only explanation for his so-called 'odd' behaviour was that, like Elizabeth Taylor, he had been distressed to lose someone he had cared about so brutally, and at just 24. Indeed, many would probably have considered Rock hard-bitten had he *not* reacted in such a manner.

The cast of *Giant*, however, was allowed little time for mourning, and not one of them attended Jimmy's funeral in Fairmont, Indiana. Jimmy's oration at the close of the film – where the effects of an all-night bender had left his voice virtually inaudible – was overdubbed by Nick Adams, his ex-lover who had appeared in *Rebel Without a Cause*.

Rock actually proposed to Phyllis at the end of October, and she agreed to marry him at once – though she must have been stunned to learn that the ceremony had *already* been arranged to take place secretly, off the coast of Nassau, on the boat owned by a friend of Henry Willson. Phyllis objected to this, having always had her heart set on a Lutheran church wedding. Rock therefore asked her to give him another 24 hours.

In her memoirs Phyllis gives the impression of being unaware that she was being set up – though cynics have suggested that she *must* have known the truth, *and* the fact that marriage at sea would have been regarded as invalid, should there be an eventual divorce and squabbling over the alimony. Whatever, the next morning Rock informed her that the ceremony had been rescheduled to take place at Santa Barbara's Bilton Hotel on 9 November . . . allowing her just ten days to get used to the idea. Rock added that all the other arrangements had also been made: the guest list, the Lutheran minister, the cake and flowers, the honeymoon in Jamaica. The reason for the hurry, Rock explained, was that he needed to be back in Hollywood by 28 November to begin work on his new film, *Written on the Wind* (1956). What he did not add was that even he had been given little say in the proceedings, that everything had been commandeered by Henry Willson with all the precision of a military coup. Phyllis *was* allowed to select her own wedding dress, though Rock chose the colour – the dullest brown. And before she could pick up the telephone to spread the word of her 'good tidings', she was told that the only guests had already been invited – a Universal cameraman who would wire pictures of the happy couple to a surprised world – and Jim Matteoni, a childhood pal from Winnetka who was to be Rock's best man.

Phyllis appears to have had reservations about the nature of Matteoni's friendship with Rock, as well as some other aspects of her intended's past:

> Later I thought how unusual it was that [Rock] had never mentioned Jim Matteoni to me. Jim had obviously been an important figure in Rock's early years, and yet Rock had never talked about him. But then, Rock never discussed his life before becoming an actor . . . He seemed bent on eliminating Roy Fitzgerald from his memory. His life began when he became Rock Hudson.

Matteoni only learned about the wedding eight hours before it was due to take place: Rock and Phyllis picked him and his wife up at the airport, but a delay collecting the marriage licence from the Los Angeles County Court resulted in Rock putting his foot down on the accelerator, and he was stopped by traffic cops outside Santa Barbara and booked for speeding. Otherwise, everything went according to plan. The ceremony lasted just fifteen minutes, and all the other guests at the Biltmore Hotel were told was that a Mr and Mrs Charles Roy were tying the knot. Neither Rock's mother nor Phyllis' parents were told about the wedding – the only other person in on the secret was Pat Devlin, Phyllis' best friend, who was matron of honour. Within minutes of Rock placing the ring on his bride's finger, Henry Willson called Universal's publicist, Jack Diamond, who immediately alerted the press. It was only after the story had been 'leaked' to Hedda Hopper and Louella Parsons that Rock and Phyllis were allowed to contact their families – reading from the script that Henry Willson had prepared to ensure that they both told the same story.

Phyllis cannot possibly have *not* known, by now, that her marriage was nothing more than a deviously arranged sham. It would take her many years to admit this – finally revealing in 1987 to Rock's friends and public what most of them had always suspected. Some of the former, too, would speculate as to whether the union had actually been consummated, or whether Phyllis had merely confirmed that it had – and they had slept together beforehand – to save face. She certainly should never be taken to task for doing so, if this was the case. And Rock, of course, was *the* archetypal heart-throb, promoted as a flawless example of super-virility.

The honeymoon got off to a bad start during the stop-over in Miami, en route to Jamaica. Henry Willson had reserved the couple a suite at the Saxony Hotel, but for some reason this has been double-booked and they were offered a cheaper room at the back of the building. Terrified of being recognised, though by now pictures of the wedding had been circulated everywhere, Rock dispatched his wife to bawl out the desk clerk, and the problem was solved. The next morning, following a brief press conference, the couple flew out to Montego Bay, where they checked in at the Half Moon Hotel, this time as Mr and Mrs Hudson.

Henceforth, according to Phyllis' revelations in her memoirs, Rock's true Jekyll-and-Hyde personality would surface. First he would risk prosecution by encouraging her to engage in passionate sex romps on the beach. Then these would be followed by a brooding period of intense melancholy which would see him rejecting her advances and yelling that he wanted to be alone – it had obviously not taken him long to locate the island's hidden gay hang-outs. She recalled, 'I had known these black moods before. But I never expected it to happen on my honeymoon.'

Rock too observed a change in his wife:

Phyllis was unbeatable. She had the greatest sense of humour in the world . . . it wouldn't quit. She loved games and *she* had to win. We had a ball together until we got married. From that day, it was all over. The white piece of paper changed everything. She became the Movie Star's wife.

Rock claimed that Phyllis had changed from a 'warm-hearted, sensitive girl' into a 'possessive spendthrift who cared for no one but herself'. He told Joan Mac Trevor, a journalist friend of whom more later, 'All my life, everybody I've met has squeezed me like a lemon – none more than my wife.'

On returning home one of Phyllis' first acts, according to Rock, had been to fire his cherished housekeeper – a woman named Truitt. A more likely reason for her dismissal would appear to have been Rock's own assertion that he would no longer *need* a housekeeper now that he had someone else to do the chores. But for all the speculation and stories surrounding the couple, Rock is believed to have genuinely cared for Phyllis.

4

Gentlemen Prefer Blonds

'Rock could be unspeakably vulgar, he cheated on me all the time and sometimes treated me like shit. Would I go through all that again? You bet!'

Massimo, Rock Hudson's Italian lover

Rock began shooting *Written on the Wind* for Universal less than 24 hours after returning from his honeymoon and immediately ran into a behind-the-scenes cat-fight. One of his co-stars, Robert Stack, had headed the credits in *Fighter Squadron* (1948), and though he would eventually count himself among Rock's closest friends, at this time he was vociferously opposed to appearing as a support to a 'two-bit' ham who had been incapable of pronouncing just one line without innumerable takes. Stack, famed for his unsmiling, tough-guy roles – some years later he would portray Eliot Ness in television's *The Untouchables* (1959–63) – was also peeved to learn, after the contracts had been signed, that Henry Willson had tried to persuade the studio to fire Stack and give Rock his part, an act that caused such a furore with all concerned that Universal's head of publicity, David Lipton, was compelled to issue an 'emergency' press statement:

> Rock Hudson would very much like to play the rich drunk, but his fans won't accept his doing anything shoddy. They like him

because he's what they want their daughters to marry, or their children's father to be like, or because he reminds them of their childhood sweetheart. If we let him break out of that sort of character, they'd howl.

In the long run, Stack would have the last laugh by winning an Academy Award for a performance that critics agreed was not a patch on Rock's. According to French singer Edith Piaf, who visited the set several times and socialised with Stack, Rock and Lauren Bacall, Stack was also homophobic. This was a front for Stack's bisexuality and the fact that at the time he was 'amorously interested' in one of Piaf's musicians.

The script for *Written on the Wind* was a controversial one, based on the tempestuous on-off love affair between Montgomery Clift and torch singer Libby Holman. Five years Rock's senior, Monty was so hung up over his homosexuality – much less ashamed of sleeping with men than of having to keep tight-lipped about this for the sake of his career – that he forced himself into relationships with any number of women in a futile attempt to determine upon which side of the fence he truly belonged, when the answer was of course quite clear cut.

Holman, who had known Monty since 1942, was an attractive, olive-skinned, doe-eyed tigress with a penchant for drink and drugs benders, black women, and neurasthenic bisexuals such as Monty and her two husbands. The first of these had been Zachary Smith Reynolds, the twenty-year-old heir to the Camel tobacco emporium, who had been found dead of a gunshot wound early in 1932. Reynolds' family had subsequently attempted to trump up a murder charge, accusing Holman of pulling the trigger, but it had emerged during the trial that Reynolds, a notorious drunk, had killed himself because he had been virtually impotent with his wife and terrified of this becoming public knowledge. Holman had subsequently inherited her husband's fortune and, two months after the trial, she had given birth to a son, Christopher, who sadly died in a climbing accident in 1950, aged 18.

The Holman–Reynolds story, a woeful pastiche of self-loathing if ever there was one, had first hit the screen as *Reckless* in 1935 with

Jean Harlow, William Powell and Franchot Tone. In *Written on the Wind* the protagonists are Lucy and Kyle Hadley (Bacall and Stack), with Rock playing Clift-like go-between, Mitch Wayne. The action begins as it concludes – with a speeding car, howling winds and swirling autumn leaves, and a fatally wounded man staggering out into the night. Then a sudden gust whips back the pages of a desk-diary to the previous year where the melodrama began.

Lucy Moore is the new executive secretary of the Hadley Oil Company, who has not yet met Kyle Hadley, the arrogant heir to its millions. Initially she becomes interested in Mitch, Kyle's best friend of whom he says, 'Mitch is just a country boy – the kind of assets *he's* got, you can't buy for money!' Before Lucy can get to know Mitch, however, Kyle takes over and, giving Mitch the slip, he persuades her into a cab and then on to his private plane. 'Am I safe?' she asks, to which Mitch who, aware of his friend's proclivities has got to the airport first, responds, 'The tanks are loaded and the pilot isn't, for a change!'

The plane conveys the trio to Miami, where only the best is good enough for Lucy: Kyle furnishes her with a suite at the most expensive hotel in town and a new wardrobe of clothes. At first she hesitates, she is not that kind of girl. But then Kyle proposes and they marry. Mitch is not happy with this arrangement; he knows that his friend is unbalanced, though the reason for this – *why* Kyle sleeps with a loaded gun under his pillow – is only hinted at in the film. 'The secret is not to pour the vermouth, but to *pretend* you're pouring it,' he says of his enforced heterosexuality. In other words, to disguise your homosexuality with straight mannerisms.

This homosexual subplot continues and matters are further complicated by the arrival of Kyle's sluttish sister, who is also Mitch's ex-lover, Marylee (Dorothy Malone). Mitch was once so disgusted by her behaviour that he washed out her mouth with soap and water. Marylee hates Kyle because he took Mitch away from her, and she is now intent on getting him back. When he rejects her, however, she eases her frustration by paying men to have sex with her – including a blond stud played by an unbilled actor with whom Rock was having a fling while the film was being made. When Marylee visits the spot next to the lake where she and Mitch used to go skinny-dipping she gazes at their initials, carved into a tree trunk, and becomes so involved with her reminiscences that she appears to be experiencing an orgasm.

For a whole year, seemingly content with his lot, Kyle remains faithful to his wife and stays on the wagon. Then things begin falling apart when the couple decide they want children, for it emerges that he is the one with the problem: a low sperm count that his doctor assures him is not a permanent affliction. Kyle takes the news badly, hitting the bottle again. When Lucy informs him that she is pregnant Kyle, believing the rumour started by the insanely jealous Marylee that the child can only have been fathered by Mitch, beats up his wife, causing her to miscarry.

For Lucy, escape is now the only option. She begs Mitch to take her away, but before this happens Kyle corners him, calls him 'lousy white trash', and pulls a gun. Marylee steps into the breach, wrestles with Kyle for the weapon, but it goes off, killing Kyle. Mitch's troubles are just beginning, however, because Marylee offers him an ultimatum: either he agrees to become her lover again or she will inform the police that *he* killed her brother. Mitch calls her bluff, and for a while she is good to her word – finding compassion only at the inquest when she confesses the truth, allowing Mitch and Lucy to be together at last.

Written on the Wind was a huge commercial success, and forty years after its release the critics were still raving about it. Tony Rayns, writing for *Time Out* on the occasion of the film's inclusion in the *BBC's Top 100 Films Of All Time*, called it, 'One of the quintessential films of the fifties, a conspicuously fierce critique of the disintegrating middle class.' Rayns concluded, 'It's not an *old* film, it's a film of the future.'

Rock, for his part, was never keen on the film and Lauren Bacall positively loathed it. In a rare television interview with Irish critic Mark Cousins in 2000, she scoffed at Cousins' affirmation that it was a masterpiece, booming over the extract in her inimitable basso-profundo drawl, '"What a man tells a woman and a woman tells a man should be written on the wind!" Soap opera beyond soap opera, a masterpiece of suds!' Bacall added that she had never understood the reasons behind Douglas Sirk's cult status, that producer Albert Zugsmith had been a moron . . . and that she had only made the film because she had been so desperate to work with Rock.

As soon as shooting had finished on *Written on the Wind*, Rock announced that he would be taking several weeks off before his next project – *Battle Hymn* (1957) – whether the studio approved or not. He was sick and tired, he said, of the media's intrusion into his private life. For two months Universal's publicity department, in collusion with Henry Willson, had made nuisances of themselves with their persistent 'insights' into the Hudsons' home life. Whenever Rock was not working or giving interviews there would be some journalist or photographer lurking around his property: he was snapped mowing the lawn while Phyllis tended to the weeding, and 'relaxing' on his double-length sofa with his head on Phyllis' lap while she pored over the latest recipe book, deciding what she would be making him for lunch. Alternatively they would be photographed at the barbecue eating one of Rock's famous steaks – one that had been prepared beforehand by Phyllis, for according to his friends Rock never barbecued anything that was even *remotely* edible. 'They had us do everything but pose in bed,' Phyllis remembered. 'And Rock, slave of the media that he was, might have consented if the photographer had asked.'

Henry Willson had tried to make up for selling the George Nader exclusive to *Confidential* by fixing him up with a studio-date and sending the pair off on a picnic with the Hudsons so that *Movie Life* could dispatch one of its hacks and report back with the headline, 'George, The Happy Bachelor Who Dates Pretty Girls And Never Loses His Heart – Or His Head!' Nader *was* photographed with Rock, but the accompanying caption could not have been more catty, 'There's a good reason why George Nader and Rock Hudson have become such fast friends. In a madhouse town where battiness is practically a vogue, these two guys are terrifically, sensationally normal!'

Throwing a few belongings into the back of their station wagon, Rock and Phyllis drove all the way to Acapulco – an exhausting five-day journey, which at least offered the couple a little privacy. But then disaster struck and Rock became ill with food poisoning, an episode which cost Universal dearly: far too unwell to drive, he had to be flown home and the driver who was hired to return Rock's station wagon to Hollywood then had to be flown back to Mexico.

After less than a week's recuperation, Rock began shooting *Battle Hymn* with Douglas Sirk, who, despite his affection for Rock, had not wanted such an affable man portraying staid preacher and war hero Colonel Dean Hess; he would have preferred a less personable actor such as Robert Stack. Some years later he wrote in his autobiography:

> Rock's talent made him cut out for an immovable role, but here I had to cast him in the part of a split character. An actor like Stack would have been much more fitting as I was unable to bend Rock's talent to this type of broken personage – the first reason being his straight goodness of heart and uncomplicated directness. Before the camera you just cannot cheat . . .

Rock's official co-stars in *Battle Hymn* were Martha Hyer (then 'dating' George Nader to keep the likes of *Confidential* quiet) and Dan Duryea, who were acted into the ground by Anna Kashfi (who was about to be married to Marlon Brando) and Philip Ahn (1908– 78), the actor son of a Korean diplomat who had died in a Japanese POW camp. Ahn was a veteran of dozens of films but probably best known as the old man in the *Kung Fu* (1972) television series.

Battle Hymn tells the true story, though not without the customary sprinkling of Hollywood invention, of how Dean Hess valiantly made amends for his fatal error during World War II when, on account of a faulty undercarriage mechanism on his plane, he accidentally bombed a German orphanage killing 37 children. 'A crime so despicable that even Hell won't have its perpetrator,' the German radio announcer rants, breaking the news to a shocked nation and obviously forgetting the horrors that *his* compatriots are wreaking on Europe. 'His hands will be stained for ever with the innocent blood of those harmless innocents.'

After the war, Hess returns to Ohio, where he marries and accepts a ministry. Even serving God, however, does not salve his conscience, and upon the outbreak of the Korean War in 1950 he re-enlists with the Air Force, hoping that participating in a non-combat training programme in South Korea will help. His men here are an uninspiring bunch, lazy and undisciplined – none more so than Skidmore (former musical-comedy actor Don DeFore), who served with him during the last war and cannot understand why he has suddenly lost his famous 'killer' instinct. What Hess does not wish Skidmore or the others to know is that he is a man of God, fearing this might lose him their respect. He soon knocks them into shape and, with the help of pretty local En Soon Yang (Kashfi) the dilapidated airbase they are repairing becomes operable once more.

At a Thanksgiving celebration for his men, Hess notices that Korean orphans are sneaking into the camp to steal scraps from the dustbins. He takes pity on them and orders the cook to feed them. 'What's he trying to do?' asks the cook. 'Prove he's got a heart of gold?' But Hess *does* have a heart of gold, and word of this spreads quickly. An old man (Ahn) he picks up on the road leads him to a bombed out Buddhist temple where more orphaned children are being cared for by En Soon Yang. Hess has the place repaired, and organises food, protection and medical supplies.

Then his cover is blown: a letter arrives from America addressed to *Reverend* Hess, and En Soon Yang is dismayed to learn that the man she is falling in love with is not only married, but about to become a father. Equally dismayed, Hess' men now regard him as a risk. Supposing he had to gun down a plane and go against the dictates of the Bible by taking a life? Yet when Skidmore is mortally wounded, he takes comfort from dying in the presence of a holy man. 'Think of life as a shadowy place, crowded with people who can't see each other very well.' Hess soothes, to Frank Skinner's superb arrangement of 'Battle Hymn of the Republic'. 'Think also of the door just beyond. When that door opens, we pass through into a wonderful brightness . . . it's just a gentle step from darkness to light!'

The agony of war has enabled Hess to find himself, something he has been unable to do until now. Then he learns that the temple-orphanage is about to be attacked again by enemy planes, and not really knowing where they are heading for he, En Soon Yang, the old man and four hundred children take to the road. In the ensuing carnage, En Soon Yang makes the ultimate sacrifice while protecting a child – she dies in Hess's arms, the nearest they have come to actually declaring their love for each other. Soon afterwards, Hess and the children are rescued by US planes and airlifted to safety, and this wonderful, thought-provoking film ends with him and his wife visiting the En Soon Yang Orphanage at Cheju-Do, dedicated to the memory of his lost love.

The film brought about a furious argument between the Hudsons when, according to Phyllis, Rock exclaimed how much he *loved* war, regardless of the innocent lives inadvertently lost in any conflict. When Phyllis challenged him over the statement, however, his response was, 'Oh, I don't think about that. I just love war!' Her reaction to this was understandably bitter: Rock, she declared, was a movie star whose word was the law. Absolutely no one dared contradict him, not even the studio moguls. And because she did not share Rock's views, Phyllis was not allowed to accompany him to Nogales, Arizona, where the battle scenes were shot. This left Rock free to engage in several not so discreet one-night stands with some of the extras.

Halfway through filming *Battle Hymn*, Rock found himself on the receiving end of a vituperous telephone call from Libby Holman, who had seen some of the rushes from *Written on the Wind*. Back in 1949, Holman had forced Montgomery Clift to turn down the role of Joe Gillis, the kept man in *Sunset Boulevard* (1950), claiming that the scriptwriter Charles Brackett had deliberately based ageing ex-movie siren Norma Desmond on her. Even though Monty had tried to soothe Libby by threatening to 'kick the fuck out of that big lump of wood', the two men became instant friends when they met courtesy of Elizabeth Taylor, who had chosen Monty to star opposite her in *Raintree County* (1957) – at a time when the studios were reluctant to employ him on account of his drinking and opiate addiction.

Raintree County had gone into production in April 1956, by which time the Taylor–Wilding marriage had reached crisis point. It didn't help that *Confidential*'s Robert Harrison had stuck his oar in by hiring a reporter to follow the couple to Morocco, where Wilding had filmed *Zarak* (1956) with Anita Ekberg and Victor Mature – and, according to John Parker's *Five for Hollywood* (Carol, 1989), had promptly, but with flimsy evidence, concluded that Elizabeth had had a fling with Mature.

Elizabeth's new film, a classic tale of the American Civil War directed by Edward Dmytryk, merely offered her union with Wilding a little breathing space. During this time Monty and the Hudsons frequently found themselves caught up in the crossfire between the feuding couple, though the dinner party at their Coldwater Canyon home on the evening of 12 May was a somewhat muted affair. Wilding was assigned to the couch suffering from agonising backache, Monty was sulking because the director had forbidden him to drink until *Raintree County* was completed – so it had been left to the Hudsons and Monty's friend, the actor Kevin McCarthy, to enliven the proceedings by cracking jokes and telling witty anecdotes. This did not work, and at around 10.30 Monty announced that he was leaving. Because he had been cautioned by the police so many times on account of his reckless driving, Monty had not been behind the wheel of his car for months and Edward Dmytryk had provided him with a chauffeur. Tonight, however, was the chauffeur's night off and Monty had driven himself to the Wildings' house – and now, apprehensive about tackling the steep, poorly lit road down to Sunset Boulevard, it was agreed that Kevin McCarthy should lead the way by driving in front of him.

On the way down, Monty suffered a blackout and crashed into a telegraph pole, suffering the most horrendous facial injuries: two fractures to the jaw, severe lacerations, an almost severed lip and a smashed nose. The ambulance took more than half an hour to reach the scene, though press photographers tipped off by the emergency services, as often happened with celebrity mishaps, were there within minutes, as were Rock, Phyllis and Elizabeth who, in no uncertain terms, threatened what would happen should anyone take so much as a single shot. Then, while Rock tried to force open the front door of the car – a complete write-off – Elizabeth crawled through the rear window to find Monty choking on two dislodged front teeth. In pushing her fingers down his throat and extracting these she effectively saved his life and, her beautiful white dress drenched in blood, she cradled Monty's head in her lap all the way to the hospital.

In the subsequent series of operations, Monty's face and teeth were completely reconstructed, and only his closest friends were allowed to see him. He refused to drop out of *Raintree County*, and this was eventually completed with his profile filmed mostly from the right – the other side of his face would remain frozen due to the severed nerve in his cheek – and the actor once hailed as the most beautiful man in America would never be the same again.

Phyllis had also accompanied Monty in the back of the ambulance, and she and Elizabeth had sat by his bedside throughout the night. Phyllis later confessed how this had caused an almighty bust-up between herself and Rock and that afterwards he had not spoken to her for days – angry, it would appear, because she had committed the unpardonable sin of speaking to the press. 'I thought I had acted selflessly, trying to be of help in a drastic situation,' she recalled. 'But he acted as if I had been guilty of some transgression. Was it because *I* had been in the spotlight and he hadn't?'

In fact, Rock was paranoid about his wife speaking to anyone about *anything* when he was not peering over her shoulder, even their closest friends, albeit that most of these knew more about his pre-stardom days than Phyllis ever would. It is therefore not difficult to imagine his reaction when he learned that she had consulted a specialist about his alleged premature ejaculation. She wrote in her memoirs, 'I realised that all husbands were different and perhaps he was just going through a phase where he couldn't control his exuberance.'

However, according to Massimo, who I met in Paris in 1992, '*If* Rock ever had sex with that woman, and it's a big if, he would have wanted to get it over with as quickly as possible so that he could save the real passion for the next guy. When it came to staying power, Rock Hudson had invented the term!'

Worse still, Phyllis discussed Rock's mood-swings with a psychiatrist – the sombre depressions followed by moments of unprecedented hilarity, such as some of the exhibitionist tricks he played on her and their friends. For example, one of Rock's 'party pieces' was to walk into a room, stark naked with his erect penis tucked back between his legs so that he looked like a woman. After executing a clumsy ballet routine he would then release it so that it slapped against his stomach. The first time Phyllis witnessed him doing this, she tried to laugh off her embarrassment by reminding him that he looked like 'one of the dancing hippos in *Fantasia*'. Alternatively he would purposely forget to shower, raise his arms and ask her, 'Wanna smell my pits?'

The Hudsons' marriage started to hit rock bottom when, shortly after Montgomery Clift's accident, Rock signed a loan-out contract with MGM for *Something of Value* (1957), much of which would be shot on location in Kenya. Peeved over the predicted success of *Giant* – the film was still being meticulously edited by George Stevens, but receiving unprecedented press interest owing to the sudden iconic status of James Dean – Universal attempted to sweeten Rock into staying with them by offering him a 'belated honeymoon' – a two-week, all-expenses-paid trip to Europe, which would take place immediately before he began filming in Africa. Rock accepted the gift, but gave no indication to Universal as to what his future plans might be. Before leaving for Europe the couple spent a few days with Phyllis' family in Montevideo – the first time the Gates had seen him. According to Phyllis, it was an irritating sojourn for Rock, who was pestered non-stop by autograph hunters and was extremely reluctant to show these people the time of day until she persuaded him otherwise.

The first stop in Europe was Paris, where the Hudsons stayed at the Plaza Athéné in its fabulous honeymoon suite – the most expensive in the city at that time. Rock was amused to study the suite's register of former guests – in 1924 and 1926 it had been occupied by Rudolph Valentino and the greatest love of his life, a handsome French reporter named André Daven, who had subsequently starred opposite him in a film and openly been installed as his 'husband' at Valentino's Hollywood mansion. But if Rock was hoping to find *his* knight in shining armour in Paris, he would be disappointed: the press and paparazzi trailed the couple everywhere as they visited all the tourist attractions and ended their first day at the plush Tour d'Argent restaurant.

Rome, however, was another matter. Immediately upon his arrival there, Rock contacted Massimo, the young Italian he had met while filming *Captain Lightfoot*. Not content with their afternoon assignations – while Phyllis was being driven around the city's shops by a studio-hired chauffeur – Rock made the very grave mistake of introducing Massimo to his wife, in full public view in the packed lobby of the Grand Hotel.

Since their last romantic assignation, Massimo had appeared in *Suor Letizia* (1957) with Anna Magnani, without any doubt the finest dramatic actress Italy produced, and it would appear that Rock – who had raved over Magnani's recent Oscar-winning performance in *The Rose Tattoo* (1955), opposite Burt Lancaster – was just as excited at the prospect of lunching with her, courtesy of Massimo, as he was of seeing more of the handsome stud.

Phyllis was aware of Rock's relationship with Massimo and devoted a whole chapter of her memoirs ('The Clash in Rome') to the following episode. In the hotel lobby she became wildly hysterical, called the Italian a 'silly little fruitcake' – not an apt euphemism, for Massimo was a big man and not remotely effeminate – and for her pains received a smack across the mouth. The blow was not a heavy one – Rock almost certainly had slapped her only to curb her hysteria – but his fingers snagged in the string of pearls she was wearing, snapping it and sending the pearls scattering across the marble floor. The incident made the front page of at least one Italian newspaper, which made only passing reference to 'Mr Hudson's actor friend', but nevertheless printed the damning claim that Rock had been drunk at the time of the 'attack' and that Phyllis had been so terrified of him hitting her again that she had asked the hotel to post an armed guard outside her room. As for Rock, he spent the night with Massimo.

News of the Hudsons' fight over Massimo was relayed to Robert Harrison, who immediately commissioned an exclusive for *Confidential*, 'Big Rock And His Roman Romeo', which though not actually stating that Rock and Massimo were lovers *did* state that he preferred being with 'the lusty Latin' than with Phyllis, which reading between the lines was of course the same thing.

Once again, the wily Henry Willson stepped into the breach, this time with what might have been Harrison's biggest ever scoop –

along with a substantial pay-off, he fed him the trashy titbit about Elvis Presley's relationship with Nick Adams, a promiscuous homosexual who had starred with James Dean in *Rebel Without a Cause*. Elvis and Adams, also a procurer of drugs and rent boys for studio bigwigs, had been photographed cruising the streets of Memphis on twin Harley-Davidson motorcycles, and Willson actually supplied the caption, 'Elvis: How I Like To Ride With The Guys'. This story would turn out to be true, though it never made the printed page – both Elvis and Rock were let off the hook when, for a second time, the scapegoat was Rory Calhoun. Ironically, Calhoun later became Adams' last lover in 1968.

The Hudsons had been scheduled to fly from Rome to Nairobi, where Rock would spend several days getting used to the climate and conditions before beginning work on *Something of Value*. Based on the best-selling novel by Robert Ruark, this told of the then-ongoing Mau Mau uprising and would provide Rock with one of his most acclaimed dramatic roles. Initially, because of the Rome incident, Phyllis refused to accompany him, and Rock was all for leaving her behind and taking Massimo instead – an idea that was quickly put out of his head by Universal's Italian representative. The last thing the studio wanted to read in the tabloids was that their golden boy had split with his wife halfway through the honeymoon *they* had paid for and gone off with a man that they had known about for some time.

Phyllis, the innocent party, was contacted – almost certainly by Henry Willson, for only he would be capable of such vitriolic action – and threatened with the exposure of a story he had concocted concerning her alleged lesbian affairs, of which he appears to have had absolutely no proof. Willson would repeat the ruse several times in the near future, and Phyllis knew only too well that in his utterly shameless world of double standards, Rock's agent would have stopped at nothing to protect his investment.

She could of course have beaten them both at their own game by exposing Rock to the media and ending all the speculation; she certainly had enough evidence. And whether, as Willson claimed, she refrained from doing so out of fear of having to forfeit the formidable luxury that came with being married to a top-name movie star, or whether she genuinely loved Rock as much as she claimed, was yet to be determined.

Whatever the reason, at the eleventh hour Phyllis was persuaded to accompany Rock to Nairobi, though on account of the escalating danger, Universal should never have allowed this. The Mau Mau, Kenya's secret militant Kikuyu guerrilla movement, had been in operation since 1952. Its aim was to end British colonial rule, a goal that would be achieved in 1960 with the granting of the country's independence and the election of Jomo Kenyatta as Kenya's first prime minister.

By the time of the Hudsons' visit, colonial government forces had set up a despicable exercise in ethnic cleansing and killed over 10,000 Kikuyu, Kenya's largest ethnic group, and the Mau Mau had retaliated with unprecedented brutality. Absolutely nowhere was safe and Phyllis, who spent much of her stay confined to her suite at the New Stanley Hotel while Rock was filming, cannot have had an easy time. Neither was there much fun to be had once the day's shooting had been canned. Phyllis got on well with Rock's co-stars, Sidney Poitier and, in a rare film outing, the distinguished British stage actress Wendy Hiller, but she loathed the director, Richard Brooks, on account of his coarseness.

Brooks was almost as renowned for his vulgarity as for his gritty scripts and supremely professional direction, but many of the actresses who worked with him – including Alexis Smith, Pier Angeli and the equally foul-mouthed Bette Davis – maintained that complaining about Brooks' anti-social behaviour only made him worse. Phyllis was having none of this and the last straw came when Brooks took Rock into the very heart of the Mau Mau country to meet some of them. As he had upset her by declaring how much he loved war, he did so again by informing her that the Mau Mau were actually 'very nice people'. Regardless of what Henry Willson or the Universal executives might say, a few days later Phyllis caught the first available plane out of Nairobi and returned to Los Angeles.

'When we take away from a man his traditional way of life, his customs, his religion, we had better make certain to replace them with SOMETHING OF VALUE.' So declare the opening credits of this harrowing, profoundly disturbing film. Rock played Peter

McKenzie, the quietly spoken white settler's son, who has watched his family struggle to maintain their farmstead, but has nevertheless enjoyed a peaceable existence. He and his Kikuyu best friend, Kimani (Poitier), attended missionary school together and until now (1945) have been more like brothers – indeed, Kimani's mother brought him up after the death of his own mother. Times, however, have changed and it is only Peter who does not look upon Kimani as just another cheap hired hand, or frown on the customs of his people: incest, female circumcision, bestiality and sacrifice, and the ritual smothering of 'demon' babies born feet-first.

Some of the Kikuyu, who outnumber the whites by 150–1, are tired of being treated like dirt by these so-called masters and are starting to fight back. 'You can't treat an African like a brother and expect to have a good servant,' Peter's brother-in-law, Jeff Newton (Robert Beatty), opines, adding, 'Blacks are blacks – not playmates.'

When Newton bullies Kimani once too often – slapping him, something even his own very strict father has *never* done – the lad realises that it is time to act and runs off to join the rising Mau Mau faction, whose leaders quickly determine that he possesses leadership potential. The story then jumps to 1952 and the eve of the Mau Mau uprising, with the Day of the Long Knives, when Peter is about to marry his long-term fiancée Holly (Wynter).

After a gruesome blood-drinking initiation ceremony, Kimani is ordered to join the party that will attack the McKenzie farmstead. Horrified, he stands back and watches his men butcher them – Newton and his two children are killed and his pregnant wife Elizabeth (Hiller) is badly injured, but Peter and Holly, who married that day, are on safari. Their being spared does not make Kimani feel any less guilty, and he disappears into the jungle.

Peter eventually tracks him down and they arrange a meeting that will hopefully bring about an end to the conflict – one which cinemagoers instinctively knew would only fail because Kenya was still in a state of emergency when the film was released in June 1957, and would remain so for another three years. A rival farmer (Michael Pate) learns of the friends' plan, gets there first with a contingency of vigilantes, and in the ensuing scuffle most of Kimani's men are killed, as is his wife. Believing that Peter has betrayed him, Kimani seeks only revenge, but in the final showdown he falls to his death on to the spikes of the lion-pit he himself has dug. An inevitably futile ending is made only slightly more satisfying by Peter's rescuing of Kimani's infant son, who will now be raised alongside Elizabeth's child, just as he and Kimani were raised, but hopefully to a better future, as the words of Sir Winston Churchill flash across the screen, 'The problems of East Africa are the problems of the world.'

On account of the tense political situation in Kenya, the locations for *Something of Value* were wrapped up in less than a month, and Rock flew back to the United States. Instead of heading straight home, he stopped off for a week in New York, later swearing to Phyllis that this had been to negotiate a film contract. She doesn't appear to have believed him, for she had long suspected that almost every one of the calls he had made to her from Henry Willson's office in the past, claiming that the studio had asked him to work over, had been but subterfuge for his 'homosexual dalliances'.

Among the pile of letters marked 'Personal' that Rock opened upon his return home was one from an eleven-year-old Australian fan, Lynette Flood. Rock was so gutted by its contents that he burst into tears halfway through reading it. The little girl was suffering from a brain tumour and had asked for a signed photograph of her idol. Rock called her family and learned that since writing the letter, Lynette had had the tumour removed and was now in remission. Though very concerned, Rock called her family and joked that this was just as well – he was extremely busy at the moment and Lynette would have to fetch the photograph herself to save him having to walk to the mailbox! He then paid for her and her parents to fly out to Hollywood, and cancelled several engagements so that he could personally drive them around Hollywood and show them all the sights. The *Sydney Morning Herald* reported, 'There are many stars in Hollywood, but if you put all their hearts together they still wouldn't be half as big as Rock Hudson's.'

On 10 October 1956 – after George Stevens had taken over a year to assemble the inordinate amount of edited footage – *Giant* received its world premiere at the New York Roxy. Rock's 'date' with

Tallulah Bankhead was to be their public outing that year. Earlier, at the Oscars ceremony, the undisputed Queen of One-Liners had uttered her famous 'I have learned that he carries a magic weapon' quip. Tonight she told a bemused young woman reporter, 'I'm here tonight because this *divine* young thing is a *giant* in every conceivable way, darling!' Twenty years on, the occasion still evoked a shiver when Rock recalled it in his interview with Gordon Gow:

> Outside the theater were thousands of people. Traffic was blocked. All of that. And I thought, 'My God, *I'm* in this movie playing one of the leads!' Jesus, it was exciting! Then I sat there in my seat and I was booed throughout the film. It was terrifying. And it wasn't until the fight near the end of the film – where the bigot I was playing was tangling with a worse bigot and getting a couple of good licks on him – that suddenly I was applauded. And it was only then that I realised that the audience was reacting so volubly to the *character*. Not to me, but to Bick.

One week later, *Giant* opened at Grauman's Chinese Theater, outside of which Rock and Elizabeth Taylor had left their hand- and footprints in the famous pavement cement. Rock was this time accompanied by Phyllis, along with the Wildings and friends Mark Miller and George Nader. Guests of honour were Clark Gable, Joan Crawford, Natalie Wood and Tab Hunter – the latter two an 'item' representing the Willson stable. The film was subsequently nominated for ten Academy Awards, two more than *Around the World in Eighty Days* (1956), the epic directed by Mike Todd, who married Elizabeth Taylor a few weeks before the Oscars ceremony. For *Giant*, Rock would be nominated Best Actor and James Dean Best Supporting Actor, though neither would win – the Oscars went to to Yul Brynner for *The King and I* (1956) and Anthony Quinn for *Lust for Life* (1956) respectively.

The missed Oscar would niggle at Rock and, according to his intimate circle, only exacerbate the arrogance that had been on the increase since the runaway success of *Magnificent Obsession*. There was, however, some compensation when he was voted Number One in Hollywood's Name-power Top Ten, a position he would hold seven years running. Although Rock was not initially thrilled with the accolade, as he explained to David Castell:

> I was earning money for the studio, that's true, but I was hardly becoming a millionaire myself. I didn't mind that so much. *What* I minded was that the studio always thought of me as a young newcomer. I had to fight and fight to get more worthwhile parts. They would say how difficult it was to get good material, but I'd say, 'I know, but other studios manage!'

On 9 November 1956, their first wedding anniversary, a huge party was thrown for the Hudsons at Henry Willson's Stoke Canyon home – all hype, of course, for the first thing Willson did once the arrangements had been made and the invitations dispatched was to inform the press how much he had spent – adding that $10,000 was but a 'snip' to show how much his boy was appreciated. Willson even hired gossip-column hacks to write about the event to reiterate to their readers that Rock and Phyllis really were the most perfectly matched pair in Hollywood, as blissfully happy now as when they had first wed, which of course was not true.

'Rock glided me over the dance floor amid the applause of the guests,' Phyllis remembered, 'and I found myself almost believing that miracles do happen.' The press, however, knew nothing about the 'fuck-buddy bash' that Willson had organised for the next evening at the same venue, to use up all the leftover food and drink. This time the guests of honour were some of the young men he had discovered, seduced and set on the pathway to fame, and a good many more who had failed to get past the initial hurdle but who were kept on Willson's books for stud and escort work – more than fifty in all.

The following year, 1957, got off to a good start with Rock completing his thirty-sixth film, *The Tarnished Angels*, reuniting the Stack–Sirk–Malone trio that had helped make *Written on the Wind* so memorable – though Robert Stack's attitude towards Rock was even more hostile than before, this time on account of Douglas Sirk's over-the-top favouritism and his insistence that Rock go off and prepare for his role as any Method actor might have done. Rock jumped at the opportunity to emulate the likes of Brando and Clift. He told David Castell:

> That should have been a terrific part, that of a drunken-out shell of an alcoholic, a newspaperman who finds a story and a romance with a flying circus. I took it very seriously and bought clothes that looked like dishrags. Douglas Sirk was very happy with my approach to the role. In those days it took two days to see the rushes. When the studio heads saw them, they threw up their hands. They couldn't have their star looking such a mess. We were ordered to re-shoot and my whole wardrobe was changed. I even had a hat with a press-ticket in the brim. After that, my heart wasn't in it.

Sirk's defence of Rock resulted in the director being given a severe ear-bashing by the chiefs at Universal. Astonishingly, they accused him of deliberately trying to sabotage Rock's career and informed him that he would never work with Rock again, and he never did.

The Tarnished Angels is a sombre, stream-of-consciousness tale set in the height of the American Depression. It was based on the novel *Pylon* by William Faulkner, the undisputed master of the genre, who regularly visited the set. Faulkner was impressed by Rock's much underrated performance as Burke Devlin, the no-nonsense, chain-smoking reporter who stumbles upon a human interest story when Roger Shumann (Stack), a renowned World War I ace now reduced to competing in carnival stunt-races, arrives in town. With him are his parachutist wife, LaVerne (Malone), their mechanic, Jiggs (Jack Carson), and their small son who, when Devlin befriends him at the start of the picture, is not sure whether Shumann or Jiggs, is his father.

Devlin is appalled by LaVerne's story of how, after she became pregnant, Shumann and Jiggs threw dice to determine which of them should wed her, since which time her husband has cared for nothing but his plane. Devlin's editor, however, is not interested in publishing this story, and fires him for losing his temper – something that makes the intrepid reporter more determined to help LaVerne and set her back on the rails, mindless of the fact that he has fallen in love with her.

Shumann will do anything to win his next big race – looping between the pylons that gave Faulkner's book its title, despite the danger towards others and himself. He causes the death of a rival (Troy Donahue), then sets his sights on the young man's wrecked plane, giving Jiggs just hours to repair it before the race. The plane is actually owned by Shumann's mortal enemy, Ord (Robert Middleton), and to acquire it Shumann thinks nothing of sending LaVerne over to Ord's hotel to prostitute herself. Devlin intervenes, promising Ord the headlines in his newspaper – the one he no longer works for! – provided he agrees to a partnership with Shumann.

The race goes ahead, but Shumann's plane develops engine trouble and instead of making an emergency landing, fearful of crashing into the crowd of spectators that had rushed on to the field, he plunges into the lake and dies the death of a hero. 'There's an old saying – nobody really dies until he's forgotten,' Devlin consoles the widow, to whom Shumann has expressed his true feelings shortly before the fatal race. Devlin then gets drunk, barges into the newspaper office and delivers a lengthy, highly charged diatribe worthy of a Welles or an Olivier. The editor gives him his job back, and he unselfishly pays for LaVerne and her son to return to her family.

The film was shot in monochrome and its final image – Rock's imposing, manly figure silhouetted against a cloudy sky – quite possibly remains his most classic pose.

Troy Donahue, twenty when he appeared in *The Tarnished Angels*, only did so because Rock had told Henry Willson that, if he could no longer go on the so-called prowl in search of lovers, henceforth he that have to supply him with a TBF – Token Blond Fuck – for the duration of the shooting schedule of every film he made, a 'tradition' that would continue well into Rock's career as a television icon. Uncannily resembling Massimo, and just as big and beefy, their on–off affair lasted longer than most and outlived his several months only marriage to Rock's friend, Suzanne Pleshette – probably because he *was* so like Massimo.

Unlike the dishy Italian, however, the rot soon set in after Donahue's failed marriage: the star of *A Summer Place* (1959) and television's long-running *77 Sunset Strip* (1958), who sent millions of teenage hearts fluttering, faded quickly as he piled on the pounds and the good roles stopped coming in. He died virtually ignored on 11 September 2001, the day of the New York terrorists attack, and on the same day as Rock's co-star in *The Tarnished Angels*, Dorothy Malone.

Though still contracted to Universal, the rushes for *The Tarnished Angels* and *Battle Hymn* led to Rock being courted by several of the other major studios. MGM offered him the ultimate lead in their remake of *Ben-Hur* (1959) – the original of 1925 had featured one of his idols, Ramon Novarro. Rock provisionally accepted the role until Henry Willson reminded him that *he* had seen enough of Rock in skirts at some of their boys-only parties without him making a spectacle of himself in a toga. Also, Willson added, there was the unmistakable homosexual subplot, albeit subdued, where the second lead, Mesala, is clearly revealed to be carrying a torch for the hero. The role, of course, eventually went to fellow Illinoisan, Charlton Heston.

Next he was considered for *Sayonara* (1957), until Willson gave this one the thumbs-down after perusing the script. There was a distinct difference between the surly, obnoxious racist in this film, Willson declared, and the Mexican-hating Bick Benedict because in the end Bick had seen the error of his ways and reformed. The part went to Marlon Brando, and Henry Willson elected that Rock's next big role would be in Ernest Hemingway's somewhat heavy-going saga of World War I, *A Farewell to Arms* (1957), which had first been filmed in 1932 with Gary Cooper and Helen Hayes. Rock's agent boasted that it would turn him into a living legend and offer Twentieth Century Fox's David O Selznick his biggest blockbuster since *Gone with the Wind* in 1939.

The production was certainly possessed of all the perfect ingredients. The screenplay was by Ben Hecht, the most versatile scriptwriter in Hollywood at that time, whose many credits, besides *Gone with the Wind*, included *Gunga Din* (1939), *Notorious* (1946) and *Wuthering Heights* (1939). Vittorio De Sica would produce, John Huston would direct, and Rock's co-stars would be Jennifer Jones (Mrs Selznick), De Sica himself, Oscar Homolka and Mercedes McCambridge.

It would be the costliest enterprise thus far in Rock's career because, although Universal would rake in a cool $450,000 for loaning him out to Selznick, Rock's salary would amount to but a fraction of this. This mattered little to him and such was their confidence in the outcome of the film that he, Willson and Henry Ginsberg (a *Giant* co-producer) had formed their own company, Seven Picture Corporation, with Rock owning 36 per cent of the shares and Ginsberg and Willson 24 per cent each. The remaining 5 per cent, they agreed, should go to Phyllis – to keep her on side now that she had discovered that her husband was 'up to tricks' again.

Phyllis certainly revealed in her memoirs how at around this time she had begun answering the telephone to 'young male voices' asking for Rock, but that when she had questioned him about these he had replied that they were fans and subsequently changed his number. Rock realised, though, that there would have to be a change of tactics, so he asked Henry Willson to begin supplying him with 'dick-fodder', most of these acting hopefuls whose reward for sleeping with Rock, besides huge payoffs providing they kept their mouths shut and ruin if they did not, would be a promise of stardom. Although Rock had condemned this practice in the past, declaring that it was much more rewarding to go off in search of his own fun, cruising for sex was now totally out of the question. Especially since Phyllis had followed up on one of the mysterious telephone calls and had had Rock trailed to an Ocean Drive leather bar where he had been observed with Troy Donahue making a pick-up. Therefore, to tide himself over until he left for Italy to film the locations for *A Farewell to Arms* – this time, he had already concocted an excuse for not taking Phyllis with him – Rock made do with Willson's paid escorts and, when his wife was not at home, seduced his hunky part-time gardener.

In the February, meanwhile, *Battle Hymn* went on general release and Rock and Phyllis, pretending to be riding the crest of a wave of wedded bliss, were asked to participate in a nationwide promotional tour. This kicked off in Chicago, where the 'local boy made big' was made a tremendous fuss of. The couple then moved on to Dean Hess' hometown of Marietta, Ohio, where the local university awarded Rock an honorary Humanities degree.

In New York, at the end of the month, there was mass hysteria at the Capitol Theater when thousands of screaming fans prevented Rock from entering the building for over an hour – he and Phyllis had to be sneaked in through a side door. According to her, Rock was incredibly shy and hated such hero worship. Just as he had in Montevideo, he refused to sign autographs. Towards the end of the tour, Phyllis was taken ill with what was diagnosed at the time as ptomaine poisoning; Rock was apparently as indifferent towards her suffering than he had been towards his fans, leaving her alone much of the time when they returned home.

In a seemingly mindless act of revenge, Phyllis took Rock's favourite collection of Levi denims out into the garden and incinerated them – something she later attributed to the effects of her illness, which was getting steadily worse. 'Maybe I thought an extreme act would get his attention,' she recollected. 'If so, it didn't work.' A few days later, Rock left for Italy, well aware that after just sixteen months his marriage was all but over and that the pretence would have to cease.

5

Requiem for a Bride

'That Gates intends to give the impression of naivety is strongly evident. Her story is a reworking of one of the staple plot lines of the Gothic novel: the heroine's "dream" marriage gradually turns into a nightmare.'

Richard Lippe, analyst, *CineAction!*

Rock was strongly advised not to do *A Farewell to Arms* by Montgomery Clift, who concluded that its production setup would endanger his sanity. Only a few years previously David O Selznick had sweet-talked Monty into making *Indiscretion of an American Housewife* (1954), with the same team of actor-director Vittorio De Sica, Jennifer Jones, extras and technicians that was to be employed for the new film. Shot on location in Rome, the production had been a nightmare from start to finish. De Sica had spoken virtually no English at the time, making it obligatory for an interpreter to be on set at all times. Jennifer Jones had put in a mediocre performance and, because she had been the boss's wife, her every whim and demand had been met, regardless of the anxieties this had caused the rest of the unit. As a result of Clift's experience with this film, self-professed megalomaniac Selznick – hugely respected by the industry, while at the same time reviled by just about everyone who crossed his path – would bear the ignominious nickname 'Interfering Fuckface' until the day of his death in 1965, courtesy of Montgomery Clift.

Rock ignored his friend's warning, but was pleased when Selznick informed him that Vittorio De Sica was to be replaced by John Huston, a director he had always admired and who, aware of his sexuality, granted his request that Massimo be given a bit part. This, he joked, would compensate for his 'distress' upon learning that Jennifer Jones' actual first name was Phyllis! He was not in such affable spirits, however, when, once the contract had been signed, Selznick told him that in order to placate a distraught De Sica, he had offered the temperamental Italian third billing!

What Selznick did not reckon on was John Huston's reverence of Hemingway and his hatred of the all too frequent 'Hollywoodising' of the classics – in this instance making the on-screen romance between the two leads central to the plot, which was not as Hemingway had intended. Huston, not content with disobeying Selznick's orders, threatened to 'beat the crap' out of him unless he started showing the author some respect – a threat which, with the directors' legendary reputation for brawling, was taken seriously. Selznick fired him.

Selznick persisted in interfering after Huston had been replaced by Charles 'King' Vidor. Rock had got away with keeping his own hairstyle – Selznick had wanted him to have a military-style, razor-cut short-back-and-sides in keeping with the period, which, Rock declared, would have made him look like Erich von Stroheim – but for some reason Selznick took an almost paranoid dislike to Rock's Adam's apple, which, when Rock was filmed in profile or feeling nervous – most of the time during this picture – was prominent and wobbly.

Unlike many of his big star contemporaries, Rock was always restrained on the set and never bawled anyone out, much preferring to slope off somewhere and sulk in the hope that this would get him his way. Selznick, however, was an intensely unpleasant, stubborn man and for weeks, until the studio make-up department solved the problem by applying a camouflaging lotion, his bone of contention was not Rock's persistent fluffing of his lines – this time through stress and not any lack of professionalism – but the offending Adam's apple.

A Farewell to Arms, subtitled 'A Romantic Tragedy of World War One', opens with Lieutenant Frederic Henry (Rock), an American serving with the Ambulance Corps, as Hemingway himself had done, returning from leave to the 'snow-capped mountains and muddy plains' of northern Italy just as the country is about to launch an offensive against Germany and Austria. Like many Hemingway characters, Henry despises the futility of war and is agnostic because he believes that no caring God would permit such horrors to take place. His friend Major Rinaldi (De Sica) suffers from permanent depression because he is used to treating the old and infirm and cannot relate to the loss of so many young lives. At the local hospital, English nurse Catherine Barkley (Jones) finds herself similarly disillusioned as her lover of eight years has recently been blown to bits by the enemy.

This psychological cocktail of trauma and bewilderment causes Frederic and Catherine to fall in love and the night before Henry's division has to leave for the Alps, he makes a pass at her. Catherine slaps him, then professes instant, almost neurotic remorse for doing so. They spend the night together, during which she fantasises that she is with her deceased lover, though by morning she is sworn to her new love. Then she sees him off, ultimately getting lost in the crowd in a scenario hugely reminiscent of the closing scene in Marcel Carné's French masterpiece, *Les Enfants du Paradis*, (1945) where Garance loses her adored Baptiste for ever.

During the ensuing battle, Henry is wounded and taken to the American hospital in Milan, where a sympathetic nurse (Elaine Stritch) cares for him until Catherine is transferred there. 'Get me a bottle of brandy and I'll marry you,' he tells her, but Catherine does not want this – wives are prohibited at the front and if she becomes his wife she will only be sent away again, so the pair opt to live in sin. Later, Henry asks her to marry him again when she announces she is pregnant, but she declines once more, not wishing to entrap him; instead, they murmur their wedding vows to each other during an afternoon race meeting. Their idyllic sojourn in Milan ends, however, when the stroppy hospital superintendent (McCambridge) catches them in a clinch. Henry is discharged from the hospital and sent to Caporetto, which is about to be besieged by the Germans.

The next segment of the film displays the carnage so vividly described by Hemingway – savage, bloody and unsparing on the eye even by today's standards. Men fight to the death for places on the overcrowded trucks evacuating the battered town; mothers lay at the roadside next to their dead babies; the hospital is reduced to rubble while the priest and those too sick to be moved are in prayer. Major Rinaldi loses his mind, and when Henry sticks up for him both are mistaken for enemy spies and arrested. Henry manages to escape and make his way back to Catherine, while Rinaldi is left to face the firing squad.

Henry and Catherine steal a boat and cross the lake to neutral Switzerland, where they settle for while. By now, though, Henry's loathing of bloodshed has been replaced by the shame and disgust that being hunted as a deserter brings. 'A coward dies a thousand deaths, the brave but once,' he opines.

From here it is downhill all the way. The birth is a difficult one – the baby is delivered by Caesarian section, and Henry momentarily resents it because it has caused its mother so much pain. When it dies he reflects upon what is happening in the world and looks upon its demise as a blessing in disguise. 'Maybe it's better to die that way than end up on a muddy road,' he says. The doctor then informs him that Catherine too is close to death – he goes to pieces, and for the first time in his life the agnostic prays, but in vain. And as the credits roll yet another dispirited young man, touched by war, is seen walking towards a bleak and empty future.

After a glorious career *A Farewell to Arms* – though visually a well-acted, evenly paced and beautifully scored (by Mario Nascimbene) film – provided Hollywood's greatest mogul with a dismal swansong, commercially and critically.

The fact that Rock was thousands of miles away from home, and would be for another five months, did not prevent his marital strife from escalating. Food poisoning had not been the cause of his wife's recent illness and within 48 hours of Rock leaving Hollywood, Phyllis had been admitted to St John's Hospital, where doctors had diagnosed hepatitis, almost certainly passed on to her by Rock. For several days she was so ill that it was feared she might not survive. Rock was contacted at once but chose to ignore the calls, possibly thinking that Phyllis was only craving attention, as had happened before whenever he had had to spend time away from home. Louella Parsons – unrivalled at sniffing out scandals, even long-distance ones – launched a defiling attack on Rock for neglecting his wife, dropping more than a few hints as to what he was getting up to once the set had closed down for the day.

Henry Willson had attempted to defend Rock *before* Parsons had published her article, when the columnist had asked him for his comments, by informing her that Rock was expected home by 25 March – a date he had plucked out of thin air. Now, he called Universal's Italian publicists and instructed them to issue a statement on Rock's behalf. The gist of this was that Mr Hudson would love nothing more than to be reunited with his wife, but his intense shooting schedule would render this far too costly, and such a delay might even prevent the film's completion. The statement ended with Rock wishing his fans to know that away from his beloved 'Bunting' he was feeling desperately miserable and dejected, but that his time in Italy would thankfully soon pass.

Nothing could have been further from the truth. By coincidence, Jennifer Jones' mother had been admitted to the same hospital as Phyllis with a suspected heart attack, and David O Selznick had given his actress wife a week off to fly home and visit her, suggesting that Rock might also take a break and accompany her. He, however, had not wanted this because he and Massimo were having the time of their lives at Rome's Grand Hotel *and* on location in the Italian Alps – with a succession of hunky extras, models and rent boys. When Rock told a French journalist, 'Without my wife, life really is a drag,' he was speaking literally, for within the privacy of their hotel suite – two rooms with a connecting door on the inside – he, Massimo and their pick-ups loved nothing more than playing 'tarts and Romans', camping it up in women's clothes and bedsheets.

The Italian tabloids commented upon how Rock had promised his 'Latin Buddy', as he affectionately called him, a headstart in Hollywood and Massimo's agent was confident that, just as he had arranged the loan-out for Anna Magnani to appear in *The Rose Tattoo*, so Massimo would be granted a temporary work permit to try his luck in the United States. Henry Willson, upon hearing this, flew out to Rome with the young man Rock had described as his 'hottest fuck in years' – Troy Donahue. Willson's plan was that Donahue would seduce Rock away from Massimo long enough for the Italian to be paid off and sent packing.

So far as Phyllis and the press were concerned, the purpose of Willson's trip was that he had an urgent contract for Rock to sign, one which would extend his time with Universal. Neither she nor they believed him, and in any case the plan backfired. Rock's and Massimo's relationship may have been intensely sexual, but they also loved each other, unconditionally and profoundly. The pair were reputed to have been having group sex with as many as six different men in any one day during breaks from *A Farewell to Arms*, and so far as Troy Donahue was concerned it was a case of the more the merrier. The hunky blond was asked to join in, and did!

European journalists had plenty of opportunities to write about Rock's unconventional love life but did not – largely because the Europeans were more sexually liberated, such things were more acceptable (and still are), but also on account of the draconian privacy laws in some countries. In the meantime, however, the American exploitative press were finally being taken to task. In February 1957, Robert Harrison of *Confidential* had been served with a staggering $2 million lawsuit by the black actress, Dorothy Dandrige – after four years of exposés peppered with innuendo, Harrison's exclusives had started living up to what their headlines and captions promised.

Dandridge had seen red after Harrison had accused her of 'perverted antics' with a naturist group, and within weeks the editor had received further writs from Maureen O'Hara and Errol Flynn. O'Hara, accused of gross indecency with a man in the back of a cinema, supplied the court with passport evidence proving she had been out of the country at the time. Flynn, alleged to have spent his wedding night with a call girl, had also been seen hundreds of miles away from where the supposed event had taken place. These and dozens of other stars, supporting each other morally and now well aware that Harrison did not have a leg to stand on, used only the costliest lawyers in Hollywood so that they could obtain substantial damages from Harrison.

Only the likes of Rock, Elvis Presley and Dan Dailey – the latter like Jeff Chandler outed for his fondness for cross-dressing – did not sue, largely because what he had implied or threatened to publish about them had been true. Lana Turner, advised by her lawyer to take Harrison to the cleaners for revealing that she and Ava Gardner had shared a man in bed, took more drastic action – she hired a hit man to kill him during a hunting trip, a mission that failed when the bullets hit a tree trunk.

By the late spring of 1957, *Confidential* had received so many lawsuits that Hollywood's public relations officer, Robert Murphy, warned the district attorney that unless the matter was resolved quickly, all the major film studios would withdraw their support from the forthcoming Republican campaign. Harrison, however, needed to keep the magazine's circulation figures as high as possible while he could, so his threats became even more menacing. So when Willson returned to Los Angeles from Italy and learned through his spies some of the headlines Harrison was planning, he called Rock in Rome and informed him that, even if Phyllis *died*, he would have to stay put until the fuss had blown over.

Willson's next 'mission of mercy' was to visit Rock's wife in the hospital, though this would be no exercise in well-wishing. Phyllis, who again must have read the newspapers and known what was happening with *Confidential,* was – according to her – told that if she persisted with her appeals for Rock to come home, *she* would be the one held responsible for wrecking his career, particularly as it was widely speculated that he would win an Oscar for *A Farewell to Arms*. She bitterly recalled:

After he left, I reflected on what a fool I had been even to mention Rock's coming home. Human feelings meant nothing to Henry. His only concern was how his clients could pour more money into his own pockets.

Phyllis spent almost three months in hospital, much of this in an isolation ward, and several weeks more at home, nursed around the clock. During this agonising period, Rock neither called nor wrote. She did receive flowers from him every few days – at least this was what she was led to believe by Henry Willson, who had arranged for them to be sent, even forging Rock's signature on the greeting tag. When she was feeling a little stronger, she began spending time with friends – the ones closest to her at this time were the Nivens (David's wife, Hjordis, had also been a patient at St John's) and Marlon Brando's wife, Anna Kashfi.

Meanwhile, with still no news from Rock, and on account of the din coming from the workmen who were renovating the property next door – Phyllis moved out of Warbler Place, taking a twelve-month lease on a beach house on Malibu's Pacific Coast Highway. For a while her only companions were a part-time housekeeper and Demitasse, the poodle Rock had given her soon after their wedding.

Here, aided by her twice-weekly sessions with a clinical psychologist, Dr Dubois, and as documented in her memoirs, Phyllis began taking positive steps to deal with her wrecked marriage. Her basic weakness, Dubois is said to have convinced her, was that as a movie star's wife she too was only play-acting instead of facing up to the reality that her husband was only interested in his career – and, when he was not working, in having fun with his friends rather than spending valuable leisure time with his wife. Furthermore, Dubois said that, in her professional opinion, the money that Rock constantly lavished on her – jewels, designer clothes, only the most expensive restaurants – was being spent for no other reason than he was trying to make an impression on those who mattered in his own, self-centred sphere.

The fact that Phyllis had at last opened up to a third party and unburdened her mind of the problems she had been bottling up since before her marriage, meant that she had started taking positive steps towards planning her own future, one that must have looked like it could *only* end in the divorce court. But, genuinely in love with Rock – and, according to his friends, the financial package that was the most essential component of his appeal – she decided that she would give him one last chance by eliminating the evil element from their lives: Henry Willson.

At the end of June the location shooting on *A Farewell to Arms* was wound up, and Rock called Henry Willson to say that he would be on the next plane home. Willson strongly advised him against this. Justice Irving Saypol, appointed by the district attorney to oversee the investigation into the wealth of lawsuits filed against *Confidential*, had announced that the proceedings – hailed by the press as 'The Trial of 100 Stars' – would open on 2 August, and that in the meantime Robert Harrison had been called upon to submit a defence and honour his magazine's motto, 'Tells The Truth And Names The Names'. In other words, the editor had been ordered to submit his files for closer scrutiny.

Harrison had no option but to comply with Saypol's instructions, though he also made a last-minute bid to ensure that his July issue – quite possibly his last – would be the best ever. The cover boasted exclusives about Eartha Kitt ('The Man Who Sat There – All Night!') and Anthony Quinn ('Caught With A Gal In A Powder Room!') – though the most potentially damaging exposé concerned arch-camp pianist, Liberace. Under the heading 'Why Liberace's Theme-Song Should Be "Mad About The Boy"!' a hack, writing under the pseudonym Hoarton Streete, detailed an alleged incident – though quite probably true – wherein the glitzy entertainer had tried to seduce a young male press agent in his suite at an Ohio hotel. According to Streete, 'The floorshow reached its climax when Dimples, by sheer weight, pinned his victim to the mat and mewed in his face, "Gee, you're so cute when you're mad!"' Liberace, however, proved no less over-the-top when suing for libel than he was in his stage act. Denouncing Dorothy Dandridge's writ as 'a piddling little trifle', he had hit Harrison with a whopping suit for $25 million *and* successfully acquired an embargo that would prohibit the media from referring to the incident again during his lifetime.

Rock was airmailed a copy of the Liberace *Confidential* article by Henry Willson, and again instructed not to leave Rome. He knew, though, that, now that filming had been completed, even the European press would begin criticising him if he did not return home to his wife soon, and in any case, had he wished to stay on in Italy he would have had to apply for an extension of his work permit, which would not have been granted because there was no longer any work for him to do. Therefore, leaving Massimo in their suite at the Grand Hotel – the idea was that his lover would wait a month or so before following on, giving Rock ample time to fix him up with an apartment, and Henry Willson a screen test and American work permit – Rock left, arriving in Hollywood a few days before the *Confidential* trial.

Once they had recovered from the Willson stage-managed meeting at the airport, with scores of reporters and a myriad of popping flashbulbs as Rock swept his wife up into his arms and carried her to the waiting limousine, Rock's reunion with Phyllis initially appears to have been successful. Phyllis recounted how they had made love the instant they had entered her beach house – and of how he had bought her dozens of presents from Italy. What she did not know was that Rock had given Massimo the money to go out shopping for these.

Furthermore, Rock is said to have made no fuss when Phyllis informed him that she had made an appointment for him to see Dr Dubois . . . or when he learned how she had investigated Henry Willson's financial dealings with the studios, suspicious that Rock's agent had been getting huge rake-offs from Universal in return for a promise that Rock would never complain that they were underpaying him.

Rock, however, seems to have already suspected Willson of short-changing him for some time, and though he kept him on as his agent for the time being, he did transfer his business affairs to the office of Morgan Maree, the man who had handled Humphrey Bogart and who more recently had rescued David Niven from financial ruin. For Phyllis, the repercussions were more severe than she had anticipated:

Henry's Machiavellian mind told him who was responsible for the switch to the Maree office. From that day forward, our relationship changed. Henry had first treated me as his protégée, then as the useful consort of his best client. Now he viewed me as a dangerous monster that he, a well-meaning Dr Frankenstein, had created . . . I didn't realise what a formidable enemy I had made. I had done the unforgivable: I had threatened Henry's relationship with Rock. Now Henry was determined to do everything possible to destroy my credibility.

For a little while, certainly from Phyllis' point of view, it seemed that the Hudsons might have patched up some of their marital difficulties. Though no amount of psychological counselling could alter the fact that Rock was, and always had been, sexually attracted *only* to men, some sort of uneasy compromise might have been effected – as had happened with the marriages of Cary Grant, Robert Taylor and Errol Flynn, to name but a few similarly indiscreet matinée idols. But Phyllis, having been brought up to respect the sanctity of marriage, was no authentic 'lavender' bride, although it can be argued that having worked for Henry Willson, she must have almost certainly been aware of Rock's homosexuality from the outset.

Any hopes that Rock and Phyllis might learn to live together were dashed when Rock took her his wife out to dinner one evening – and forgot to latch the gate. Phyllis' poodle, Demitasse, got out into the road and was killed by a truck. All the suppressed anger and frustration of the last few months came forth with such venomous hysteria that a doctor had to be summoned to sedate her.

The death of her beloved pet meant that Phyllis no longer wished to live at the beach house so, once Rock had assured her that he would seek help for his 'problems', she moved back to Warbler Place. For Rock, this would lead to a gruelling, wholly unnecessary period of psychological torment – he was more or less expected to don the proverbial hair shirt for a trait which he did not even *wish* to rectify, *and* to make a futile but genuinely heartfelt attempt at keeping Phyllis by his side the only way he knew how . . . by showering her with intermittent affection and more material possessions.

Many years later, George Nader repeated to Sara Davidson what he claimed Rock had confided in him, 'I have tried thinking of razor-blades. I have tried thinking of black widow spiders. I have tried thinking of snakes . . . It doesn't do any good. Nothing works.' Nader added, doubtless in defence of his friend's good name, that he had been unsure of Rock's exact implication, suggesting that he may have been referring to his premature ejaculation – if indeed he had ever suffered from the condition. It was not out of the question, though, given the fervour with which Henry Willson had poisoned his mind against her (of more later), that in his despair Rock might have been trying to *frighten* Phyllis out of his life. Worse still, that at some stage he had thought of killing her. Willson himself certainly would have been capable of anything – he is known to have had at least two unwilling partners 'roughed over' for not complying with his regime.

These outbreaks from Phyllis, interspersed with alleged moments of out-of-character brutality from Rock, only escalated once he had been to see a psychologist and made to discuss his supposed sexual and behavioural shortcomings with a total stranger. Phyllis recalled an incident when they were out driving with friends. Rock was speeding, and when she touched a decidedly raw nerve by accusing him of 'trying to do a Jimmy Dean' he gave her a backhander across the mouth.

Henceforth the couple would spend more and more nights sleeping in separate rooms, though there was one last bid to patch up their differences when, early in October, Phyllis accompanied Rock to Hawaii for the location work on his next film, *Twilight for the Gods* (1958).

Rock's morose mood enabled him to add a little Method to his portrayal of David Bell, the shabby-looking, hard-drinking captain of a steamboat, whose license has been revoked on account of an accident and whose job now amounts to ferrying around a weird assortment of characters, including criminal Cyd Charisse. The story was by Ernest Gann, who had written *The High and the Mighty* (1954) for John Wayne. Rock, however, made *too* much of the part and when the head of Universal saw the early rushes he ordered Rock to 'clean up his act' or risk being suspended from the picture – defeating director Joseph Pevney's objective, for Bell's persistently tawdry state and erratic behaviour had been essential to the plot and in the revised takes Rock looks grotesquely out of place.

For a little while, in their suite at the Royal Hawaiian Hotel, the couple appeared to be getting on rather well, although Phyllis was still weak following her recent hospitalisation and unable to participate in their usual sporting–fishing activities. Her semi-indisposition, however, soon offered Rock the perfect excuse to leave her resting at the hotel while he went off in search of male company. However, matters reached crisis point when the film was finished and they returned home, when, within hours of their return, Phyllis made another appointment for Rock to see her psychologist. Rather than keep the date, on 17 October, while Phyllis was out shopping, Rock packed his bags and moved into the Beverly Hills Hotel under an assumed name.

It seems quite likely that Phyllis Hudson's steadfast refusal to accept Rock as he was, instead of interfering with what was for him perfectly normal human nature, contributed more to the collapse of their marriage than any of his or Henry Willson's machinations. The note pinned to the kitchen door at Warbler Place was almost an open invitation for visitors to get in touch with the scandalmongers – 'I'm going to the Beverly Hills Hotel. Let's keep it quiet' – in this instance resulting in Louella Parsons, the woman he would subsequently refer to as 'the Paganini of Piffle', exploding the whole saga across the front page of the *Los Angeles Examiner*.

The Parsons piece appears to have been behind Rock's next move, two weeks after the split, to take Phyllis out to dinner and suggest reconciliation. She, however, could not resist imposing a crucial condition: he would have to see her psychiatrist this time, a Dr Rankin, and come clean about even his most innermost thoughts and secrets. Not unexpectedly, Rock refused, and a few days later he moved into a furnished apartment on Crescent Heights. Within a week he had more furniture than he knew what to do with – Phyllis had called in the removal men and rid the house on Warbler Place of any evidence that her estranged husband had ever been there. She had even had the place redecorated.

An early visitor to the Beverly Hills Hotel had been Rock's Italian lover, Massimo, but when he now turned up at Crescent Heights and announced that Henry Willson had secured him a work permit and a number of auditions, Rock would have nothing to do with him. He was lying low, he said, and did not wish to be reminded of his 'murky' past. The so-called 'Trial of 100 Stars' was in full swing and over the previous few weeks Hollywood had seen a mass exodus of anyone – from major stars down to the extras and studio personnel – who might have had something to hide, no matter how trivial.

Two weeks into the proceedings there was a major drama when one of Robert Harrison's key witnesses – a sub-editor named Peggy

Gould, who was scheduled to take the stand the next morning – was found dead in her hotel room. It emerged that Gould had been going to testify *against* Harrison and that she had double-crossed him by selling *Confidential*'s headlines, ahead of publication, to the district attorney. The verdict was suicide. Shortly afterwards, Harrison's editor-in-chief, a former member of the Communist Party named Howard Rushmore, shot his wife dead in the back of a New York taxi, then turned the gun on himself.

Although the jury were out for fourteen days before all the issues were unanimously resolved, the trial resulted in little more than a large number of out-of-court settlements. Liberace came off better than most – donating his $40,000 payoff to charity once he had discharged his legal fees, and urging everyone else to do the same. Few of the other settlements amounted to more than $10,000 – even so, collectively they were enough to force Harrison out of business and put an end to his hated publication.

Within weeks of the trial, Harrison, the bane of the film world for so long, found himself the subject of a scurrilous Hollywood movie. *Slander* (1957) opens with a shot of the New York skyline over which are superimposed the names of several fictitious muck-raking magazines: *Lurid, Smut, Dirt*, which are edited by an outrageously effeminate, mother's boy publisher inaptly named H R Manley, whose personal motto reads, 'Ye Shall Learn The Truth – And The Truth Shall Make You Free!' Rock, and many of those persecuted by *Confidential*, were tickled that Manley was portrayed by Steve Cochran, a gay actor who had also been menaced by Robert Harrison. Secretly they also wished that Harrison's own mother might have followed the example of her on-screen incarnation – and blown his brains out.

Massimo, meanwhile, was deeply hurt to have been used so cruelly by the man he had loved. Had he been possessed of any genuine feelings for the young Italian, of course, Rock might have suggested a temporary lying-low at least until the *Confidential* dust had settled. However Rock was starting to show his true colours, and he made it clear to Massimo that he had been merely one more notch on the Hudson bedpost. Massimo had been aware all along of Rock's promiscuity – indeed, he himself had been no less sexually charged during Rock's sojourn in Italy – but, the fact that such precise arrangements had been made for his relocation to the United States lulled Massimo into believing that of all Rock's men, he was the one who mattered most. Yet when he begged Rock to show just a little compassion, the door was slammed in his face and the next day he was visited by two Willson heavies who warned him that, unless he wanted to spend the rest of his life in a wheelchair, he had better keep away from Rock Hudson.

Massimo enjoyed several minor successes in Hollywood over the next few years, mostly in what Rock had called 'tits and sand' movies, but he was hampered by his limited English and in 1962 returned to Europe and better things. Astonishingly, he forgave Rock for treating him like dirt, and over the next ten years their love affair would be briefly revived several times – twice when Massimo visited Los Angeles for a holiday, and then again in London and Rome. They last met in 1985 when Rock was very ill. Strikingly handsome well into middle age when I met him, Massimo died in Paris, aged 69, in 2002.

The Hudsons' split cost them a number of friends, as their camp divided into two factions. Rock's Hollywood cronies, spurred on by an increasingly spiteful Henry Willson, would have nothing to do with Phyllis – not that she cared, she said, because she had always found most of them shallow and phoney, educated in nothing but the trappings of their self-centred little sphere. Rock, too, lost the respect of some of those who had admired him – top of the list being George Nader and Mark Miller, who didn't speak to him for a year.

Rock, meanwhile, attempted to shelve his problems by immersing himself in his work. *This Earth is Mine* (1959) was directed by veteran Henry King, who since *Tol'able David* with Richard Barthelmess in 1921 had churned out a veritable stream of classic movies, usually with strong rural themes. One of his most celebrated was *The Song of Bernadette* (1943), with Jennifer Jones, and for a while there had been talk of her appearing opposite Rock in this one – a coupling he was not looking forward to, after the Italian fiasco. He was relieved therefore when King informed him that his co-star would be English rose actress Jean Simmons.

Just as *Giant* would spawn *Dallas*, so *This Earth is Mine*, based
on Alice Tisdale Hobart's novel *The Cup and the Sword* (1942), may
be regarded as a precursor of the television drama series, *Falcon
Crest*, (1981–90), which featured Rock's former co-star Jane
Wyman as the scheming matriarch, Angela Channing. The opening
scene, too, is reminiscent of *Giant* – this time the passenger on the
train is Elizabeth (Simmons), on the last leg of her journey from
England to California, where she is to stay with relatives she has
never seen. These are the aristocratic Rambeaus, ruled over by the
ageing Philippe (Claude Rains), a stubborn individual who
nevertheless takes to his 'new' granddaughter at once – as does her
pushy cousin John (Rock).

Philippe is a fiercely proud, moral man who has built his empire
from scratch, starting with a small plot of land where his beloved
wife is now buried. What Elizabeth does not know is that she has
been brought to America because he has arranged for her to marry
the heir of a rival vintner, a union which he declares will result in the
Rambeaus becoming the most powerful vineyard owners in the
country. The old man, however, is not living in the real world. This
is 1932, the twelfth year of Prohibition, yet rather than sell his
harvests to bootleggers, what grapes cannot be sold for the table
Philippe purchases at rock-bottom prices from his tenants and
ploughs back into the ground for fertiliser. 'The grape is living proof
of the existence of God,' he opines, while John faces the very real
fact that if they do not sell their vast wine stocks to his bootlegger
contacts in Chicago – even though this is breaking the law – the
company will go bankrupt.

Unable to sway his grandfather, John persuades his tenants to
allow him to sell their grapes for ten times the amount they will get
from Philippe, terrorising the ones who refuse into doing so, though
they thank him in the end. Philippe and his domineering daughter,
Martha (Dorothy McGuire), have meanwhile convinced Elizabeth
that arranged marriages are often more beneficial than conventional
ones, in that they are rarely impeded by personal emotions. She has,
however, fallen in love with John, though before she gets around to
expressing her feelings, he accuses her of prostituting herself for the
sake of gain in agreeing to marry a man incapable of returning her

love. Elizabeth slaps him, and in a fit of pique he goes off with Buz (Cindy Robbins), a local girl who is only interested in him because her racist father will not allow her to see her Italian sweetheart . . . a sub-plot that Rock said reminded him of the way Universal had tried to come between him and Massimo, though the real culprit behind their split had of course been Rock himself.

John leaves for Chicago, but Elizabeth catches up with him as he is boarding the train. She confesses that she loves him, and swears that she will wait for him, although she changes her mind when Buz turns up at the Rambeau house and announces she is pregnant and, having convinced Philippe and Martha that the child is John's, extorts money from them. Subsequently Buz goes against her father's wishes and marries her lover – only to have him suspect that the child is not his when she eschews the Italian names he has suggested and insists upon calling him John.

John returns home after a year's absence, and drives out to be reunited with Elizabeth in his grandfather's favourite part of the Rambeau vineyards – the 'sacred' earth where his wife lies. On account of the baby, which John knows cannot be his, Elizabeth will have nothing to do with him. Angry, John tosses aside the cigarette he has been smoking, which then sets fire to the vines, and sets off after Buz. She confesses that her father forced her to lie about her child and promises that she will tell Elizabeth the truth, although this does not prevent her husband from wanting to fight with him. John, always the pacifist, effects a getaway but his opponent shoots at his car and a bullet lodges in his spine. Elizabeth visits him in the hospital and begs his forgiveness for wishing something terrible might happen to him.

Matters are further complicated when Philippe dies, bequeathing the greater part of his estate to Elizabeth, the 'outsider', whereas Martha – who has spent a lifetime waiting on him hand and foot – is left only the house. To John he has bequeathed his 'sacred' earth, his dearest possession that the young man destroyed and that he must now cultivate from scratch, the way he did all those years ago. Thus the story has turned full circle, and *This Earth is Mine* ends with John on his knees, planting his vines as Elizabeth brings him cuttings from the vines in her valley, the way his grandmother did Philippe.

Repeating her exact words as they work side by side, hopefully towards a more prosperous future now that Prohibition has ended, she tells him, 'To make good wine, you wed the right vines, as good bloods are blended to make a good family!'

On 18 December 1957, when Rock attended the televised premiere of *A Farewell to Arms* alone, the whole of America realised that rumours in the press about his marriage being over must have been true. Henry Willson had tried to press-gang Phyllis into attending, declaring, 'We need some upbeat publicity. Having you at Rock's side for the premiere will do it.' This time the ruse failed to work, though whether Phyllis' absence actually had anything to do with him not getting the Oscar is not known – though in the age of the so-called 'moral majority' not unlikely.

He may not have won the Oscar, but he certainly created something of a stir at the 1958 ceremony. A few weeks before the event he had been asked to sing a duet of 'Baby, It's Cold Outside' with an actress of his choosing. Everyone expected this to be Jane Wyman, his former co-star, who had had several hit records with Danny Kaye and Bing Crosby, but Rock selected the most infamous movie siren of them all – 66-year-old Mae West. This turned out to be an unforgettable experience and the highlight of the evening, as Rock explained:

> Of course, I'd seen her in films since I was a kid, so I was pretty staggered by it all. We went down to her house for rehearsals . . . she was always in a sort of pale beige negligee with a train about twenty-feet long. We'd stop for a breather, sit and talk. She was plain and simply a sweet old lady who told me marvellous stories about her life. But the minute we'd start rehearsing, all of a sudden she was Mae West – giving me all that thing she did. We never got through the song. And we didn't on the show, either, because she gave me the giggles. She thought that all the sex-queens in movie history were bullshit. She said that if they didn't have a sense of humour with it, it wasn't worthwhile.

Phyllis, meanwhile, filed for divorce. Taking a leaf out of Henry Willson's book she had elected to fight power with power, hiring Jerry Geisler, one of the shrewdest, most accomplished and costliest attorneys in Hollywood. In 1943 Geisler·had successfully defended Errol Flynn in his notorious rape trial. The previous year he had succeeded in getting Charlie Chaplin acquitted of an underage sex charge, and other top-name clients had included Lana Turner and Marilyn Monroe.

In 1987 Phyllis spoke of her horror, real or invented, over Jerry Geisler's revelations:

> Driving home, I tried to grasp the enormity of what he had told me. The whole thing was too nightmarish to comprehend. Was Rock a homosexual? I couldn't believe that. He had always been the manliest of men. Though our lovemaking had often been brief, we had also known moments of sexual passion. Had our marriage been a cover-up for Rock's true nature? Impossible . . .

It did not take Geisler long to find out about Massimo and all the others and, added to the sworn statements by friends who had witnessed Rock hitting his wife – including her matron of honour, Pat Devlin – he built up a case that, had some of the details been leaked to the press, would have resulted in Rock's career ending in a blaze of public shame. Henry Willson would also have been brought down because Geisler had unearthed all the juicy details of how Rock's agent had not only 'lip-serviced' every single one of his male clients – even the straight ones – but had some of these or their associates beaten up, and once threatened by shotgun-toting thugs, for not toeing the line.

Willson, only too well aware of the lead Geisler would be taking – though even he could not have imagined that the attorney was pressuring Phyllis to name the hapless Massimo as co-respondent – tried to stop Geisler in his tracks by warning him that if Phyllis did expose Rock's sexuality, then he would call a press conference and announce that the real reason for the Hudsons' failed marriage was that Phyllis was a promiscuous lesbian whose only interest in Rock had been in getting her hands on his money.

Geisler stuck to his guns, though he advised Phyllis not to refer to Rock's homosexuality – if his popularity with the box office slumped on account of such revelations, then so would his earnings and the percentage of these he would be forced to shell out in alimony. Willson was then ordered to drop his unproven allegations against Phyllis, if not, Geisler vowed, he would present the press with a list of names of all the actors in Hollywood with whom Rock and his agent had had sex. Willson very quickly came to his senses. Rock for his part exacted his revenge on Phyllis by closing their shared bank and credit accounts, leaving her with no income at all.

Over the next few months she was supported by friends: Pat Devlin, the Nivens, Marlon Brando and his wife Anna Kashfi. And when someone – Jerry Geisler, most likely – informed the press that Brando had sent Phyllis a $1,000 cheque 'because the lady had no money to eat', few people in Hollywood had much sympathy for Rock Hudson. Rock even yielded her health insurance policy – something she would only learn about the following year when she received a hefty bill for hospital treatment and had no funds to pay it.

Once the threats and double-dealings had subsided, the divorce itself was relatively straightforward. Phyllis filed her petition on 22 April 1958, citing extreme mental cruelty and actual bodily harm. Rock did not contest this, nor did he appear in court until the final hearing at the Santa Monica Superior Court on 13 August, when he agreed to an alimony settlement fixed at $1,000 a month for ten years. Phyllis got to keep the house at Warbler Place, the Ford Thunderbird Rock had recently given her, and her 5 per cent share in Seven Pictures Corporation.

The film and fan magazines, then as now in whose eyes no movie star could do wrong, were merciless towards Phyllis and depicted her only as the grasping, insensitive wife who had taken this 'homely Midwestern boy' for a ride. Some sent photographers to spy on her – several pictures appeared in the press that had been taken from ladders against the windows. To rid herself of this intrusion Phyllis bought an Alsatian guard dog. What the media did not know, aside from the obvious, was that within weeks of the divorce settlement Rock and Henry Willson began stripping her of her Seven Pictures

Corporation assets – like the health insurance, something Phyllis only found out about when it was almost too late.

In 1961, when Phyllis learned that Rock had transferred her holdings to his other production company, Gibraltar, without her consent – ostensibly so that Henry Willson could squeeze out their third partner, Henry Ginsberg, with whom he had fallen out – she took Rock to court, this time without the help of a lawyer. Prior to the hearing he was told that if he failed to pay what she said he owed her, she would reveal everything about their sham marriage in a kiss-and-tell book she was thinking of writing. Rock knew not to argue – he paid her an additional $130,000.

The couple would neither see nor speak to each other again. In 1964, Phyllis went to court again, this time to change her name back to Gates. Rock and Henry Willson, however, had managed to acquire one victory over her – Phyllis was compelled to sign a legal document which forbade her to publicly discuss or write about her marriage while Rock was alive.

6

One-way Street

'Usually I can smell a failure as soon as I read the script. I can't smell a hit, though. If I could do that, I would be a multi-millionaire!'

Rock Hudson

Rock got over his divorce – and at the same time flaunted his indiscretions in Massimo's face – by renting a stilt-house, not far from the Italian's Malibu bedsit and directly overlooking the gay section of the beach. Here, during his first few weeks of newfound freedom, he entertained a succession of muscular, tanned hunks. As had happened in Rome, he is reputed to have had sex with as many as three different men in a single day, celebrating the fact, he declared, that the likes of *Confidential* could no longer harm him. For three months, he later told friends such as Mark Miller – on account of his being trailed everywhere by Phyllis' private detective and her spies – he had lived a life of enforced celibacy, and now was the time to make up for all the fun he had missed out on.

In this respect he was probably being paranoid: as has been established already, Phyllis seems to have had no desire to out Rock publicly because of the disastrous effect this would have had on her own financial situation. Therefore, there would have been no point in her even caring what he had been getting up to – all that had mattered had been getting rid of him and resuming a more stable life.

Similarly, given his quite phenomenal sexual appetite, one finds it hard to imagine Rock abstaining from sex for more than a few days, let alone for three months.

Many of these casual partners, Rock once confessed, were reluctantly passive – not that he always liked 'to be on top', he said, but because so many of them were so overwhelmed to be in his presence, let alone be privileged to have sex with him, that they were too nervous to achieve erections. Jon Epstein, the producer friend who worked with Rock in the *McMillan and Wife* series (1971), recalled how he had once lamented, 'I wish I could go to bed with a bag over my head – because when people go to bed with Rock Hudson they're so nervous, they can't do anything!'

Rock's career did not suffer on account of his failed marriage, though even his most cloying critics were forced to agree that, despite his continuing status as Hollywood's Name-power Number One, his only truly great roles had been in *Magnificent Obsession* and *Giant*. Other than these, for five years he had been little more than an over-hyped studio-manufactured automaton and decorative B-movie actor – and not always a very good one. There was already a clear indication that if he persisted with his current trend of 'squeaky-clean beefcake' roles, he would soon be relegated to the status of has-been. Ross Hunter, the producer of *Magnificent Obsession*, who had risked his own reputation by putting Rock into his first dramatic vehicle, similarly recognised within him a rich source of hitherto untapped, natural humour and to this end approached Henry Willson during the summer of 1958 with a view to Rock appearing opposite – he hoped – Doris Day in *Pillow Talk* (1959), Stanley Shapiro's and Maurice Richlin's light-sex comedy.

Both Rock and Doris Day were as sceptical about accepting their parts in the film as Universal were about backing a venture for which they only had Ross Hunter's assurance that it would be a success. Rock told journalist Gordon Gow:

> When they gave me the synopsis to read, I said I really couldn't do the film. It seemed to me dreadful. But then, a synopsis is not really a fair thing. It only gives you an inkling of what the story

is about. When I read the script I felt differently. The dialogue
was really sharp.

Rock also had reservations about working with Doris Day, having an
'insider's knowledge' that her off-screen reputation as a hard
taskmaster did not match up to the sweetness-and-light image she
projected in her films, though he felt that there was good reason for
this. He explained to David Castell:

> It's true that Doris can come on strong. But like most people
> who come on strong, what she's really saying is, 'Help me'.
> And if you help her, everything's just fine.

The film reunited Rock with Nick Adams, the good-looking but
shifty actor he had met on the set of *Giant*. At that time Rock had not
shown any interest in him on account of Adams' reputation for
causing trouble, so why Rock wanted to be involved with him now
is not known. Since James Dean's death, Adams had boasted to all
and sundry that he and Jimmy had been lovers, and his relationship
with Elvis Presley had caused Elvis' guru manager, 'Colonel' Tom
Parker, untold problems and forced him to pay *Confidential* a small
fortune in hush money.

Whatever the reason, Rock went out of his way to secure Adams
a part in *Pillow Talk*, though virtually none of the cast and
production staff could stand him, and to a certain extent this helped
revive Adams' flagging career. Between 1959 and 1963 Adams
starred in two cult television series, *The Rebel* (1961) and *Saints and
Sinners* (1962–3), but afterwards, with little work coming his way
and his lavender marriage on the rocks, his mental health
deteriorated. In February 1968 he was found dead of a drugs
overdose, aged just 36.

Rock was told, too, that he would have to sing in the film,
something that terrified him because he had always considered
himself tone-deaf. And, though he was renowned for his ribald and
perverse sense of humour and fondness for playing practical jokes,
Rock was not sure that he would ever be capable of making
audiences laugh – certainly not in the 'Cary Grant tradition'

expected by the scriptwriters. And despite Ross Hunter's much-publicised comment that she was possessed of 'one of the wildest asses in Hollywood', Doris Day refused to believe that anyone could perceive her as sexy.

It was Henry Willson who convinced Rock that he was funnier, not to mention better-looking, than Cary Grant, arguing that after only a few minutes of screen time Grant's harsh, nasal inflections tended to wear on the nerves, whereas Rock's deep, manly drawl had never failed to send shivers down the spines of both sexes. As for Doris Day, her last two films had flopped after being savaged by the critics and she was more or less pushed into the project by her third husband–manager, Marty Melcher, a man who was every bit as grasping and manipulative as Willson. He told Hunter, once Doris had agreed to do the film, that she would only sign the contract providing he was engaged as co-producer, his fee for which would be a 'mere' $50,000.

Melcher's deviousness did not stop at his wife for, once Rock had accepted the part of over-sexed songwriter Brad Allen, Melcher pounced on him, strongly advising him to drop Willson and engage him as his manager. Rock's response – 'Henry only screwed me for fun, not professionally!' – suggests that he already suspected Melcher of being a crook. Unfortunately though, Doris Day did not discover that he had been embezzling her funds until his death in 1968, when he left her $500,000 in debt.

Throughout shooting, which began early in February 1959, Rock fought it hard to conceal his hatred of the man. What he never knew, however, was that after a vicious row with Ross Hunter over Melcher's appointment, Willson had enforced a deal wherein he would pocket $25,000 – to be deducted from his client's salary – for his role as Rock's 'adviser'.

Pillow Talk launched the most popular, perfectly matched and, above all, most credible comedy partnership of the sixties: the randy, loquacious but loveable rogue and the dotty, standoffish perennial virgin who wears a succession of daft hats. The film opens with a close-up of New York interior designer Jan Morrow's shapely legs – at once dismissing Doris Day's own theory that she was unsexy. Then the screen divides into three segments: Jan is

compelled to share a party line with Brad Allen, whom she has
never seen, and hears him serenading his latest flame with the song
he claims he has composed especially for her. The song is
'Inspiration', whose lyrics he amends time and time again
throughout the scenario so that they include the name of whichever
easy lay he is hoping to get into bed, at one stage he even croons in
French as he reaches for the control box next to the couch: one
switch automatically locks the door on his conquests, dims the
lights and operates the record player; another converts the couch
into a bed. Jan butts in and bawls him out: he is hogging the line,
and this is hindering the running of her business. Brad accuses her
of being a bore, to which she yells, 'If I could get a call through
every once in a while, my life wouldn't be so drab!'

Jan complains to the telephone company and is told that she can
only have a private line in the event of an emergency – such as her
becoming pregnant. All the same, an inspector calls on Brad – a
pretty girl who immediately succumbs to his charms. Brad finds out
who has reported him, and calls Jan to give her a piece of his mind,
'Get off my back, lady. Stop living vicariously on what you think I
do. There are plenty of warm rolls in the bakery. Stop pressing your
nose against the window!'

Next to enter the fiasco is Jonathan Forbes (Tony Randall), Jan's
client and Brad's thrice-married millionaire sponsor, who hopes that
Jan will become wife number four, regardless of the fact that she
does not love him and finds him intolerably dull. Neither Jan nor
Brad are aware that Jonathan knows them both, and when each tells
him of his/her telephone antagoniser, he does not suspect what is
going on between them. Brad is sceptical, however, when Jonathan
expostulates the joys of wedlock, and philosophises:

Before a man gets married he's like a tree in a forest. He stands
there independent, an entity unto himself. And he's chopped
down. His branches are cut off, he's stripped of his bark and
thrown into the river with the rest of the logs. Then this tree is
taken to the mill, and when it comes to he's no longer a tree.
He's a vanity table, the breakfast nook, the baby crib, then the
newspaper that lines the family garbage can!

Having fallen for Jan, who still does not know his true identity, and becoming aware of how much she loathes him, Brad invents an alter ego – Texas magnate Rex Stetson, a home-loving country boy who owns a mountain. They meet, and as they ride in the back of a cab on their first date, we hear aloud their respective thoughts – the properly raised girl who is interested in marriage, the totally unscrupulous playboy who only has sex in mind:

> SHE: What a marvellous-looking man! I wonder if he's single?
> HE: I don't know how long I can get away with this act, but she's sure worth a try!

Rex sweeps Jan off her feet after rescuing her from the clutches of a client's drunken son (Nick Adams). 'We have a saying back in Texas,' he reprimands him. '"Never drink anything stronger than you are – or older!"' And, during their next party-line spat, Brad tells Jan what a scoundrel Rex is, claiming that he has overheard them talking on the phone. 'Don't let that yokel act fool you. This ranch-hand Romeo's just trying to lure you into the nearest barn!' On their next date, aware that his gentlemanly behaviour is forcing Jan to make a play for him, Rex of course proves a model of respectability.

> I'm not one for making fancy speeches. But I get a nice warm feeling being near you, ma'am. It's like being round a pot-bellied stove on a frosty morning.

Now she is really hooked and the next time we see them chatting on the party line, Brad and Jan are in their respective baths, suggestively touching toes where the vertical line divides the screen down the middle. Later, in a tableau where he almost bumps into her at the hospital and blows his cover, Brad dashes into the nearest room – an obstetrics clinic – where he demands an examination. He tells the nurse, 'I haven't been feeling too well – probably just an upset stomach, but a fellow can't be too careful!' The doctor thinks he is pregnant, especially when a few minutes later he sees him dashing into the ladies' room! Then he calls Jan again and attempts to put her off Rex by suggesting that the Texan may be gay. 'There are some men who are very devoted to their mothers,' he says. 'You know, the type that likes to collect cooking recipes and exchange bits of gossip?'

On their next date Rex attempts to follow this up with stereotypical 'lavender' gestures, but bottles out and devours her with kisses, very nearly bringing her to the point of orgasm. That same evening, Rex asks Jan to spend the weekend with him in the country. She complies because she trusts him. They canoodle in front of the hearth and he declares that she is no longer a pot-bellied stove, but an out-of-control forest fire. A little later she sings her thoughts aloud – 'Possess Me' – and is on the verge of giving into him when she stumbles on a copy of the sheet music of his seduction piece, 'Inspiration', which she has heard many times when eavesdropping on Brad's conversations. 'Bedroom problems,' she scathes at a photograph of the irascible fake Texan. 'At least mine can be solved in one bedroom. Yours couldn't be solved in a thousand!'

Packing her bags, she is about to leave when Jonathan Forbes turns up. Jonathan drives Jan back to New York and she cries all the way, including in a roadside diner where an angry customer mistakes Jonathan for a cad and punches him out. 'I never knew a woman who had so much water in her,' he gripes. Brad's machinations to have Jan to himself have, however, backfired. Jonathan has paid him a small fortune for a new batch of songs, but Brad feels so guilty over the way he has duped Jan that he can no longer compose. And Jonathan, who now knows the true identities of the protagonists, realises that for the first time in his life, Brad Allen is genuinely in love:

> The mighty tree has been toppled. For years I've been waiting to hear them yell 'Timber!' over you. You love her and she can't stand the sight of you. What a beautiful sight – the great Brad Allen, chopped down to size, floating down the river with the rest of us guys!'

Jonathan urges Brad to rectify the situation, but Jan will have nothing to do with him. He tries to worm himself into her affections via Alma, her hard-drinking maid (Thelma Ritter), who suggests that

Brad should hire Jan to decorate his apartment – then promptly drinks him under the table. Jan takes the job only because she believes she can handle him.

> Once I had the mumps. It wasn't very pleasant, but I got over it. I look over Brad Allen like any other disease. I've had him, it's over. I'm immune to him.

Jan turns up at Brad's place, discovers his control box and tells herself, 'He's like a spider. He wants me to decorate his web!' Brad instructs her to turn his apartment into a place she would feel comfortable in, gives her carte blanche, and moves out while she gets to work . . . and while he spends much of this interim period ringing around old girlfriends to say goodbye, Jan transforms the apartment into a harem and even installs an ancient fertility symbol.

Brad is livid. Bursting into Jan's apartment he drags her out of bed, carries her kicking and screaming through the streets to his boudoir, flings her on to the bed and announces that he wants to get married. At first she seems shocked, and he is about to leave when she flicks the switch on the readapted control box. The door locks, but instead of smoochy gramophone music it operates a whorehouse pianola – her way of saying yes. The action then jumps forward three months and we see Brad bumping into the same doctor and nurse who previously believed he was pregnant. 'I'm going to have a baby,' he cries, before they whisk him off to the examination room and the credits roll!

Within days of starting work on *Pillow Talk*, Rock and Doris Day had baptised each other Roy Harold and Eunice Blotter, nicknames they would use for the rest of Rock's life, and in this and their subsequent films together so many meant-to-be-serious scenes ran way over schedule because of their clowning. Their love scenes were provocative for their day, though never over the top. *Time* magazine observed:

> When these two magnificent objects go into a clinch – aglow from the sunlamp, agleam with hair lacquer – they look less like

creatures of the flesh than a couple of Cadillacs parked in a suggestive position.

Their regular foil, Tony Randall, opined to Sara Davidson that Rock was supreme at playing romantic leads because he truly believed in romance.

In the trade, the Hudson–Day comedies quickly acquired the nickname 'DFMs' – Delayed-fuck Movies – on account of their protagonists not being allowed to sleep together until after they were married. In them, however, Rock was only indirectly expressing his homosexuality, as his friend Armistead Maupin, of whom more later, has explained:

> Most of the guys I knew really like to see the old Doris Day films, and I think one of the reasons we laughed at them so hard was that there was a real gay 'in-joke' occurring in almost all of those light comedies – because at some point or another, the character that Rock Hudson played posed as gay in order to get the woman into bed. It was tremendously ironic because here was a gay man, impersonating a straight man impersonating a gay man!

As soon as he had completed *Pillow Talk*, Rock gave up his stilt-house and relocated to Newport Beach, where he bought a boat, the *Lady Claire*, from the actress Claire Trevor. Changing its name to the *Khairuzan*, Piper Laurie's cross-dressing character in *The Golden Blade*, he hired a two-woman lesbian crew and sailed with them to local beauty spots such as Catalina Island, where picnics were laid on with at least one beach boy 'for dessert'. Henry Willson reprimanded him for his recklessness. *Confidential* may have been defunct, but the likes of Hedda Hopper, Louella Parsons and Elsa Maxwell – the undisputed doyenne of double-standard, herself gay, whom Rock had met in Rome when she had been 'paying homage' at the courts of Maria Callas and Anna Magnani – would never be silenced.

This time, however, Rock refused to do his Svengali's bidding, and Willson reciprocated by asking Universal to loan Rock the money for a twelve-month lease on a large, Spanish-style house that had taken his fancy at 9402 Beverly Crest Drive. Its owner, the producer Sam Jaffe, was spending a year working in Europe. Rock was urged to move into the property at once – if he could not control his sexual urges, Universal's William Goetz concluded, coughing up the cash, then at least he would be able to conduct them much more privately.

Rock's next film, *The Last Sunset* (1961), began shooting in Mexico early in 1960, and was directed by Robert Aldrich of *Autumn Leaves* fame. His co-stars were Dorothy Malone, looking more radiant than ever, and Kirk Douglas, immediately prior to the release of *Spartacus* (1960), who gets to croon a couple of songs, including the beautiful 'Cu Cu Ru Cu Cu Paloma'. The fine score was by Ernest Gold: there were even a few chords from his *Exodus* theme, which would prove a huge hit around the world the following year.

The film, however, was not as successful as everyone hoped, quite simply because, hot on the heels of *Pillow Talk*, the public were expecting more of the same and not what a sarcastic Universal (whose advances Rock had spurned) called in a press statement 'another two-bit glossy potboiler'. In fact, Rock had been given no choice but to return to tried-and-tested standard movie fare: when *The Last Sunset* began production, *Pillow Talk* was still being edited, and at this stage no one at Universal had any clear indication of how the critics and public would react to it, only that Ross Hunter was having a tough time persuading cinema chains to take on a film that was so far removed from anything Rock or Doris Day had done before.

Today *The Last Sunset* may be regarded as an above-average Western, but in his 1961 autobiography even director, Robert Aldrich, dismissed the film as mediocre, though through no fault of its star, as he explained to Jimmie Hicks:

> Rock Hudson, of all people, emerged from it more creditably than anyone. Most people do not consider him a very accomplished actor, but I found him to be terribly hard-working, dedicated and very serious. If everyone in the picture from producer to writer to other actors had approached it with the same dedication, it would have been a lot better.

'I need some horse-shoe nails,' drawls sheriff Dana Stribling (Rock) as he rides into a desolate Mexican town in search of his arch enemy O'Malley, whom he has never met. O'Malley (Kirk Douglas) – a black-clad, reportedly half-deranged but philosophical gunslinger, who, it emerges, had killed Stribling's brother-in-law – is on a personal mission of his own: he wishes to reclaim Belle Breckenridge (Dorothy Malone), 'the pretty little girl in the yellow dress' he loved many years ago, but who now has a settled life as a rancher's wife with a fifteen-year-old daughter, Melissa (Carol Lynley).

Belle's husband (Joseph Cotten) is about to embark on a cattle-drive to Texas: he needs a fast gun and a trail boss to get him safely across the perilous Indian country and hires O'Malley, who suggests that only one man is capable of heading the operation – Stribling – well aware that once they have crossed the border and are out of Mexico, he himself will be arrested by the sheriff and tried for murder.

The tetchy relationship between the protagonists changes when Belle's husband is recognised as a deserter from the Civil War, and killed . . . and when O'Malley falls for Melissa, knowing that old flame Belle is in love with Stribling. The hardened killer saves the lawman from death in the quicksands, even though he is sure that this will not affect Stribling's determination to hand him in. The two also fight side by side when a trio of hired hands attempt to kidnap the women to sell them as white slaves. Then we learn why Stribling's kinsman was killed, for the argument between him and O'Malley had evolved over Stribling's sluttish sister. 'A free-drinking house – nobody ever went home thirsty,' is how O'Malley denounces her before Stribling and O'Malley fight, emerging from their altercation a little more understanding of each other when Stribling tells O'Malley that, after the death of his brother-in-law, his sister became so distressed that she hanged herself. Later Stribling confesses to Belle how he had lost his wife and daughters during the war . . . and in a tender scene hugely reminiscent of Rock's own arranged marriage, he tells her that he is intent on her becoming his wife:

BELLE: Will I have anything to say about this marriage?
STRIBLING: Not until I ask you. And I can't until I square things up with him . . .

O'Malley plots to stay on in Mexico with Melissa – a country where he may co-habit with an under-aged girl without breaking the law – until Belle drops the bombshell that they can never be together because Melissa is his daughter . . . something he is reluctant to take in until he sees her wearing her mother's yellow dress. The film then concludes with the inevitable showdown across the Texas border. Stribling no longer hates his quarry – he may even respect him, yet he cannot shirk his responsibilities and after he has gunned him down he realises that, unable to face the future without the girl he loves, O'Malley has fought a duel with an empty gun.

Meanwhile, in October 1959, *Pillow Talk* was released, and much to everyone's surprise proved one of the year's biggest hits and Universal's top money-earner to date. Even *Box Office*, a magazine that had been generally dismissive of Rock's performances over the years, observed hypocritically, 'Hudson is as suave, self-possessed and convincing as though he has been delineating lighter roles all through his distinguished career.' As a result, he and Doris Day were contracted to make two follow-ups over the next four years and Henry Willson joined him in forming the aforementioned Gibraltar Productions, a venture that would see them buying shares in every future Hudson film. Combined with his regular salary, this placed him in the same $1 million-plus per film earnings bracket as Tracy, Brando and Grant.

The first of these follow-ups, Rock was told, would be *Lover Come Back* (1961), with Doris Day, which was pencilled in for shooting at the beginning of 1961. In the meantime – 'For the want of something better to do,' he said – Rock flew to Rome to make *Come September* (1961), another Shapiro–Richman sex comedy, with Italian legend Gina Lollobrigida and teen idols Bobby Darin and Sandra Dee.

Rock may have felt apprehensive about filming in Rome because Massimo was there on vacation with the Hollywood actor he had recently taken up with. Rock had also heard rumours of Gina Lollobrigida's apparent reputation for being difficult to work with. Within days of checking into the Grand Hotel, however, he had fallen for a young blond actor who was appearing in the film, and as for his leading lady, as had happened with Doris Day, the pair got along famously and concluded after just one scene that they were having such fun, a second film would definitely have to be on the cards.

La Lollo, as she was affectionately known, was without any doubt the most exciting co-star Rock ever had. In recent years she had starred opposite Burt Lancaster, Gerard Philipe, Errol Flynn and Tony Curtis – each time walking away with the production – and she very nearly did so in this one. A firebrand of sparkling talent she was, like Rock himself, a natural wit in what was for her a rare, cherished comic role – though it is possible, with her then-limited English, that she might not have quite understood the wealth of gay 'in-jokes' and intonations that peppered the script.

In *Come September* Rock plays millionaire businessman Robert Talbot who, once a year – always September – spends several weeks at his Italian villa with his beautiful but temperamental lover, Lisa (Lollobrigida). She, however, is weary of playing 'girl of the month' and has decided to marry a man she believes she loves – it is only July, and by September she will have plucked up the courage to tell Robert they are through.

Lisa's plans – and the machinations of Talbot's butler, Maurice (Walter Slezak) – are thwarted when, this year, Robert makes his trip to Italy earlier than usual surprising both Lisa, who is trying on her wedding dress, and Maurice, who is caught on the hop. For eleven months of the year, these past six years, Maurice has taken advantage of his boss's absence by transforming the villa into a hotel, not for dishonest reasons but to use the proceeds for the upkeep of the place. Robert's sudden appearance forces Lisa to tell her fiancé that the wedding is off, while Maurice desperately tries to restore the villa to its former self.

What the butler cannot do, however, is get rid of the latest batch of guests – a party of female students and their chaperone, who has fallen in love with him – and matters are made worse by the arrival of a quartet of young bloods. They have already encountered Robert on the road outside Rome, taunting him over his expensive car, only to be recompensed by Robert's (Rock's) bemused, homoerotic stares – hardly surprising, perhaps, for one of the men was portrayed by

Rock's current lover, though in fact he had flings with all four during the making of the film. When they turn up at the villa, they catch Robert in a passionate clinch with his sweetheart – his shirt is unbuttoned to the waist and he is wearing her pink, feathered picture hat. Tony, the troupe's leader (Darin), greets him with a wolf whistle then bends down suggestively, levelling his backside with Robert's crotch as he unloads the luggage.

One of the girls, Sandy (Dee), having been told that Robert only thinks he owns the villa because he is suffering from shell shock, puts her student psychology skills to good use by coaxing him on to the analyst's couch, but rather than effecting a cure lets slip what Maurice has done. Robert fires the butler and orders everyone to leave. 'Teenagers are much like the H-bomb,' he says. 'When they go off it's much better to observe them from a distance.' Then, while he is celebrating their imminent departure with champagne, the girls' chaperone slips on the cork and ends up in traction. Lisa talks Robert into allowing the girls to stay, but the young men end up pitching a tent outside the villa's gates.

By this time, all the students have paired up and, fearful that he will be prosecuted for breaching Italian morality laws, Robert and Lisa elect to chaperone their unwelcome, under-aged charges. 'The bedroom is like a wedding gown,' he tells one. 'It's bad luck for a fellow to see it before you're married.' Henceforth, the youngsters fail in their attempts to wear the couple out so that they may get down to some serious necking. When they hire motorcycles to explore the steep hills of Rome, Robert and Lisa still have plenty of energy left despite riding a hundred miles to out-dance them throughout the night – executing the mambo with unaccustomed brilliance – and for Robert to drink them under the table afterwards.

Lisa, however, resents her lover's sudden moral platitudes, particularly as he has never practiced what he preaches – taking advantage of her for just one month each year, when she has no idea what he is getting up to the rest of the time. 'I'm tired of being a free sample,' she screams, before storming off. 'The market's closed – you'll have to start shopping somewhere else!'

Robert and Maurice go after her: his car gets a flat tyre, so he steals a truck filled with live geese and when the police arrest him –

Robert does not speak Italian – Maurice fabricates a story that Robert is an escaped master criminal and that Lisa is his accomplice. He is thrown into a police van – she is flung there with him after being arrested at the church, having decided to go ahead with the wedding she was planning at the start of the film. But if she still loves him, Robert wants nothing to do with her, and when the police realise he is innocent and release him, he heads for the railway station to catch the next train to the airport. Lisa rushes after him. The train is about to leave and the guard will not allow her past the barrier – until she borrows a baby, pushes her way through the crowd and holds it up to the window, miming to Robert that the child is his – raising a good many eyebrows because she is still wearing her wedding dress! The film ends with the couple returning from their honeymoon, only to discover that Maurice has ignored their instructions and turned the villa into a hotel again – this time taking in a party of nuns! Superb stuff!

Lover Come Back, Rock's second film with Doris Day, proved even more successful than *Pillow Talk*. Coming hot on the heels of Universal's wave of second-rate productions and major flops, it resulted in Rock becoming one of the highest-paid and most popular movie stars in the world. Furthermore, his box-office prestige is said to have saved the studio from bankruptcy. Even the *New York Times'* acerbic, make-or-break film critic, Bosley Crowther – certainly no Hudson fan – liked it. Crowther called the pair, 'Delicious . . . he in his big, sprawling way, she in her wide-eyed, pert, pugnacious and eventually melting vein.'

The rivals-cum-lovers in the film are Jerry Webster and Carol Templeton, who work for enemy advertising agencies and whose methods of winning over prospective clients could not be more diverse. 'In all beehives,' the voice-over proclaims, 'there are workers and there are drones.' Carol represents the former: a by-the-book, hard-working, conscientious and decent girl who (like Doris Day's character in *Pillow Talk*) wears a succession of silly hats. Then the camera cuts to the drone: Jerry in the back of a cab, half-sozzled, a pretty girl clinging to his arm.

Wealthy entrepreneur J Paxton Miller (Jack Oakie) has recently arrived in New York and is anxious to spend $5 million advertising floor wax. Carol arranges a morning meeting in Miller's hotel suite and her homosexual assistant, helping her assemble a suitable package, shows her his colour chart. 'Leonard, who has a lilac floor in their kitchen?' she asks, to which he replies with a flourish, 'I do!' Jerry, meanwhile, gets the upper hand when he learns that Miller hails from Virginia. He reads up on the role the state and Miller's ancestors played in the Civil War then whisks him off to a burlesque and, while the band plays Dixie tunes, spins Miller a yarn about their grandfathers fighting for the same side in the same battle. Finally, he fixes 'his' client up with an orgy in his hotel suite.

When Carol arrives for her meeting early the next morning, Miller is still roaring drunk and all about him is wrecked. Horrified, she urges her boss to have Jerry charged with unethical conduct, only to be told that this will be a waste of time:

> BOSS: He's like a common cold. You know you're going to get it twice a year . . .
> CAROL: There are two ways to handle a cold. You can fight it, or you can give in and go to bed with it. I intend to fight it!

Next we are introduced to Jerry's wimpish, neurotic employer, Peter Ramsay (Tony Randall), who, having received Carol's complaint, turns up at Jerry's apartment intent on sorting him out. Jerry retaliates by boasting how good he is at his job – 'Give me a well-stacked dame in a bathing suit and I'll sell aftershave lotion to beatniks.' Then when Ramsay orders him to call Carol and reassure her of his company's 'high moral character', Jerry offers an 'apology' that only makes matters worse between them:

> JERRY: I'd like to ask you a favour. Will you kindly keep your big fat nose out of my business? If the competition's too tough, get out of the advertising profession.
> CAROL: You aren't even in the advertising profession, and if I weren't a lady I'd tell you what profession you are in . . . Let me put it this way, I don't use sex to land an account.
> JERRY: When do you use it?

CAROL: I don't . . .

JERRY: My condolences to your husband!

CAROL: I'm not married . . .

JERRY: That figures . . . a husband would be competition. There's only room for one man in a family.

CAROL: [clenching her fist] Let me tell you something, Mr Webster. I wish I were a man right now . . .

JERRY: Keep trying. I think you'll make it!

Carol is really mad by now. She calls the burlesque and lets off some steam with Jerry's favourite floozy there, Rebel Davis (Edie Adams), who in turn threatens to report this philanderer to the Advertising Council: Jerry swore to Rebel two years ago that he would make her the Miller Wax Girl, and she realises that in all this time he has been stringing her along with promises of television stardom to get her into bed. Jerry gets himself off the hook by confessing that it has taken him this long to find the perfect product for her to plug – 'The key which will open the gold gate to Hollywood'. Rebel is ashamed of herself for ever doubting him, and begs him to give her another chance; she will do anything, she emphasises. Jerry nods, checks his watch, and they head for the boudoir.

On the table there is a newspaper with the headline 'VIPs Arrive For Convention', and this gives him a brainwave: Rebel will henceforth be known as 'The VIP Girl', and the scene changes to show her posing for the cameras in skimpy outfits, promoting a product that does not exist.

Confident that his career – and his neck – have been saved, Jerry instructs his producer to file the film and forget about it. Then he sends Rebel along to the Advertising Council meeting, which Carol has arranged to discredit him. As a token of appreciation he has given her his army good-conduct medal, which he has asked her to wear next to her heart. Rebel shows this off, giving each of the all-male committee an eyeful of her ample cleavage, and offers Jerry's apology for not being there – 'He is with the Red Cross,' she says, 'donating blood.' Carol cannot resist the quip, 'They wouldn't take his blood. It's 86 proof!'

Having been made aware of the non-existent VIP account, Carol now decides to play her rival at his own game by putting in a bid for it herself – while Peter Ramsay, advised by his psychiatrist to adopt a positive and responsible attitude towards his life and career, makes his first ever executive decision, releasing the VIP film of Rebel to a television station – resulting in a huge demand for a commodity that must now be invented to save his company from financial ruin. He and Jerry attempt to remedy this by enlisting the services of Linus Tyler, an eccentric chemist who Jerry ends up impersonating when Carol – who has never seen Jerry, not even in photographs – turns up at his laboratory, hoping that she might woo Tyler into duping Webster and giving her his account.

The ensuing mayhem is hilarious and the shy, old-fashioned and inexperienced-with-women 'scientist' berates Carol for attacking Jerry:

> JERRY: As my uncle the missionary used to say, 'If thou canst not speak well of a man, speak not at all!'
> CAROL: You make me feel ashamed of myself . . .
> JERRY: It's just that I cannot presume to judge my fellow man. I am but a humble chemist.
> CAROL: Oh, no. You're a genius and a great humanitarian, and I want to know you better. Doctor, there's so much I could learn from you.
> JERRY: As my father the philosopher used to say, 'Knock at my door, and I shall take you in!'
> CAROL: Doctor Tyler, I'm knocking.
> JERRY: Miss Templeton, I'm taking you in . . .

The phoney academic's ploy – to get this teetotal virgin between the sheets – almost succeeds when Carol meets Jerry again, this time as himself, and starts lavishing him with attention courtesy of her expenses account. Over dinner she overconfidently confides, 'A woman instinctively senses when a man can be trusted,' just as the pufferfish in the aquarium behind them gulps down its live prey. Then she takes him dancing, she looks like a million dollars while he turns up in a grotesquely outdated suit. They visit the burlesque where Jerry takes all of his clients, though Carol keeps her eyes tightly closed while the stripper is on stage. Then they go golfing, cycling, sailing and swimming – when Carol tells him not to be bashful – he looks truly wonderful in his bathing trunks, holding in his stomach and flexing his biceps. And finally she teaches him how to kiss, cooing, 'I think this may be your best subject!'

Carol is so infatuated with her beau, and so sure that he can be trusted, that she allows him to sleep in the guest room at her apartment. He maintains the charade by camping things up, telling her that he will never marry because he is not possessed of Jerry Webster's finer qualities. Carol reminds him that he knows how to kiss, to which he replies gruffly, 'A kiss – what does that prove? It's like finding out you can light a stove. It still doesn't make you a cook. Forget me, Carol. You need a man, not a mess of neurotic doubts!' Then he flings himself face-down on the bed and pouts – and just as she is about to surrender and seduce him, the phone rings. It is her boss, warning her that she is entertaining an impostor.

Initially, Carol does not let on to Jerry that he has been rumbled. She asks him to go for a midnight dip – he has no trunks, but she replies that these will not be necessary. Then she drives off, leaving him naked on the beach where they first kissed, and he is picked up by a furs van and dropped off at his hotel wearing nothing but a mink coat. 'Hey, Fred,' cracks one of the two old men who seem to have been everywhere that Jerry has been up to his womanising capers, 'he's the last guy in the world I would have figured!' – not a sensible line, considering how Universal had fought for over a decade to prevent Rock's 'other life' from becoming public knowledge.

Carol next instructs the Advertising Council to prosecute Jerry because he has conned the public by promoting a non-existent product. He ostensibly proves her wrong by turning up at his 'trial' with a box of VIP – sweets that the real Doctor Tyler has eaten and that, when eaten, enter the bloodstream as pure alcohol. The committee, along with Jerry and Carol, scoff the lot and end up drunk . . . and the scene cuts to the former protagonists in bed, in Maryland, with a marriage certificate affixed to the mirror! Unaware as to how this has happened Carol screams the place down, and demands an annulment.

The action then moves forward and Jerry is visited by representatives from the liquor industry who complain that they are losing money because one VIP, selling at ten cents, equates to three martinis. Jerry is offered a huge payoff to take his product off the market – which he requests should go to Carol. Then he receives a call from the hospital. Nine months since their wedding, his ex-wife is about to have a baby. Jerry therefore acquires a special licence, and he and Carol are remarried while she is being wheeled into the delivery room!

Rock always maintained that of all his comedy films, *Lover Come Back* was his personal favourite. He told Gordon Gow:

> The advertising man in *Lover Come Back*, like the composer in *Pillow Talk*, was a ne'er-do-well. And playing a ne'er-do-well is terrific . . . I guess it's because it's what we all wish we were but don't have the guts to be . . . the advertising executive who plays around all the time, who was bored until he met Miss Day and said to himself, 'That would be rather interesting to toss in the hay – but I think I'll see if I can get her to go on the make for me!' Now, that's fun and it's very playable!

While making the film, Henry Willson 'leaked' the news to the press that Rock was amorously involved with the actress–singer Marilyn Maxwell, who had recently separated from her husband. Though not a love affair, there would be a strong affinity between the two over the next decade, though why Rock should become interested in a woman whose lifestyle was poles apart from his own remains a mystery. He was at the peak of his profession, while Maxwell was struggling to keep afloat. Four years Rock's senior, she had begun her career at sixteen singing with a dance band, moved on to films, but after a relatively successful spell with MGM her blonde bombshell had faded. Soon after meeting Rock, Maxwell would be stripping in burlesque shows.

The press reported Rock and Maxwell as 'going steady' in June 1961 when, just days after completing *Lover Come Back*, he flew out to Surinam for the location shooting of *The Spiral Road* (1962).

Rock had already told Maxwell that he was gay – more than this, he had introduced her to a bit-part actor from the film he was involved with, and when he called from Surinam and confessed that he and this young man were sharing a hotel suite, Maxwell replied that this was fine by her – adding that he would soon get over these 'fads' once he was married to a real woman! Rock accepted this somewhat unconventional proposal at once, declaring that he would be delighted to make her the second Mrs Hudson, though there would have to be one condition: she would have to allow him his 'other' life. This Maxwell could not do, but though the pair ceased being 'lovers' – the press were informed of a fictitious rift – they would remain close friends for the rest of Maxwell's life, and Rock often came to her aid financially. The first time was in 1963 when he paid her medical bills after she very nearly died of an ovarian cyst. And although he would continue to hide his particular light under a bushel, Rock would never openly admit that he was in love with a woman again.

7

'Wanna Have Some Fun?'

'He was a master of illusion, devious and secretive, capable of being extremely kind and utterly heartless. Like the Trickster, he appeared to different people in different guises.'

Sara Davidson, biographer

At the end of 1961, the house that Rock had been renting from Sam Jaffe was unexpectedly put on the market – the asking price a non-negotiable $167,000. Rock had become so fond of the place and the shelter it had afforded him from an inquisitive world that he instructed Henry Willson to draw up the necessary documents – since his divorce he had transferred his business interests from the Maree office back to his agent – only to be informed by the man he had been gullible to trust once more that he, Universal's biggest star, did not have that kind of money to spend.

Rock launched an immediate undercover investigation into Willson's dealings, but again, because he was fearful of Willson exacting his revenge by exposing his sexuality to the press, he agreed to keep the subsequent findings secret, though this time he did drop Willson once and for all. Over the next few months, many of Willson's other top name clients followed suit, and his career as an agent eventually slumped beyond recognition. Alcoholic and near destitute, Henry Willson ended his days in the Motion Picture Home in November 1978 aged 67, and in common with most of the great names he had launched, used and abused, Rock neither commented publicly on his passing, nor sent flowers to the funeral.

Universal remained tight-lipped over any deal, legitimate or otherwise, that they may have struck with Henry Willson to deprive Rock of a salary comparable with his worth and the vast profits his films were bringing their way, though they did console him by purchasing the house on his behalf. In return his new agent, John Foreman, negotiated a five-year extension of his Universal contract, at the end of which the deeds and full ownership of the property on Beverly Crest Drive would revert to Rock.

For a little while, Rock was content to share his home with his dogs (seven, at the beginning of 1962), a middle-aged gardener named Clarence, and Joy, his black housekeeper, who had been engaged by Robert Wagner and his wife Marion, to whom Universal had sublet the house while Rock had been overseas shooting *The Spiral Road*. Rock spent the rest of his life in the house on Beverly Crest Drive and set in motion a mammoth restoration programme that dragged on for twenty years, setting him back an estimated $700,000.

When Tallulah Bankhead, one of the first visitors to the Castle as it would henceforth be known, asked Rock why the massive front security gate had been left unlocked, he replied truthfully, 'Because if any good-looking guy decides he wants to fuck Rock Hudson, I don't want him climbing the gates and wearing himself out first!' He also told Tallulah, whom he was frequently escorting around Hollywood at this time, that when the interior decorators had asked him for his preferred style, he had responded, 'I want everything doing Early Butch with a Mexican flavour!'

From these gates, one crossed the car park to what appeared to be a front door but opened on to a wide, red-tiled patio that connected to the main U-shaped building. Each of the rooms was done out in a different colour and given a Mexican name in keeping with the 'macho' environment Rock had created – an almost Moorish-style fortress, which would camouflage his sexual leanings at a time when gay men were still regarded in most circles as effete, nervous Nellies who favoured pastel shades, silks and an over-abundance of kitsch. Everything about the Castle was rugged, straight out of Hemingway:

foot-thick hewn oak ceilings and beams, huge doors and fireplaces, candelabra, six-seater sofas, massive statues of animals and birds, African artefacts, zebra-skin rugs. The Tijuana Room, where special guests stayed, was decorated red in the style of a Mexican bordello. Rock's bedroom was royal blue, and had as its centrepiece a four-poster bed, which he joked could have slept six, though so far as is known since returning from Italy after meeting Massimo he had not gone in for group sex.

His favourite room, as with his former homes, was his den. This contained a bar and a fully equipped theatre, and housed his vast, catalogued record collection, his 'gadgets' – only the best, most expensive movie equipment, juke box, hi-fis, cinema-screen television – and an exhaustive film library. Over the years Rock acquired not just a 16mm print of almost every film he appeared in, but also the scripts and hundreds of stills from each one.

The Castle's patio area was equally gargantuan: a 40-foot pool 'guarded' by a lion's head fountain and surrounded by more Mexican statues – mostly naked, frolicking youths, with pride of place going to allegedly the largest stone barbecue in Hollywood at that time. Ferndell, the tropical area behind the pool, was designated an unofficial *pissoir* for those who could not make it back to the house in time . . . and for those guests who wanted a little indiscreet fun, Rock had created 'Assignation Lane', a narrow, lantern-lit pathway threading through the dense cliff-side vegetation, which – she claimed on account of the vast number of ejaculations that took place there – Tallulah Bankhead re-baptised 'Liberace's Passage'!

Chez lui, Rock became almost Garbo-like, inviting only the privileged into his domain. Most of his guests, certainly during his early years here, would be expected to sit through his old movies, though they would usually be offered a choice, as he explained to *Photoplay*'s Mike Webb in 1969:

I guess I've run *Giant* fifty times since settling down in the house. Well, the movie's three-and-a-half-hours long and this doesn't include the time it takes to change reels. The intervals run quite a bit as people repair themselves to the bathroom and you mix fresh drinks and all that, so it's usually four or five in the morning before they take off home, everybody bombed. Alternatively, I surprise them by showing *Tomahawk* or *Taza*. Then they're in a spot because the movie's terrible and I'm terrible and they say futile things like, 'You were marvellous!' when I know all the time I was absolutely lousy.

Rock also took up a new pastime – needlepoint! – creating some quite beautiful pieces of embroidery, which would be universally admired. And for the first time in his life, perhaps, he had found inner peace:

> My house is the only place I really have any privacy. Outside the house, everything I do is watched and talked about, but once I come in those gates I can relax and let go. I love to work on my house, to tear down walls and lay bricks. And for real relaxation, there's nothing like gardening. When I'm thinking about career decisions and working out new roles in my head, I like to go out in the garden and sweat . . . Sometimes I'll just pull weeds for hours and be totally lost in my thoughts. If I had it all to do over again, I'd probably be a landscape gardener.

'I hate domineering females!' Rock explodes in *Man's Favorite Sport?* (1964), which began shooting in the spring of 1962. The film was directed by Howard Hawks, a member of Hollywood's 'royal family' who, from his humble beginnings as a Famous Players-Lasky props assistant, had gone on to produce and direct such movie milestones as *Scarface* (1932), *Red River* (1948), *Bringing Up Baby* (1938) and *Gentlemen Prefer Blondes* (1953). Hawks was equally at home working with intense drama as he was screwball comedies such as this one.

However, barring a few hilarious mini-tableaux and despite the presence of 23-year-old Paula Prentiss, *Man's Favorite Sport?* was in comparison with his recent comic exploits, second-rate. With her own brand of madcap humour, Prentiss had tickled audiences in a series of films with Jim Hutton, notably *The Honeymoon Machine* (1961), but unlike Doris Day and Gina Lollobrigida she did not quite 'click' with Rock, and this was reflected at the box office.

Rock played Roger Willoughby, the lumbering assistant in a department store fishing equipment section, who has compiled the best-selling book, *Fishing Made Simple*, solely through eaves-dropping on his customers' conversations. Because of his 'experience', the store manager enters Roger for the prestigious Wanapoohee Lake Contest, sponsored by the father of wacky Abigail Page (Prentiss), who, having learned the truth, threatens to expose him as dishonest unless he takes her with him to the camp. 'Dishonest?' he barks. 'Does a man who sells canaries have to learn to fly?'

Reluctantly, Abigail agrees to teach Roger the finer points of lake-fishing – even though he cannot swim, handle a boat, nor stand to see, touch, smell or eat fish. His apparent stupidity, however, does not prevent her from falling in love with him, though initially he does not reciprocate because he already has a fiancée . . . though when he gets around to kissing Abigail the earth moves, quite literally, as the camera cuts to old back-and-white footage of trains crashing head-on, before she goes into a trance!

Eventually, following a series of mishaps involving a bike-riding bear and an irate fiancée who dumps him after finding him in a compromising position with Abigail and her closest friend, Roger wins the competition . . . only to announce that he is a phoney. He is fired by his department store boss, who is eventually forced to give him his job back following protests from the other competitors who maintain that, fake or not, Roger still knows more about fishing than the rest of them added together. Roger also gets his girl, and the film ends with them being swept into the middle of the lake on Abigail's canopied camp-bed after he had crept into her tent to shelter from the rain – there is a repetition of the earlier train smash and for some reason Abigail impersonates Cleopatra, which, according to most of the critics, only proved what an utter waste of talent and time the whole exercise had been.

Man's Favorite Sport? inadvertently introduced Rock to a new lover, his first regular relationship since Massimo. Lee Garrington was a 24-year-old trainee stockbroker from Atlanta. Four months previously, having completed his military service, he had arrived in Hollywood, bitten by the acting bug, and had been fortunate to have been hired as an extra in the hugely popular television Western series, *The Virginian* (1962).

According to the interview he gave to Sara Davidson after Rock's death, Garrington had been obsessed with Rock for some time and, not sure how to go about getting an introduction, had begun hanging around outside Rock's cottage, pretending to be reading a newspaper, in the hope that his idol might notice him. Garrington concluded that his only reward had been a cursory, over-the-shoulder glance one day as Rock left the cottage and walked straight past him.

In fact, Rock had noticed the young man, but immediately come to the not unexpected conclusion that the dishy blond 'giving him the eye' might have been some sort of reporter/*agent provocateur*, though he had been sufficiently interested to go to the trouble of hiring a gay-friendly private detective – not for the first time, apparently – to find out if this stranger was 'clean' . . . in other words, gay. The detective delighted Rock in reporting back that Garrington was indeed gay, but already spoken for and living with a man. Rock was unperturbed: never one to break up a relationship when there were obviously so very many fish in the sea, he paid the detective to monitor the situation and asked him to inform him should Garrington become available.

Several months later, once the inevitable split had occurred, Garrington was contacted by an intermediary and a meeting arranged. He also appears to have been told that Rock would be expecting him to have sex on their first date. According to Garrington, however, this was no great shakes – as Rock himself later confessed, the new man was in such awe over being in bed with Rock Hudson that he was unable to rise to the occasion.

Lee Garrington is said to have been Rock's most cherished lover since Jack Navaar. Having given up acting and reverted to stockbroking – and unafraid of public opinion because homophobia was less rife in his line of work – Garrington was also completely out and, concerned that this might affect Rock's career, he refused to move into the Castle when asked. Again, there was talk of Rock's willingness to risk everything for the man he loved – and no Henry Willson around to persuade him otherwise.

For a while they behaved like any other couple: they travelled extensively, never on separate planes or trains, and always shared a hotel room, mindless of the gossips; they socialised cheaply because Garrington valued his independence and insisted on paying his way. But like any Hollywood 'marriage', there were setbacks. Garrington later confessed how initially he had found Rock a disappointing lover because, despite his great size, he was a gentle man and preferred to be the passive partner, whereas Garrington hankered after domination. Soon into the relationship, when Rock made the discovery that his new beau liked picking up rough trade, there was an argument and Rock told him that they would have to stop going steady. However, the pair remained close for more than ten years and regularly resumed their sexual relationship whenever one of them was between lovers.

Immediately after completing *Man's Favorite Sport?*, Rock began shooting *Send Me No Flowers* (1964), his third and final film with Doris Day and Tony Randall. In it he played hypochondriac George Kimball, who is too enveloped in his imaginary ailments to know much about the outside world. We see him taking his temperature under the shower, then at the breakfast table where he devours a plate of pills from the pharmacy he keeps in the bathroom. 'Men of my age are dropping like flies,' he tells Judy (Doris Day), his scatty, long-suffering wife, who supports his habit by grinding sugar to make fake 'Seconal' sleeping pills. 'Do you ever read the obituary page? It's enough to scare you to death!'

George consults his doctor about his chest pains – the doctor assures him that he is merely suffering from indigestion, and adds that he only wishes all his patients were as healthy as he is. Then George overhears the doctor discussing another patient over the phone. 'Bad news,' he says. 'Not much you can do when the old ticker goes.' Believing that he may have but a few weeks to live, George confides in best friend Arnold (Randall), who promises to write the eulogy and handle the funeral arrangements – and promptly copes with his grief by hitting the bottle. George then becomes concerned for his widow-to-be – he does not want Judy running off with the first man she sees – so he sets about finding her a new husband and buys a burial plot for the three of them!

The publicity shot for *Iron Man* (1951) which earned Rock the nickname 'Baron of Beefcake'.

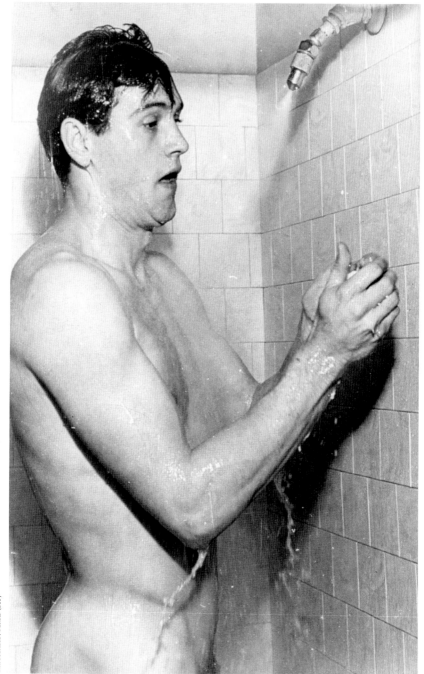

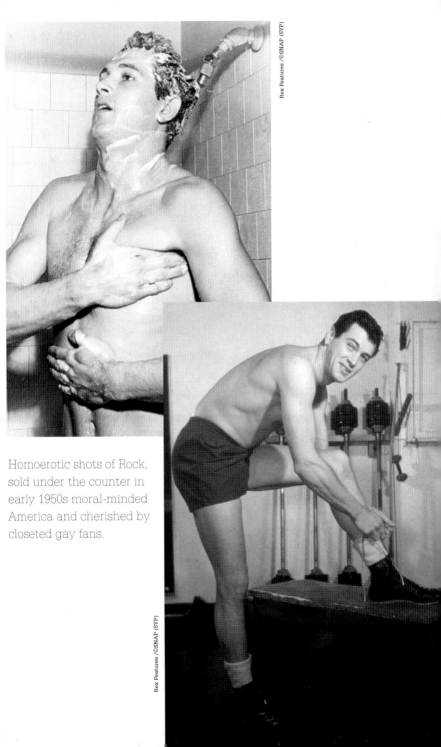

Homoerotic shots of Rock, sold under the counter in early 1950s moral-minded America and cherished by closeted gay fans.

Rare shots of Rock with lovers, before the studio intervened. At the gym with Bob Preble *(below)*; *(opposite)* with Scott Brady *(top)* whilst shooting *I Was a Shoplifter* (1950); with *Iron Man* co-star Jeff Chandler *(below)*.

(Above) Rock's least favourite but otherwise excellent 'tits and sand' role, *Taza, Son of Cochise* (1954).

(Opposite) With Yvonne de Carlo in *Scarlet Angel* (1952).

One of Rock's most acclaimed roles, opposite Jane Wyman in Douglas Sirk's *Magnificent Obsession* (1954).

With close friend Elizabeth Taylor, on and off the set of *Giant* (1956). Since Rock's death, Taylor has tirelessly campaigned to raise money for AIDS charities.

With Edith Piaf at the Mocambo (1956). Piaf told the cameraman, 'One of Rock's legs weighs more than my entire body!'

Without any doubt, Rock's most revered co-star, Doris Day (1959).

(Opposite) With Marilyn Monroe at the 1962 Golden Globes shortly before her death. The following year Rock would ask to narrate the documentary, *Marilyn*.

With Gina Lollobrigida in arguably his
campest film, *Come September* (1964).

Despite the warm smiles, Rock
disliked working with Jennifer Jones
in *A Farewell to Arms* (1957).

Engaged in 'girl-talk' with Anthony
Perkins on the set of Perkins' 1958 film,
This Angry Age. Despite the rumours,
they were never lovers.

(Opposite) In Cannes, with Princess
Grace of Monaco (1957). Holding the
glass (right) but removed from the
photograph, is Rock's long-term Italian
lover Massimo.

With Julie Andrews in *Darling Lili* (1970). Rock hated working with her.

Several candidates are considered, but fate lends a helping hand when Judy is literally swept off her feet by horseman Bert Power, her former college sweetheart (Clint Walker), when he rescues her from a runaway golf cart. Power is a super-smooth charmer who announces that he is in town for his latest swindle – and, looking George in the eye, adds that the real reason for his permanent bachelor state is that, since being dumped by Judy all those years ago, he has never been able to settle for second best. Arnold considers Power ideal husband material, and George does his utmost to push the pair together, though secretly he despises his smarmy rival.

This leads Judy into believing that George is cheating on her – until he informs her he is dying. Then she pampers him: in the very next scene he is ensconced in a wheelchair, talking to his favourite tree! Judy is about to book him into a costly private clinic when his doctor turns up at the house and she learns about the mix-up. The doctor tells her, 'George Kimball will outlive us all – unless he worries himself to death!'

Judy plots her revenge – certain that George is having an affair and that he has invented his terminal illness as a cover-up. She locks him out of the house, empties his beloved pills out of the window and bursts a hot-water bottle over his head. George moves in with Arnold. The spare room is being redecorated, so they sleep in the same bed and bicker like a long-married couple. Arnold is peeved because his friend is no longer dying – he has spent three days getting drunk and penning George's eulogy, all for nothing. The story ends happily, however, when Judy learns about the proposed plot in the cemetery: realising that there never was another woman, she forgives him and Power is sent packing.

Although he and Doris Day had tremendous fun, as usual, making *Send Me No Flowers*, Rock later denounced it. He told Gordon Gow:

Right from the start, I hated the script. I just didn't believe in that man for one minute. Making fun of death is difficult and dangerous. That scene where I went out and bought a plot for myself in the cemetery – to me it was completely distasteful.

During the mid-sixties Rock, along with many other major Hollywood stars, suffered a temporary, but nevertheless distressing, slump in his career. The problem for most stars was that television had robbed the studio system of much of its mystique. In the so-called Golden Age of Hollywood true megastars such as Garbo, Dietrich, Gable, Bogart et al commanded the unflinching respect of their fans because, despite the complexities of their private lives, they had been seen as regal, untouchable beings – deities almost – created and nurtured by insensitive moguls and immature, sycophantic movie magazines for those who wished to escape the drudgery of the real world, particularly between the two world wars. Now, some of these luminaries had been 'demoted' and had been brought into the living rooms of America to advertise soap powder, junk food, shampoo and less useful paraphernalia.

In the meantime, cinema screens played host to a new breed of grittier star: Faye Dunaway, Al Pacino, Jack Nicholson, Warren Beatty, Robert Redford . . . stars who would never be in the matinee idol class as their predecessors, but who were held in awe by their fans because the more realistic roles they played demanded considerably more than glamour alone.

At this time, Rock made *Blindfold* (1965), a lukewarm comedy thriller directed by Philip Dunne and co-starring Claudia Cardinale – already, at the age of just 26, the veteran of over thirty films, including *Rocco and His Brothers* (1960) and *The Pink Panther* (1963). Just as lovely as Sophia Loren and Gina Lollobrigida – either of whom Rock had wanted to be in the film – like Loren she owed much of her success to marrying the producer who had discovered and launched her. Unlike Loren and La Lollo, however, her abilities as a comedienne were limited, and though she has her moments here, much of the time she makes for little more than pretty scenery.

There were rumours, particularly in some of the Continental tabloids after the film's release, that Rock and Cardinale had been amorously involved – a story probably instigated by Rock himself, who is said to have had an 'unreciprocated interest' in another co-star, thirty-year-old Alejandro Rey, whom he had admired three years earlier when Rey had flexed his not inconsiderable muscles as a champion diver opposite Elvis Presley in *Fun in Acapulco* (1963).

Whether he got around to propositioning the handsome – and straight – Spaniard is not known, but thought to be unlikely, though he did have a fling with a young actor who played a sailor in the film.

'Just because I have suffered several disappointments, you seem to be under the impression that I am emotionally shallow,' Dr Bartholomew Snow (Rock) tells the secretary who keeps photographs of the eight women he has been engaged to in her diary, as mementos. 'On the contrary, it is precisely the warmth of my emotions that causes all of these difficulties. Mine is a tender spirit, eager for love, easily wounded.' Sadly, this is as witty as it gets. Snow is a psychologist who is shanghaied into treating neurotic young scientist Arthur Vincenti (Rey), a former patient now working on a top-secret government mission. Snow is blindfolded and escorted by car and plane on a regular basis to a mysterious location, and learns that Vincenti is about to be kidnapped by foreign agents. Vincenti's sister, Vicky (Cardinale), purposely crashes her bicycle into his horse while he is out riding, and together they hatch a rescue plan.

Henceforth the story becomes contrived and confusing – lots of double agents in homburgs and raincoats, a psychotic mule, and a dilapidated house in the middle of an alligator-infested swamp, which the re-blindfolded Snow locates by memorised sounds from his earlier journeys – enabling him and fiancée number nine to outwit the crooks and pluck Vincenti to safety in a denouement straight out of a James Bond spoof.

Blindfold saw Rock slip to Number Two in the Name-power chart, offering his pride such a battering that he decided – as Ross Hunter had decided for him immediately before *Magnificent Obsession* – that a complete change of direction might be the only way forwards. As a loan-out from Universal and acting on his new agent's advice, he accepted the part of Antiochus Wilson on John Frankenheimer's *Seconds* (1966), a curious but entertaining exercise in *Grand Guignol*, which succeeded in dumbfounding the critics. Depending on one's point of view, the film was a masterpiece, the best drama Rock had done since *Written on the Wind*; or just unadulterated, puerile hogwash! It certainly challenged his abilities, proving to detractors once and for all that he could act as well as the very best of them and carry a picture virtually without any support from his co-stars. Of these, only Frances Reid is remembered. Indeed, she would soon become a household name as matriarch Alice Horton in America's longest-running soap, *Days of our Lives* (1965–) – a role she is still playing, 35 years on.

Seconds provided strange fare indeed, and was most un-Hudson-like: naked romps, authentic (as demanded by Frankenheimer) drunken outbursts and frequently incomprehensible dialogue. Accompanied by Jerry Goldsmith's raucous score, many of the scenes were shot – by veteran cinematographer James Wong Howe – through fish-eye lenses, in triptych or reflection, and the weird angle-shots and special effects create grotesquely deformed features and elongated limbs that are not always easy on the eye. Perseverance, therefore, is the order of the day in what is ultimately a rewarding experience.

In an obliquely disorientated scenario that would have done Kafka proud, sixty-something banker Arthur Hamilton (John Randolph) feels that personally and professionally he has reached the end of the road, when a stranger in the railway station shoves a scrap of paper into his hand. This contains a telephone number that puts him in touch with an organisation dealing in 'reborns' – sad, disillusioned souls like himself who have benefited from being surgically, psychologically and even vocally reconstructed to become perfect, younger, life-loving specimens.

Like the hapless Joseph K in Kafka's 1925 novel *The Trial*, Hamilton does not appear to have much say in future events. The telephone call he goes on to make connects him with Charlie (Murray Hamilton), his former tennis doubles partner, whom he thought had died years ago when there had been talk of them turning professional. Charlie persuades Hamilton to enlist although his reasons for doing so are only clarified at the end of the film.

Saying goodbye to his wife, Emily (Reid), he drives to the unnamed organisation's headquarters, where the Cadaver Procurement Section arranges for his estate to be divided between it and his relatives. His death, he learns, will take place in a hotel fire after he has attempted to rape a young woman, and no one will realise that the corpse is not his. He is then handed over to surgery, emerging almost a foot taller and twenty years younger as Antiochus Wilson – Rock making his appearance, scarred and confused, forty minutes into the film.

Initially, once his scars have healed, Wilson the former workaholic drudge is content with his transformation. He finds himself suddenly at the centre of a new, optimistic circle of friends and acquaintances who are already cognisant with his new identity as a successful painter with a beach house and studio in Malibu. He even has a pretty mistress, Nora (Salome Jens). However, it does not take long for him to feel as disillusioned as a 'reborn' as he did when he was Arthur Hamilton. Still thinking as his former sex-starved self, he at first abhors the bacchanalian revelry that follows the harvest at a local vineyard. Then his revitalised libido takes over and he participates in an all-out orgy – Rock's first ever adult scene where, after being stripped naked by the men, he leaps headfirst into the huge vat of mushy grapes with twenty others and lets it all hang out, so to speak.

When Wilson discovers, however, that everyone in this new world 'reborn' like himself, he is appalled. Breaking away from them, and feigning to have been a friend of Arthur Hamilton's, he visits his widow. Naturally she does not recognise him, though Emily is shocked by how much he knows about herself and her late husband. And when Wilson realises how egocentric he was in his former life – 'Arthur had been dead a long, long time before they found him in that hotel room,' Emily says – he desperately wants his procedure to be reversed so that he can return to his wife and make amends for neglecting her. But of course, as with Joseph K, there is to be no turning back.

Wilson is recaptured by his sinister minder, John (Wesley Addy), returned to the organisation headquarters and ushered into the 'schoolroom' he accidentally stumbled into when he first arrived – the area where discontented 'reborns' are confined while awaiting the next stage of their programme – not the advancement they have been hoping for, but death itself, so that their bodies can be reconstructed by the Cadaver Procurement Section and used as doppelgangers, as happened with Arthur Hamilton during the hotel fire, and enable other unfortunates to have their deaths faked and become 'reborns'. Thus Wilson is finally wheeled into the operating theatre, strapped to a trolley and screaming in terror, while the doctor switches on the electric drill that will bore into his skull and give him a fatal cerebral haemorrhage.

Unspeakably grim but thought-provoking, *Seconds* was one of Rock's favourite films. Cynics have suggested this is because of the name 'Wilson' [sic], as Henry Willson had brought about Roy Fitzgerald's rebirth, only to be destroyed by his creation, with Rock's Antiochus Wilson hating the society he had been thrust into (ostensibly, Hollywood itself). Ten years after the film's release – and subsequent failure – he told Gordon Gow:

> What I liked was that the story wasn't really told until the film had been seen. Or in my case, until I had finished reading the script . . . For some strange reason it's only truly told when you think back on it. I mean, that clinic is a death clinic. But as you watch the movie you don't feel that. You're thinking of these unfortunate people who can't grapple with life the way they are. So they change for a better life – for nothing! Meanwhile the clinic's gotten rich from the assets of the clients – just flat rich. That's what made it terrifying to me. And equally, that's what made it intriguing to do!

In the middle of 1966, Rock made *Tobruk* (1967), directed by Arthur Hiller and co-starring George Peppard and distinguished British actor Nigel Green. Ironically, Rock's swansong for Universal proved his best for the studio for some time, though he professed, also to Gordon Gow, how much he had hated it:

> Did you ever start to read a book and never finish it? Well, it's like that with me if I'm stuck with a poor script. It just feels as if there's no point in continuing. I could name you many examples from the movies I've made. The most recent would be *Tobruk* or *Showdown*. If you're not gripped by the first fifteen minutes of a movie, the movie's in trouble. Likewise,

I'll give a book 75 pages and if it doesn't hold my attention by then I stop reading. But on the other hand, what a joy it is to be hooked on page two of a book. Or a film begins, and bang! Something happens and it's electric!

In the film Rock played Major Craig – a role originally intended for Laurence Harvey – a fictitious Canadian hero of the ill-fated British campaign that failed to recapture the Libyan port from the Germans in September 1942, but nevertheless paved the way for Montgomery's defeat of Rommel at the Second Battle of El Alamein.

Craig has been captured in Algiers by the Nazis, but he is rescued by Captain Bergman (Peppard) – a German Jew serving with the British Special Identification Group – and shanghaied to Kufra in the Sahara, where he is ordered to launch an attack on the enemy fuel dumps at Tobruk, something he wanted to do earlier when the task would have been easier, only to then be refused permission. Now, Craig is given a small detachment of men, disguised as prisoners of war being escorted by Bergman's column – and just eight days to complete his mission across eight hundred miles of blistering desert, which he knows like the back of his hand.

'He looks so calm, you'd think he was planting daisies,' one soldier observes as he prods around in the sand with his bayonet in search of mines.

Craig's party encounters all manner of danger – attacks by British planes, the destruction of their transmitters, Nazi secret agents, aggressive Arabs, and a traitor amongst themselves. Yet after an awkward beginning to their relationship the agnostic (Craig) develops a fondness for the outsider (Bergman) and in one scene, which Rock later confessed had brought him to the verge of tears, Craig attempts to understand his companion's predicament of being German and Jewish:

CRAIG: We all know what's going on in Europe.
BERGMAN: There must be a little of the Jew in you . . .
CRAIG: They say there's a little of the Jew in everyone.
BERGMAN: Ja, and a little of the Nazi, too!

CRAIG: Your war's going to last a lot longer than mine, Captain . . .
BERGMAN: It's two thousand years old now. For the first time since Jesus we're beginning to think and feel as a people. The days of the wandering Jew are coming to an end. We're going home – Israel, where we belong.

When Craig's party – now disguised as wounded German soldiers – finally reach Tobruk, they are horrified to find Rommel's reserve about to make its move on El Alamein. Most of Craig's men are massacred in the ensuing skirmish, Bergman included, but Craig succeeds with his mission, driving a captured enemy tank up against the fuel dump and blowing it to bits . . . a decidedly Pyrrhic victory for only he and three comrades have survived their ordeal and, as the credits roll, they rush towards the sea to be rescued by a British ship.

So far as Rock's association with Universal was concerned, *Tobruk* had been the last straw. Although he had got along well with the other actors and crew, as usual, he felt that he had been snubbed by the studio executives – many of whom despised his versatility in an era when movie stars were pigeonholed into type, even more so than today. He told David Castell:

When I was playing drama, there was always surprise that I could do comedy. When I left the comedies to appear in *Seconds*, everyone was amazed that I could tackle dramatic parts. People in Hollywood had awfully short memories. When I finished *Tobruk*, I had to pay for my own party. I asked everyone from the front office, but nobody came. When it was over, I drove my car up and down the streets of the lot, out through the gates and said, 'Right, I'm never coming back here!'

For the first time in fourteen years, Rock was free to please himself, to pick and choose his roles. He also became the legitimate owner of the Castle. However, far from feeling content, he suddenly became paranoid about his future, wholly convinced that without the support of the studio that had launched him no more decent parts would ever come his way. He began drinking, though not yet heavily enough for it to affect his health. He was also getting through two packs of cigarettes a day, but still looked astonishingly fit and saw no reason to give up on his so-called vices. He told *Photoplay*'s Mike Webb:

> I love to smoke and I keep hoping someone will discover it's a healthy habit because the smoke kills all the germs in your system. I love to drink, but I hate exercise. I don't mind going outside on the hill and chopping down a tree, but I hate organised exercise. I built a gym in my house, but I never use it. I don't even like to walk through it!

Then, out of the blue, in the summer of 1967, Rock received a call from MGM, offering him the part of Commander James Ferraday in the screen adaptation of Alistair MacLean's 1963 novel, *Ice Station Zebra* (1968). The plot was complex, with a wealth of frequently tedious, repetitive technical jargon. A nuclear submarine – the true star of the picture – travels under the icecap to the North Pole on a rescue mission when the staff of a weather station radio distress signals. On board the sub are three secret agents (Ernest Borgnine, Patrick McGoohan, and former footballer Jim Brown), and for over two hours of screen time it is impossible to discern which is the villain, or to work out why Ferraday's mission is taking place. Effectively Ferraday is trying to recover a capsule, dropped by a Soviet satellite, which contains film taken of every nuclear missile base in the northern hemisphere. The ending – a Russian para-troopers versus American and British confrontation, where again it is sometimes impossible to tell who is who – is confusing to say the least. Even so, the more than moderate success of the film helped revive Rock's flagging career . . . and introduced him to the man who would replace Lee Garrington in his affections.

Jack Coates was an outgoing, 23-year-old anthropology student at the UCLA, who had been making ends meet by working as a gas-station attendant and bit-part actor for MGM. As with Garrington, Rock is said to have checked him out – discovering that Coates was living with an older man. This time, however, he had no intention of hanging around until Coates was free. Too shy to make the first move, or perhaps fearing a rebuff, he began stopping off at the gas station where he 'innocuously' studied the object of his desire while Coates was filling his car – then taking it home, siphoning off the tank and returning for more gasoline, until Coates finally took the hint and asked him out on a date!

Coates, however, was no easy prey, and despite being asked to move into the Castle he refused to walk out on his lover – whom he had been with since the age of eighteen – having been warned by friends that, though undoubtedly a good 'catch', Rock Hudson had a notorious reputation for discarding his men on a whim because there were always so many more waiting in the wings. Absolutely true, of course, though Coates soon changed his mind when Rock presented him with a rather silly ultimatum: unless Coates submitted, Rock would tear up all his Hollywood contracts and never work again. Coates swallowed the ruse and moved in – the first lover to live at the Castle in twelve years and the pair, though never monogamous, are said to have enjoyed five blissful years together without so much as an angry word passing between them. Rock also refused to allow Coates to give up on his studies, even though his being at college meant that they could only see each other at weekends or during the holidays.

In the spring of 1968, Rock flew to Paris to make *Darling Lili*, arguably the last of the truly great Hudson vehicles, with Julie Andrews and directed by her husband Blake Edwards, who had triumphed with *Days of Wine and Roses* (1962) and *The Pink Panther* (1963). 'I needed someone tall and handsome, dashing and hero-ish,' Edwards is quoted as saying by Jimmie Hicks (*Films in Review*, May 1975). 'They gave me a long list of names, but not one fitted the specification. Then I realised that I needed Rock Hudson to play Rock Hudson.'

Sadly, the film would prove nowhere near as successful as everyone anticipated – through no fault of its stars who put in quite exemplary performances: Rock is superb as the charismatic hero, although it is Andrews' film from start to finish. Vocally, she is in even better form than she was in *The Sound of Music* (1965), which is indeed saying something.

Although Rock got along well with Edwards and the rest of the cast, he is reputed to have loathed his leading lady, who reminded him on the first day of shooting that of the two, she was by far the bigger box-office draw. She was certainly made a great fuss of, for while Rock had to make do with an entourage of just two, Andrews had dozens of people to wait on her hand and foot. There was also a much-talked about argument between the two stars, when Andrews is alleged to have screamed at Rock that, aside from sharing the same profession, they had absolutely nothing in common. 'Rock quietly told her that they had, and exactly what this was,' a Paramount spokesman, who insisted upon remaining anonymous, told me in Paris in 1997. 'He told her in front of a whole group of people, and that lady's face turned so green, it's no small wonder he didn't get fired from the picture on the spot!' Even so, none of this animosity shows in their scenes together, even in the most intimate ones, which more than suggest that Rock's 'Roy Harold and Eunice Blotter' days (as Rock lovingly referred to his partnership with Doris Day) were far from over.

Lili Schmidt (Andrews) is a German spy masquerading as British music hall star Lili Smith during World War I, though her approach owes more to the great French chanteuse Damia (1889–1978) than anyone who graced the London stage – particularly in her use of the then innovative single spotlight highlighting just her face and hands. Her opening number, 'Walk Me Back Home, My Darling', is also a Damia standard, cleverly re-arranged by Michel Legrand, fresh from producing an album of French chansons for Barbra Streisand. Lili works for the sinister Colonel Kurt von Ruger (Jeremy Kemp), and as the film opens is about to leave for France where, for some unexplained reason, she is to be awarded the *Légion d'Honneur*. Enter two bungling French Army Intelligence agents who are searching for the female spy in their midst, and dashing American aviator Major Bill Larrabee (Rock), whom Kurt has ordered Lili to befriend because he is supposedly in the know about an imminent Allied invasion.

Lili has grown weary of meeting stuffy, middle-aged generals and majors and is in no hurry to get to know this one, who has been worshipping her from afar since watching her entertaining wounded soldiers at the front. We first see Larrabee engaged in an aerial dogfight with the infamous Baron von Richthofen (Ingo Mogendorf), though it is a good half-hour into the film before he pronounces his first lines: accompanied by a band of gypsy musicians, he turns up at Lili's Paris lodgings at three in the morning and asks her out on a picnic. For her it is love at first sight, though for now she maintains a professional stance and attempts to seduce him solely for the acquisition of military secrets, which, of course, are never forthcoming because he is always one step ahead of her. When one of Bill's drunken friends (Lance Percival) lets slip that her beau is involved with 'Operation Crepe Suzette', she relays this information to Kurt – who responds that if he, the head of their spy ring, has never heard of it, then it is either extremely top secret, or non-existent, in which case Larrabee is on to them.

In a country hotel, Larrabee, who has thus far proved unseducible, turns on the charm. 'I think you're the most provocative, exciting and desirable woman I've ever met,' he drawls, while Lili persistently interrogates him about his mysterious mission – in effect, to end his relationship with stripper Crepe Suzette (Gloria Paul) so that he may be free to be with her, though he does not tell Lili this. Instead he lies that Operation Crepe Suzette will prove the biggest military exercise since the Battle of the Marne, and that a few evenings ago he personally discussed tactics with General Haig – unaware that Lili was with the commander on the evening in question! Outraged, Lili storms out of the hotel and heads back to Paris in a downpour, while a background choir sings 'Smile Away Each Rainy Day'. Larrabee rushes after her, and eventually corners her in her bathroom. 'You bastard,' she snarls at him for spinning her a yarn, while he reprimands her by holding her under the cold shower. And the response is pure Roy Harold:

> So I'm a liar. What would you rather be – a traitor? The lives of hundreds, thousands, of men depend on Operation Crepe Suzette being kept a secret. So, what in the name of hellish vanity makes you think I'd compromise that in the name of your adolescent, narcissistic ego?

> . . . Sure I lied to you. And you know what? I think you're
> glad you caught me lying . . . I think maybe you have to come
> up with excuses just to avoid the moment of truth. In a word,
> Miss Smith, I think it's just possible you're a virgin!

For the *grande horizontaliste*, being called a virgin is the supreme
insult. Lili slaps Larrabee's face, he kisses her brutally, and of course
'it' takes place. The next day, wearing Lili's scarf as a token, he
fights the Red Baron again, and again he gets away (Richthofen was
eventually shot down in 1918, having bagged 80 planes). Lili,
meanwhile, has learned the truth about Crepe Suzette, and visits a
salle des beuglants (music hall) to watch her in action. Incensed that
Larrabee could be involved with such a vulgar creature, she emulates
her in her next show – shocking her society audience by stripping
naked during the otherwise innocuous 'You Don't Need Three
Guesses'. Afterwards she tells Kurt, 'You can take it from me that
Operation Crepe Suzette has never existed except in bed – and no
doubt he's operating right now!'

When Lili and Larrabee meet again, he has been slightly wounded
and confides that he has stolen Richthofen's legendary Fokker
triplane. Naturally she scoffs, until she learns from Kurt that he
really has done this, and begs him to forgive her. When he leaves on
his next supposed vital mission, however, she follows him and sees
him meeting Crepe Suzette. At last he has got around to telling her
that it is over between them, but Lili misinterprets the situation and
organises for damning evidence to be planted in Suzette's apartment,
and she and Larrabee are arrested for treason. This fails, and afraid
that her own cover as a spy has been blown, Lili joins Kurt who is
about to face a court martial, and the pair board the train for
Switzerland to evade arrest – pursued by a fleet of angry German
aviators who are after Kurt, and Larrabee who thinks Lili has been
kidnapped. The ensuring scene is stirring stuff: the enemy planes are
shot down, and the slow, closing-in shot of Lili running across the
hillside to wave her lover goodbye is straight out of the opening
credits of *The Sound of Music*.

The film ends as it began, with Lili Damia-like on the stage,
performing the same song at a victory benefits concert. Ruefully,

she conjures up the ghostly images of soldiers lost in action, including Larrabee it would appear – until he walks in, safe and well, and they are tearfully reunited, compelling us to reach for our handkerchiefs.

While shooting *Darling Lili* another reunion took place – with Massimo – but even this did not stop Rock from pining for his new lover, and he asked Paramount's French representative to make arrangements for Jack Coates to be flown out to the set, arguing that he and Massimo had conducted an open relationship in Rome without creating a fuss. The studio's Hollywood executives, however, were virulently against this. They had cautioned Rock before assigning him to the film because, they accused, he had allowed his sexual indiscretions to get increasingly out of hand since leaving Universal and ridding himself of Henry Willson. Now, they threatened to tear up his contract and recall him to Hollywood, should he persist in this career suicide.

As had happened with Jack Navaar, Rock was ordered to get rid of Coates, and on top of this he was told that if he was fired from *Darling Lili* at this late stage (the production had already been shooting for several weeks when Rock joined it, and would acquire other problems along the road, which would delay its release for two more years) Paramount would sue him personally for compensation. Rock, whose hatred of Julie Andrews was by this time said to have been such that he would have done anything not to keep on working with her, nevertheless called the studio's bluff – they capitulated, and Jack Coates was sent over on the next available flight. 'It was a tough time for us all,' the aforementioned studio technician observed, 'but Rock kept himself ticking over – a couple of nights with me, and bedhopping between his Italian stud and a 22-year-old technician called Jimmy.'

Rock's letting down of his guard caught up with him in the October when he flew home for the premiere of *Ice Station Zebra* – and a repeat performance of what had happened at the first night of *Magnificent Obsession* when a heckler at Hollywood's Cinerama Dome stepped out of the crowd, faced him, and bawled 'Fag!' This time Rock's friends had to hold him back to prevent him from hitting the man, and he swore never to attend another such event again.

Darling Lili was quickly followed by *A Fine Pair* (1969), his second coupling with Claudia Cardinale, part-filmed in Italy and enabling him to catch up once more with Massimo, and *The Undefeated* (1969), a much underrated film with John Wayne. Rock was initially excited about this particular project, not just about working with 'The Duke', but with director Andrew McLaglen, another tall man, 'I was hoping working with those two would do wonders for my posture after years of stooping down on my co-stars,' he told David Castell.

Rock soon revised his opinion of John Wayne once shooting got under way, and he later declared that the whole experience of *The Undefeated* had been a nightmare. He should have realised what he was letting himself in for – spending weeks on location in Durango, Mexico, with a man whose homophobia was almost as legendary as his no-nonsense approach to the tough-guy parts he played. In 1946, upon being told that Montgomery Clift was having an affair with third-lead John Ireland, Wayne had gone berserk and tried to have Monty fired from *Red River*. This so upset the younger star that their fist-fight in the film had been for real, with Wayne coming off worst for once. Rock was therefore told by Andrew McLaglen that under no circumstances would Jack Coates be allowed into Mexico, let alone near the lot.

Throughout shooting, Wayne had Rock watched like a hawk, monitoring his movements and even his telephone conversations in search of the slightest indiscretion. He learned that Rock was amorously interested in one of his co-stars, a young blond actor who, according to some sources, might have reciprocated had the circumstances been less fraught. Worst of all, Wayne treated him like an inexperienced subordinate, as Rock explained to Professor Ronald L Davis:

Wayne started giving me suggestions. 'Why don't you turn your head this way? Why don't you hold the gun like this for the close shot?' They sounded like good ideas, so I tried them.

Then that night I started thinking, 'Am I going to be directed by this guy? Is he trying to establish dominance, or something?' So the next day I said to him, 'Why don't you turn your head this way?' Wayne pointed his finger at me. 'I like you!' he said.

Because Rock had stood up to him – inasmuch as Montgomery Clift had done – John Wayne began respecting him, though Rock's admission that the pair became firm friends is only partly true. Wayne would nurture a lifelong resentment of homosexuals and frequently refer to them as 'fairies', even though most of the ones he mocked were every bit as butch as his legend proclaimed he was. Rock also howled when told that Monty had bawled Wayne out on the set of *Red River* with the classic put-down, 'Me a fag, Mr Wayne? Aren't you the one who was baptised Marion, dear?'

In *The Undefeated*, Wayne pulls out all the stops to monopolise every scene he shares with Rock – out-swaggering, out-drawling, traits which aid rather than hinder their on-screen rivalry, though Rock – despite a suspect Southern accent – comes across as the more charismatic of the two. It is 1865 and Robert E Lee has surrendered to Grant, news that is relayed to Unionist Colonel John Henry Thomas (Wayne) following a skirmish where losses to both sides have been heavy. Now that the war is over, Thomas' men do not want to leave him and he accepts a commission to capture wild horses to replace those lost in the conflict – these are to be sold to the US government and the proceeds shared out amongst his soldiers in repayment for their loyalty.

Meanwhile, Confederate Colonel James Langdon (Rock) returns to his Southern plantation. His son and brother-in-law have been killed in the fighting, and his future looks grim when Union agents turn up and try to force him to sell his land for next to nothing an acre – it is either this, or it will be taken from him. Langdon frees his slaves, murmurs 'Goodbye, old lady' to his house – then torches it so that no one will have it. Then, joined by his entire local community, he and his family hit the trail for the Mexican border. Here, war is raging between the supporters of Hapsburg usurper Emperor Maximilian and the deposed president, Benito Juárez, who two years from now will retake control of the country, be restored to the presidency and have Maximilian executed. For reasons that are not explained here, Langdon and his company are to be met in Durango by Maximilian's representatives and escorted to Mexico City.

The Unionists' and Confederates' paths cross when Thomas captures 3,000 wild horses and both US and Mexican government officials want to buy. The Americans, however, are only interested in part of the herd, whereas the Mexicans need the lot to augment their revolution. Thomas has seen far too much bloodshed in recent years to be interested in politics so he sells to the highest bidder, then changes direction and heads south. One of his men asks, 'You ain't expecting trouble are you, John Henry?' To which Thomas replies:

> Trouble? Well, let's see. We have Maximilian on one hand, Juárez on the other hand and bandits in between. On top of that, we're Americans in Mexico, taking a caddy of horses to a very unpopular government. Why should we expect trouble?

The hostilities between Thomas and Langdon are, however, surprisingly muted – whenever things look like becoming too heated, a bemused sergeant (Bruce Cabot in one of his last roles) quells tempers by producing a whisky bottle. Then romance blossoms between Langdon's daughter and Thomas' adopted Cherokee son (Melissa Newman, Roman Gabriel) and, at a more leisurely pace, between Thomas himself and Langdon's widowed sister-in-law, to whom he has apologised, having learned that his cavalry may have been responsible for her husband's death. This immediately reunites the rival factions.

After several adventures – a hoedown and friendly brawl, a failed ambush by bandits – the allies reach Durango. Langdon is the first to enter the town, where he is greeted by General Rojas (Antonio Aguilar), who tells him that he is an adherent of Maximilian and invites Langdon, his men and their families to a welcoming feast. This is a trap, for Rojas supports Juárez: Langdon is forced to watch a group of French prisoners face the firing squad, then told that he and his company are also prisoners of war, who will be shot unless

Langdon can persuade Thomas to hand over his horses. Until now it has been against Langdon's principles to ask a Yankee for anything and, he argues, would Thomas give up his horses to save the lives of men who not so long ago were mortal enemies? He asks, all the same, and Thomas – who was going to give Juárez his horses anyhow, though not for nothing – tells his men that they must decide what to do, not him. Unanimously they conclude that under the circumstances Christian values must be applied (Juárez was infamous for his anti-Christian policies), and following a skirmish with a detachment of French rebels – who are annihilated by the stampeding horses – the situation is resolved. Rojas gets his horses, but pays the going rate, and everyone heads for home – Thomas and his new love back to his Oklahoma ranch, Langdon and his family back to Washington, where he is planning on a seat in the House of Representatives.

In the autumn of 1969, Rock flew to Rome to make *Hornets' Nest* (1970) for United Artists and, as had happened with *Darling Lili*, he made arrangements for Jack Coates to join him once he had settled in at the Grand Hotel. After Gina Lollobrigida and Claudia Cardinale, he was tremendously thrilled at the prospect of working with another Italian beauty – Sophia Loren – but she inexplicably dropped out of the production at the last minute and was replaced by the equally voluptuous but less charismatic Yugoslavian star, Sylvia Koscina. There were many on-set problems, and while Rock's leading lady screamed her disapproval over director Phil Karlson's tough shooting regime in the scorching heat, Rock sloped off to have a little fun with his latest indulgence – a twenty-year-old bit player named Guido, who was the very spit of Massimo. As had happened before, the new amour was given a part in the film . . . and Jack Coates was contacted and told to stay put in America.

8

'That F-ing Oblong Box!'

'Television is the monster of all time that eats everything and everybody. When they wanted McMillan and Wife *to go to two hours, I said, "Why? The thing doesn't even hold up for ninety minutes!"'*

Rock Hudson

In February 1970, Rock flew to London – not to make a film this time, but to enter a recording studio and cut a 45rpm single and an album of songs by the American poet–*chansonnier* Rod McKuen. The album was called *Rock Gently*. Rock had particularly admired McKuen's English adaptations of the works of Jacques Brel, and his reworking of George Moustaki's (who had composed 'Milord' for Edith Piaf) 'Solitude's My Home', which had recently been covered by Dorothy Squires.

Rock had sung in several of his films, though he had never taken it seriously. He was, however, possessed of a pleasing, controlled baritone – Tallulah Bankhead was not far out in suggesting that he sounded a little like Perry Como – and he was not the only one who genuinely believed that he might have a successful singing career ahead of him. Rod McKuen himself told the *Daily Express*' David Wigg, 'I think he'll make Number One without any trouble. He has a unique sound and an octave-and-a-half vocal range.'

Rock told a British press conference that he had been taking singing lessons off and on for three years and enthused, 'Singing's something I always wanted to do. Finally I've got the chance to do it. I'd much rather hear a scene sung than spoken.'

Unfortunately, the recordings were eventually assigned to a mail-order company, and even Rock would denounce them as disastrous, though effectively he was selling himself short. 'There are closets full of them back home,' he would tell interviewer David Castell – bringing the interjection from his then lover Tom Clark during their interview, 'Nonsense, there are *warehouses* full of them!'

In this year too Rock played his first and last psychopath – Michael 'Tiger' McDrew in *Pretty Maids All in a Row* (1971), based on the novel by Francis Pollini and subsequently denounced by all the critics who reviewed it as the worst film Rock ever appeared in. It was directed by French master of titillation Roger Vadim, who was specially imported by MGM. Rock told Robert Colaciello of *Interview/VIEW*:

He's a marvellous director. He has this capacity that any good or great director I've worked with has – his just being there makes you try harder. You trust him, you lean on him and he gives you the go-ahead. Go, baby, go!

Making the film, however, was not all plain sailing. In a distinguished career, Vadim had directed some of the world's most beautiful women including Catherine Deneuve and past and present Mrs Vadims, Brigitte Bardot and Jane Fonda – stars who, in those days, had no problems with nudity scenes. Rock, however, would not prove such a pushover. When Vadim showed him the script where he was supposed to appear full-frontal in one scene, Rock threatened to tear up his contract, telling the somewhat surprised Frenchman, 'If *you* want to take a look at my dick, that's fine by me, but I'll be darned if I'll flash it for all the fucking world to see!'

Pretty Maids All in a Row was a decidedly unpleasant film, and its storyline – Tiger is the high-school counsellor who seduces only the prettiest girls on the campus, then murders them when they become too clingy – has ensured that it will never figure in any Hudson television retrospective owing to the increasing number of such real-life stories in recent years. And if the film's advance publicity – suggesting that Rock was as much the super-stud off-screen as he was on – was a feeble attempt to curb the rumours circulating once more about his personal life, MGM looked like they were in for a disappointment. According to the tabloids, Phyllis Gates was about to publish a kiss-and-tell account of her marriage to Rock . . . and this time there was no Henry Willson or all-powerful studio to offer payoffs or 'other' protection – in other words, threats.

Convinced that he was about to be 'sold down the river' by his ex-wife, Rock contacted a journalist with whom he had had a brief affair – a man who was now employed by the influential *Screen* magazine. Money exchanged hands, and the former lover arranged for an interview to be published in September 1971 – ensuring that his own name was excluded from the piece. Rock began by declaring that he had no idea what Phyllis could possibly find to write about him that his fans would find the least bit interesting. Ninety per cent of Hollywood marriages, he avowed, ended in divorce – a figure that was probably representative of the United States in general. He added that being a single man also had its advantages, in that he did not have to worry about leaving his family behind when filming abroad. Then he got down to the so-called nitty-gritty:

Yes, I think I *would* like to marry again. Probably not an actress or a career girl. Two lives pulling in different directions cannot help but put a strain on such bones. Hollywood is crowded with young, beautiful, available girls. I enjoy taking them out. Generally, I'm happy with my life as it is right now. There are few men I envy, or with whom I would trade places. But I *could* meet somebody today and get married tomorrow.

Rock's interviewer – or maybe the man who had organised this latest charade – could not resist concluding, sarcastically, 'Nobody who knows Rock Hudson *well* would wager on that!'

Ignoring any sly hints, nothing proved quite so humiliating as the very open public debate, conducted during the summer of 1971, when a Hollywood gay group – not unlike the so-called 'outing' movements of the present day who wrongly believe that society will be more tolerant of homosexuals if major celebrities come out or are forced out of the closet – sent out a large number of invitation cards that had been inscribed, 'To Celebrate The Wedding Of Mr Jim Nabors And Mr Rock Hudson.' Jim Nabors was a popular television host who, like Rock, had battled most of his career to prevent his sexuality from being exposed to the media. Rock had guested on his CBS variety show, and Nabors is thought to have stayed at the Castle on a number of occasions, though not as a lover – once was while his house was being cleaned up and refurbished after a fire. The announcement, however, was taken seriously by at least one gossip columnist who, though not actually allowed to name names for fear of prosecution, might just as well have done when he wrote, 'One is like the Rock of Gibraltar, the other is like your neighbour.'

The incident spilled over on to a number of radio and television chat shows, and for weeks the gates at the Castle were besieged by reporters, most of whom knew the *real* Rock Hudson but were afraid of putting pen to paper. Rock's good-humoured but flippant comment – 'It's over! I've given Jim all his diamonds and emeralds back!' – did not help, but if the newspapers were unable to get a sensible answer out of the 'groom and groom', there was no shortage of witnesses who were more than willing to offer first-hand and frequently graphic accounts of the nuptials, for suitable remuneration of course.

No two stories matched as alleged guests spoke about the ceremony, which had variably taken place in New York, Carmel, Las Vegas, Vancouver and Chicago – and at a Hollywood party hosted by Carol Burnett – though how or *why* the 'union' came about has never been explained. Rock and Jim Nabors were never lovers and most importantly – certainly at this stage in Rock's life – Nabors was neither blond nor muscular. What is virtually certain is that there *was* some sort of ceremony, serious or otherwise, though if a later report in the *News of the World* – conveniently published after Rock's death – is to be believed, the location was London, where the event was witnessed by 'a beautiful model' who, conveniently, only gave her story to the newspaper on condition that her identity should not be revealed:

The setting was the plush, candle-lit living room of a luxury house in Belgravia. And the odd couple made the vows before a 'priest' and eighteen guests. Most were men, with a sprinkling of glamour girls including the ex-*Vogue* model. 'I was an innocent fifteen-year-old at the time and was stunned by the whole thing,' said the model. 'I'd gone to the wedding with a friend of Rock's, thinking it was going to be a normal one between a man and a woman . . . I can't remember what responses Rock and Jim made to the priest. What I do remember is that the whole event took place in great seriousness, as though it was a man and a woman getting married in church . . . Most of the guests were designers and models, and nobody else seemed to think it unusual.'

The outcome of the scandal was that Nabors' television show was taken off the air, and at the end of 1971 – buckling under the unprecedented media pressure – Jack Coates packed his bags and went back to his family in Arizona. Later, he would tell Sara Davidson that he had left the Castle because he had been unable to stand the intrigue and in-fighting amongst Rock's courtiers, adding, 'Everyone wanted to be the movie star's best friend, and because I had pillow talk, they tried to get to the throne through me.'

The 'wedding' fiasco came close to ruining Rock's long-standing reputation as a romantic leading man, and matters were only aggravated when *Pretty Maids All in a Row* went on general release. A change in publicity now billed this as a black comedy, but the critics did not find the story of a man who went around bumping off young girls particularly funny – if this was the best Rock could do, one declared, then perhaps he should call it a day and go back to driving trucks. Rock himself confessed that some of the reviews for the film were the worst he had ever read. Salvation, however, came from the very worst source, as he later recalled to David Castell:

Universal asked me to do a little Movie of the Week entitled *McMillan and Wife*. I said no. They upped the money and still I said no. More money, still no. Finally, they offered me so much that it would have been absurd to decline. I would have been cutting off my nose to spite my face. I agreed to do it. Of course, it turned into a television series that tied me up for another seven years. I think perhaps Universal and I were *fated* to work together.

Rock was paid $120,000 an episode – more than anyone had ever received for a television series. The 70-minute comedy-dramas, ten to begin with, were to be screened at three-week intervals as part of the *NBC Mystery Movie* season with *McCloud* (1970) and *Columbo* (1971). In Britain, the series was called *Murder, Mystery and Suspense* and also included *Banacek* (1972). Rock was told that if required the series could be shot around any film schedule, that he would have full script approval, and that he would be able to choose his own leading lady.

Though he had never wanted to do television – which he scathingly referred to as 'that fucking oblong box in everybody's living room' – Rock is said never to have once complained on the set, though he did confess to the *Guardian*'s Bart Mills how he had hated the series' tight shooting schedule:

The villain in all this is time. There's not enough time. A movie, for instance, is made with some care. When I made *Seconds* with John Frankenheimer it was shot in four months. A *McMillan and Wife* segment is shot in three weeks, for the same amount of screen time [sic] as *Seconds*. They're made back-to-back, one after another, with no development of character, always the same. It's grounds for alcoholism! For five years I had to remain an all-knowing, superhuman son of a bitch who never went to the bathroom!

After auditioning seven potential 'wives' by taking them out to dinner with series producer Leonard Stern, Rock selected a virtually unknown 25-year-old, husky-voiced actress named Susan Saint James – reputedly because like himself she hailed from Illinois, and because she had been born with the same surname as his best friend, Mark Miller.

McMillan and Wife was ostensibly a seventies version of *The Thin Man* (1934) starring William Powell and Myrna Loy. Sally, the daughter of an eminent criminologist, proves the perfect, if somewhat naive, spouse for the laid-back, non-smoking, ladies' man Police Commissioner Stewart McMillan, and together they are drawn into innumerable cases – mostly homicides – aided by Mack's plodding, equine-faced sidekick, Sergeant Charles Enright (John Schuck). 'I'm not grinning,' Enright says in one episode, 'that's the way my mouth is!' Completing the line-up is Mildred (Nancy Walker), the sharp-tongued housekeeper whose cooking fills Mack with dread, and who never misses an opportunity to chide him for his would-be womanising. When Sally says, 'Mildred, you know that I trust Mack completely,' she cannot help the acid response, 'That's why we make such a good team. I don't trust him at all!'

The series has dated more considerably than the William Powell–Myrna Loy films of the thirties. Susan Saint James frequently looks like a teenager in her 'Flower Power' costumes, and Rock is sometimes ungainly and unappealing in wide-lapel suits, kipper ties, and every now and then a moustache, which does not suit him. The pilot show, *Once Upon a Dead Man* (1971), had most of its interior scenes filmed at the Castle, and was an instant hit not just in the United States, but around the world, where it was dubbed into more than a dozen languages.

As with Rock's comedy films, there are a lot of in-house gay jokes and references, and another precedent was set – that of the 'token fuck'. The requisite, easily identified, blue-eyed, fair-haired hunk who appears in almost every *McMillan and Wife*, with whom Rock was involved only while that particular episode was being made: the speed cop, the Highland dancer, the musician, the cowboy extra, the corpse . . .

The early shows varied in quality from the passable to the frankly appalling. In *Terror Times Two* (1972), credibility is stretched beyond the limit when Mack is kidnapped and a double whose mission is to kill one of the witnesses called against an underground gang is substituted in his place. 'I've been fleeing women since I was fifteen,' the real Mack quips, an obvious double entendre slipped in by Rock, a fact that is proved when even Sally cannot tell the difference between her husband and the fake.

In *Blues for Sally M* (1972), the pair investigate the attempted murder of a young jazz musician (Keir Dullea) who has dedicated a new piece to Sally, something she cannot comprehend because she does not know him. It then emerges that he is a split personality who has attempted suicide to gain attention – his 'other half' is the partially sighted, elderly critic Sally has been reading to in her capacity as part-time social worker and, despite the ten-cent wig and beard, she has not recognised him.

For much of the time in *Two Dollars on Trouble to Win* (1973), Rock himself looks like he is wearing a wig, while he searches for the crook who is trying to provoke Sally's skinflint racehorse owner uncle (William Desmarest) into having a heart attack. There are so many holes in this plot that it is no real surprise when the baddie emerges as the stable's top jockey.

In this first series of *McMillan and Wife*, Rock gives a good impression of bonhomie, as if he is genuinely enjoying the light-hearted romps that had returned him to the zenith of his popularity. He was, however, putting on an incredibly brave face to camouflage his burgeoning depression and disdain.

'The whole thing is lamentable,' he told Joan Mac Trevor, the Hollywood correspondent of the French magazine *Ciné-Revue*, who had been a close friend of Rock's since *Giant* and to whom he opened up his innermost thoughts, surprising even himself. 'The characters have the consistency of cigarette paper and the intrigue's only of interest to drunks and fools.' The scripts, he declared to just about anyone who interviewed him on the subject, were corny and the hours way too long. He also professed to hating his co-star Susan Saint James, who, well aware of the fact that Rock was gay, was apparently not averse to boasting to friends that she had fallen in love with him, and that he had initially reciprocated her crush by letting her sit on his lap – something he denied. But what really incensed him was her thrice being nominated for her role, and she *was* quite remarkable as the long-suffering Sally, while he was not even in the running when the nominations were put forward.

Rock's shaky equilibrium took a savage blow in March 1972 when his friend and former fiancée Marilyn Maxwell died suddenly of a heart attack brought on by a pulmonary ailment. Some years later Rock's agent, Dale Olsen, revealed to Joan Mac Trevor just how much this had affected his client:

> His grief drove him to alcoholism. He became like a wounded animal, seeing no one, refusing to even pick up the phone, which at the time was ringing nonstop. Occasionally he would go out, drive around for a few hours, then stop off absolutely anywhere and down a dozen drinks, one after the other. *That* was the period when he'd become determined to wreck his health, and he didn't give a damn about the consequences.

Rock paid for Maxwell's funeral, and was one of the pallbearers. He moved her fifteen-year-old son, Matt, into the Castle and looked after him while the estate was being sorted out – and when a reporter referred to Maxwell's once being considered as the second Mrs Hudson, he levelled, 'Marilyn Maxwell was the only wife I ever *wanted*.' Then, setting his grief to one side, he flew to Mexico to make *Showdown* (1973).

Rock's co-star in the new film could not have been a worse influence on his alcohol problem – Dean Martin, one of the few people capable of drinking him under the table. One afternoon – to the relief of the studio's insurers, both were sober – Rock was rehearsing a scene in which he had to drive an antique motor car when the brakes suddenly failed and he crashed into a concrete wall. He sustained a broken leg, two fractured arms, a cracked rib and severe concussion.

Shooting was held up for six weeks while Rock recovered, firstly in hospital, then at the Castle. He was barely up on his feet again when he received news from Mark Miller that George Nader had been blinded in one eye and forced to give up his acting career. Putting aside his own plight, Rock rushed to his friends' side, offering not just moral support but financial assistance: once Nader was well enough to look after himself, Mark Miller was put on to the Hudson payroll as Rock's personal secretary, ostensibly so that he would be able to support the partner who had supported him for more than thirty years.

Again, there was a new man in Rock's life. Oklahoma-born Tom Clark was a former actor and MGM publicist whom Rock had known for some ten years, but the pair had never become involved, he said, because someone else had always been in the way. Clark was also several steps away from the Hudson stereotypical lover – big, but neither muscular, blond nor even good-looking. Also, unlike most of the others, he was around the same age as Rock, and a heavy drinker. Most importantly he was possessed of the same offbeat sense of humour – and if Rock needed anything right now, it was cheering up. Soon after becoming an item the couple flew to Australia to collect Rock's 'Logie' – the country's equivalent of a BAFTA or an Emmy – beginning a series of round-the-world jaunts that would raise many eyebrows, although 'officially' Clark was Rock's publicist and personal manager.

The 1973 *McMillan and Wife* season was a distinct improvement on its predecessor, although some critics were unkind in referring to Rock's 'latest prop' – his midriff, which prompted the studio into ordering him to diet. 'What I *would* like is three hamburgers and a big bowl of spaghetti,' he told *TV Times* reporter Ken Martin when they met for lunch at the Universal canteen. 'But what I'm *going* to have is a salad and black coffee.' Rock was amused when Martin cracked, bravely perhaps, 'Go ahead and have the hamburgers, Rock. You could always be the first fat superstar!' He was not so tickled, however, when he read the finished article, within which Martin observed, doubtless in light of the Nabors scandal:

Maybe it is fear of questions that are too probing that makes him insist on a Press agent being present each time he gives an interview – though you only have to spend a week in Hollywood to find out all you want to know about him from friends and colleagues. You'd think by now he wouldn't worry about privacy, because audiences these days are too intelligent to care if a star's private life is different from his on-screen roles – and Hudson has proved that his popularity can survive anything.

Meanwhile, in *Freefall to Terror,* there was almost a repeat of the car-exhaust murder attempt that had occurred in an earlier episode – and lip-readers got to see Rock mouthing 'Oh fuck!' In the same episode, in a scene that the producer wanted to pull but Rock insisted stay put, Mack collapses with a fit of the giggles. What viewers did not know was the reason for his mirth – his 'man of the moment', playing a policeman, had unexpectedly opened his raincoat and flashed at him! Neither does Rock contain his laughter in *The Fine Art of Staying Alive*, when, during a flashback where he and Sally propose to each other, we are party to Sally's appalling table manners.

The in-jokes continued in *No Hearts, No Flowers*, when Sally tells her husband, 'I just want to be as satisfied as any other woman you have to handle.' But along with the jokes there were endless repeat sequences. In *Death of a Monster . . . Birth of a Legend*, for example, the action begins with the same car chase that ended the previous episode – Mack, almost nonchalantly catching another criminal before jetting off to Scotland with his entourage. 'Wonder if the Scotch is any good here,' Mildred poses, as they arrive at Mack's uncle's castle just in time to hear the old man being shot dead in *another* locked-room murder. The ensuing story then covers every possible Scottish theme: the Highland games, sword-dances, bagpipes, loch monsters, clan feuds and what Scotsmen wear under their kilts, with Mack not unexpectedly giving everyone an answer to this popular poser – and an eyeful. There are also some dodgy accents, most excruciatingly from Roddy McDowall, who tells Mack after someone has taken a pot-shot at him, 'You're lucky you're not on your way to be stuffed and mounted!' Like Rock, McDowall was secretly gay, and the scene required numerous takes because the pair kept cracking up. And finally our hero gets to look resplendent in tartan and warble a few lines from 'Just a Wee Jock and Doris' before waylaying the killer.

By far the best episode of this series was *Cop of the Year* (1972), which centred around the murder of Sergeant Enright's ex-wife – in yet another locked room, with his own gun, while they are having a row. In a flashback, where the McMillans are en route to meet Enright's 'other half' at the ceremony where he is to receive his Cop of the Year award, Mack poses the then very risqué question, 'What makes you think we're meeting a she?' When Enright becomes the chief suspect, his superior stands by him, despite the fact that the chances of proving him innocent are slim. In the course of the enquiry Mack visits a Hollywood studio – real-life director George Seaton is putting his actors through their paces for *Showdown*, the film he had just completed with Rock! Seaton, an acknowledged expert on guns and ammunition, provides the commissioner with the missing link that enables him to solve the case: Enright's ex-wife, who was terminally ill, hated him so much that she took her own life and framed him to make it look like he had murdered her.

Before these episodes were televised, Rock and Tom Clark flew to South America, where the first series of *McMillan and Wife*, dubbed hilariously into Spanish, was high in the television ratings. Rock had been signed up to make several personal appearances in Buenos Aires, and one television station had signed an agreement with Universal to film *The Rock Hudson Story* – a tell-all documentary, which of course would be anything but. Such was the hysteria among Rock's fans that the pair had to be escorted everywhere by the military police – until they moved to Rio de Janeiro, where Rock had hired a suite overlooking the gay stretch of Copacabana Beach. When they returned to Hollywood, Tom Clark took up residence at the Castle.

In March 1973 Rock was contacted by his friend Carol Burnett, claimed by many to have been matron of honour at his 'wedding' to Jim Nabors. Burnett had, some little while before, revived the musical *I Do! I Do!* and having raved over his album of Rod McKuen songs now proposed that *he* should be leading man when the new production went into summer stock. This was a tremendously difficult, if not potentially hazardous, venture for a man who, though more than capable of doing so, had never sung or danced in front of an audience other than the half-hearted crooning of 'Baby It's Cold Outside' at the 1958 Oscars with Mae West. And now he would be expected to perform *seventeen* numbers and routines! Burnett, however, would not take 'no' for an answer, and . without stopping to think what he might have been letting himself in for, Rock consented. He told David Castell:

I figured, after all, that I had nothing to lose and everything to gain, including experience. I learned the lines in one week, the score in the second, then we had three weeks in rehearsal. They say it's the most difficult of all the American musicals to do because there's nobody else on the stage except this couple and they age fifty years during the evening – so that even during the costume changes you have to keep talking, and when you go off stage you still have a microphone to carry on the conversation.

The complicated dance routines for the show were choreographed by one half of one of the most important American double-acts of the mid-twentieth century, Gower Champion (1919–80), who with his wife Marge had thrilled audiences with their dazzling dance displays in films such as *Showboat* (1951) and *Till the Clouds Roll By* (1946). The plot, based on the play *The Four-Poster* (1964), centred around a couple who have been married fifty years, and who in a series of flashbacks re-enact the ups and downs of their life together. The premiere, in San Bernadino on 13 June 1973, saw Rock so affected by stage fright that he twice missed the cue for his opening song – fortunately, the audience were still cheering his entrance and few noticed. The reviews, however, were not as good as he would have liked, though every subsequent performance was a sellout, and the play transferred to Los Angeles.

At the end of the year, Rock and Susan Saint James began shooting a further series of *McMillan and Wife* – reluctantly, it would appear, for he was starting to tire of what he called the show's serious lack of professionalism. He told Ron Davis:

In television you have to remember what you're doing will come out of a little box. So you have to exaggerate and play everything bigger than life. You can't be subtle or your character will get lost. On the big screen the slightest move – the lifting of an eyebrow, the curling of a lip – comes across like a blasting horn because it's magnified twenty times. The same thing will register zero on TV. We also had a different director on every show and he'd say, 'Come in the door, go over to the fireplace and put a log on.' And I wanted to say, 'Well, I *can't*

do that. I just did that on the last show with the other director!'
So I went down to the office and told the producer, 'The
director's doing stuff that I don't think is any good.' And *he*
said to me, 'You don't understand – *you* have to direct!' And
the scripts became progressively worse as the seasons wore on.
They weren't particularly funny and we had to ad-lib a lot of
them. That's dangerous. Comedy should be proven, well-
worked out – not done off the cuff.

Rock later said that only two episodes of this entire series had been
worth watching. *Reunion in Terror* (1974) sees Mack return to his
old college after twenty years for a football team reunion, where, not
surprisingly perhaps, several former players are murdered – in
sequence with the numbers they wore on their shirts.

In *The Devil You Say* (1973), the action takes place during the run-
up to Halloween when Mildred witnesses a murder at the hospital
where Sally works: prior to this, Sally has been called by the victim
– whose body has mysteriously disappeared in yet another locked
room – and warned that her life is in danger. We then learn that for
several years, each October, she has received anonymous gifts – a
bell, a garter, an ancient Egyptian medallion and ring – which she has
passed on to Mildred. What she now discovers is that they have been
sent by a devil-worshipper who believes her to be a fourteenth-
century goddess he loved in his former life! In one scene, the most
hilarious in the show's four-year run, the killer almost meets his
match when he barges into the McMillans' house and is accosted by
Mildred – dressed as a witch, she throws everything at him she can
lay her hands on, stopping short only of the essential whisky
decanter. He gets away, however, kidnaps Sally, and drags her to the
sacrificial altar upon which she must die by midnight in order for his
cult to survive. Mack gets to her a few seconds before the dagger is
about to be plunged into her heart – and all she can find to say is,
'Like my hair?'

In the summer of 1974, Rock and Carol Burnett took *I Do! I Do!* on
the road. There were short seasons in Washington, where they took
an evening off to perform some of the song-and-dance routines at the

White House, and in St Louis, where some of Rock's relatives lived. Tom Clark arranged for Rock's mother to be flown out from California, and organised a family reunion, which is said to have made Rock cringe because, for Kay's sake, he had been forced to acknowledge a bunch of comparative strangers. Clark would later repeat (to Sara Davidson) a conversation he claimed he had had with Kay at around this time, which intimated that Roy Scherer may not have been Rock's father. Whether Rock himself knew this is not known, though he was certainly aware of his mother's flighty past and probably would not have put anything past her.

This sudden appearance of so many family members he had never heard of until now – people who could legally make claims on his estate, should anything befall him – filled Rock with such trepidation that upon his return to Hollywood he contacted his lawyers and had them draw up a will leaving virtually everything to Tom Clark or George Nader and Mark Miller, should Clark predecease them. And in the event of all three dying before him, Rock's will included a codicil instructing that his estate should be divided amongst his favourite charities.

Rock's next film, a *Grand Guignol*-meets-Machiavelli *schlockfest*, which saw him belatedly following in the horror footsteps of Joan Crawford and Bette Davis, was *Embryo* (1976), directed by Ralph Nelson. His co-stars were a wooden but decorative Barbara Carrera, the Nicaraguan former model, who in 1983 played Fatima Blush in the Bond film *Never Say Never Again* – and Diane Ladd, who after Rock's death portrayed his mother in the television biopic, *Rock Hudson* (*see* Appendix). 'There's a little bit of Frankstein, a little bit of Svengali, a little bit of *Seconds*,' he told David Castell, 'but overall it's like no other film I've been offered. Obviously there is some horror, some bloody moments, but only where the script absolutely calls for it.'

Like *Pretty Maids All in a Row*, on account of the insensitive handling of its subject matter, *Embryo* is hardly likely to appear in Hudson retrospectives. It is tacky, tasteless, camp in the extreme during its closing scenes, but nevertheless compulsive viewing if one is fortunate enough to obtain a copy. The opening credits inform us that what we are about to see is not all science fiction but 'based on current foetal growth outside the womb medical technology'. Speeding on a stormy night, scientist Paul Holliston (Rock) knocks down and badly injures a dog, which just happens to be pregnant. He takes the animal to the home he shares with his spinster sister-in-law, Martha (Ladd), and installs it in the lab he has not entered in the three years since the death of his wife. At the time of her death, having suffered three miscarriages, the pair were working on an experimental growth hormone, placental lactogen, which they hoped would help others facing a similar dilemma.

Now Paul's long-idle brain goes into top gear. He calls his son, Gordon (John Elerick), and asks him to bring medical supplies, and tells Martha, 'Get me some k-9 plasma from the refrigerator'. He fights to deliver the puppies before the mother dies. He saves one, injects it with growth hormone and within days it attains adulthood, is super-intelligent on account of the drug's side effects, but has no emotional feelings whatsoever. Paul baptises it 'Number One', tells everyone that it is the mother who has survived and decides that his next experiment will be on a *human* foetus. A doctor friend provides this (the fourteen-week foetus of a suicide victim) and while Paul collects this, Number One lets herself out of his car, kills another dog and dumps the body in the bushes.

Paul hides the foetus in his lab, feeds it the growth hormone and she grows at an unexpectedly alarming rate, two years for every 24-hour period, stopping when she reaches 25. He calls her 'Victoria', prepares her for the outside world and is astonished at her capacity for learning. She reads the Bible in one sitting and denounces it as illogical; she becomes an expert chess player after merely studying the rules and she spot-reads Paul's notes and learns how she came to be, realising that effectively she is a non-person.

Paul invents a persona for his protégée, takes her to a party and introduces her as his new research assistant but refuses to say what he is researching. She appears to bond with Gordon's wife, Helen (Anne Schedeen), but aside from Number One, nurtures feelings for no one and only alienates Paul's friends by being more expert in their particular field of interest than they are. Back home after the party, wearing a see-through negligee, Victoria waylays him as he is undressing for bed and tells him, 'I want to learn, to experience. Would you teach me?' Paul obliges and, after he has made love to her, Victoria goes into another room and pleasures herself – a scene that was cut from most prints of the film for its brief run in American cinemas. She then realises that the ageing process has recommenced and that only hours after having intercourse, she is several weeks pregnant. Not knowing as much about growth hormones as the man who created her, Victoria realises that she needs an antidote to prevent her from ageing too far: an infusion from the pituitary gland of an unborn child. She also falls foul of Martha, who has checked her out and found no trace of her ever having been born. No problem, for Victoria administers a lethal injection, which causes her to have a fatal heart attack en route to Gordon's place.

From this point *Embryo*'s *schlock* content goes into overdrive. While Paul is out of town attending Martha's funeral, Victoria destroys his notes so that no one will ever discover the truth. She then reads up on how to perform a Caesarian section and pays a pregnant hooker to come home with her. The girl 'doesn't do dykes' but for $200, she'll learn to like it! Victoria has just delivered the child when Helen turns up. Why she is not with the rest of the family at the funeral is not explained. Having flung the dead whore downstairs, Victoria opts to procure another foetus as a spare. Paul, meanwhile, is heading home having learned that his sister-in-law was murdered. He meets up with Gordon and they find Helen about to be operated on – and the Keystone Cops take over. Hoping to kill her, Paul plunges the growth hormone syringe into Victoria's neck so that she begins re-ageing one side at a time. But not before she has finished Gordon off with a scalpel and he falls, up-tipping the experimentation tank and sending the baby bouncing like a rubber ball across the laboratory floor. Then off she speeds in her car with Paul and the police in hot pursuit, crashing into a ball of flames at the edge of a lake. Paul manages to drag her free and is in the process of drowning her when the cops pull him off. She has told him that she is dying but as she convulses at the roadside, the stupefied paramedic announces that this old crone is actually about to give birth: to Paul's baby. And as the credits prepare to roll, Paul goes completely insane and screams for both mother and baby to die.

Meanwhile, there was an allegedly not-so-friendly parting of the ways between Rock and Susan Saint James when her Universal contract expired and she refused to negotiate another unless the studio agreed to a substantial salary increase. Some reports at the time alleged that Rock had threatened to boycott the series unless she was *forced* out, though there is no evidence to support this. Nancy Walker also left the show, and John Schuck announced that he only wanted to appear in the occasional episode.

Rock's own contract with Universal still had one year to run, and initially the studio considered supplying him with a replacement Sally. This, he declared, in the days when character face-changes in American soaps were not as commonplace as they are today, would succeed only in making the series less credible than it had already become. Therefore an uneasy compromise was reached. Sally was killed off in a pre-episode plane crash.

Retitled *McMillan*, the series featured a new-look Mack: chain-smoking, hard-drinking, a little greyer around the temples, and more often than not falling in love with a different girl at the end of each episode . . . though off the set Rock was still enjoying his 'token fucks' with blond studs who seemed to be getting younger. There was a new sidekick: baby-faced Steve DiMaggio, played by Richard Galliland, who later starred in *The Waltons* (1972–81) . . . and the ubiquitous housekeeper, Mildred, had been replaced by her equally dominating sister, Agatha, brilliantly portrayed by comedienne Martha Raye. The fact that Raye, a top name in Hollywood for forty years, had received a special Oscar in 1969 for entertaining the troops in the Korean and Vietnam Wars went a long way towards Rock suggesting her for the part.

All Bets Off (1976), the first *McMillan*, sees Mack taking a break in Las Vegas – eight months after Sally's death, and not referring to her once – with tennis-pro girlfriend Donna Drake, played by Jessica Walter, whom Rock had admired as the psychopath opposite Clint Eastwood in *Play Misty for Me* (1971). In *Coffee, Tea or Cyanide* (1977) Mack is on vacation again, this time on a flight to Hawaii, when one passenger is poisoned and another stabbed to death. The episode featured crooner Jack Jones, Pier Angeli's sister Marisa Pavan, and Julie Sommars as a nosy reporter whose engaging personality while helping Mack to solve the crime very nearly led to Universal offering her a regular part in the show – save for the fact that Rock could not stand her. If he was to have an additional sidekick, he said, it would have to be Stephanie Powers, who played his deputy district Attorney love-interest in *Affair of the Heart* (1977). She, however, was committed to a number of projects, including the *Hart to Hart* (1979) television series with Robert Wagner. And so, after filming the episode, Rock announced that the current batch of *McMillan*s would be his last.

9

Threes on Their Knees

'He would try to pass himself off rather touchingly as being interested in gay rights whenever I was around him. Clearly, Rock didn't have a clue about gay rights.'

Armistead Maupin, writer and friend

In November 1975, Rock's friends organised an extravagant bash at the Castle to honour his fiftieth birthday. Guests were instructed to wear fancy dress and for some reason most of them turned up as Arabs. A few hours before the bash, Rock and Tom Clark had had a lovers' tiff, and though they had made up at once, Clark had laughingly sworn that he would have his 'revenge'. When all the guests were assembled, Rock descended the staircase – camp-like, to the strains of 'You Must Have Been a Beautiful Baby', wearing nothing but an oversized diaper. Later he opened Tom Clark's present and put this on – a tee-shirt that had been customised at the last minute with the slogan, 'Rock Is A Prick'.

A few weeks later, Rock took *I Do! I Do!* to London – on the face of it not a wise move, for some critics were still recoiling from the abysmal revival at the Lyric seven years previously, starring Anne Rogers and Ian Carmichael. Rock was not to know this, and in any case most of the tickets had been sold before he had boarded the plane in Los Angeles, ensuring that the curtain would not come down prematurely on this production as had happened before. It opened on 21 January 1976 at the Phoenix Theatre – in a so-called 'Hollywood' season that included Louis Jourdan in *13, Rue de l'Amour* and Charlton Heston in *Macbeth*. Carol Burnett had opted to take a break from the production and Rock's leading lady was Juliet Prowse – his second choice after the London-based American actress Lee Remick, who was unavailable. The reviews were exceptional, even if the star very quickly became bored with it all, as he explained to David Castell, halfway through the eight-week run:

Juliet and I have got to the point where our minds wander during the songs. I remember Carol [Burnett] giving me some advice. She said that one night she was in the middle of a number and she caught herself wondering about what to buy in the market. She was so shocked that she wrenched herself back to the show, and it was only then that she blew the lyric. The advice was, always go with the dream. So I find myself thinking, 'Shall I eat Italian tonight? Shall I start with avocado?'

Rock's customary geniality was tested during the London run by one unnamed critic, who observed, 'Hudson wasn't as bad as I hoped he would be.' 'That's really below the belt,' Rock told Castell, 'and that's just where I'll hit him if we ever meet up. I don't know why there are critics at all, let alone why they should be paid for exercising their egos.' And with another journalist – distinguished British film critic and historian Roy Pickard, then writing for *Photoplay* – Rock was less interested in discussing the play than he was in confessing that he was still in mourning for James Dean:

The last words I said to Jimmy Dean came from a line I said in the movie because after that very shot he had to get away from the set and race his 'little spider' up the freeway to get killed. 'You're through, finished,' was the line I said to him. 'You're all washed up!' I've often wondered, you know, if Dean had stayed alive whether he would have remained the cult figure he became so quickly. What would have happened to him? Would he have developed as an actor? Somehow I don't think so. But those words were a bit prophetic, weren't they? Even now, twenty years later, they still give me a shiver.

As had happened in Rome, while he was in London, Rock became obsessed with discovering the city's gay nightlife, dashing off with Tom Clark to a different pub or club most nights after the show. One of his favourites was Bang Disco in Charing Cross Road where, according to Peter Burton – then working as the establishment's doorman, but today one of British gay culture's most illustrious writers and representatives – he made no attempt whatsoever to conceal his identity.

People would point and exclaim, 'Wow, it's Rock Hudson!' Then they'd walk up to him for a chat and always find him so utterly at ease and charming. There was absolutely no pretending. Everyone respected him for that.

After London, *I Do! I Do!* played a three-month season in Toronto, and though most of the reviews were again poor, all that mattered so far as the promoters were concerned was that the box office was doing big business. Not so, however, Rock's next venture: *John Brown's Body* (1976), based on Stephen Vincent Benet's Pulitzer-prize-winning poem of 1929, and the play that had brought about Rock's infatuation with Tyrone Power. Co-starring Leif Erickson and Claire Trevor the production was a miserable failure – not through any fault of the cast, for the notices were quite exceptional, but simply because it toured at the wrong time, the summer of 1976, stopping off at all the wrong venues, such as college campuses, which were closed for the holidays.

Meanwhile, Rock's fans were treated to the final episodes of *McMillan* – the end of an era, and the critics agreed that these were the best ever. In *Have You Heard About Vanessa?* (1977), Mack, aided by a pretty photographer, investigates the apparent suicide of a top fashion model. In fact, she is not dead at all: the victim turns out to be a lookalike friend whom Vanessa has pushed from a balcony because the girl has stolen her lover . . . the scene where Vanessa 'returns' from the dead, wearing exactly the same clothes she has on in the home-movie Mack is watching when she walks into the room, is the most farcical in the whole series.

In *Dark Sunrise* (1977), Mack is away on a fishing trip, when he reads about his own 'murder' in a newspaper: his apartment has been blown up, killing himself and a pretty student – played by a very young, very plain-looking Kim Basinger one year before her Hollywood debut. The victim turns out to be a 'Mack-sized' college professor with whom she was involved – his body burned beyond recognition, enabling the real Mack to don a feeble disguise and solve the crime, committed by a bogus priest who has buried a cache of gold under the church altar! And in *Phillip's Game* (1977) our hero investigates the murder of a crooked building inspector who is about to testify against a disreputable contractor. Mack gets his man, but woven into the plot is his involvement with yet another old flame – played by singer Shirley Jones, who coerces him into a nice duet of 'Bye Bye Blackbird'. This episode was actually the second *McMillan* to be filmed but amongst the last to be screened – hence the belated news of Charles Enright's promotion to lieutenant, Mildred's 'defection' to the East after inheriting a diner, and several references to the late Sally, who has been forgotten until now.

Universal are known to have offered Rock a substantial salary increase for 'just one more' series of America's favourite, sexiest detective, regarded as a welcome antidote to the cynical Banacek and grungy Columbo, but Rock rejected the deal, declaring that enough was enough.

Rock threw caution to the wind by accepting the part of King Arthur in the stage version of the musical *Camelot* (1978). Richard Burton and Julie Andrews had triumphed with this on Broadway in the mid-sixties, though the film version had been a woeful exercise in miscasting when they had been passed over in favour of Richard Harris and Vanessa Redgrave – artists hardly noted for their musical abilities – affording the production a place in Michael Medved's famous movie compilation volume, *The Golden Turkey Awards*. Rock's interpretation of the play's most celebrated songs 'If Ever I Should Leave You' and 'How to Handle a Woman' were, however, in a class of their own. *Camelot* opened in Dallas, then played seasons in Massachusetts and Long Island, and most of the critics agreed that this was the best thing he had done on the stage so far.

As the tour of *Camelot* was drawing to a close, Rock called Mark Miller and asked him to organise a 'Beauties' party at the Castle, the likes of which had not been seen at the home of a Hollywood star since Rudolph Valentino's all-male love-fests of the twenties. Fifty of the dishiest hunks in town were hired to splash around the pool, or just 'drape and drool' around the adjacent garden areas wearing the skimpiest, flimsiest swimsuits. And there were no prizes for guessing which closeted Tinsel Town lovers from way back Rock was referring to when he told Armistead Maupin, 'The brunettes are all called Grant, the blonds are called Scott!' (He was referring to the famous long-running love affair between Cary Grant and Randolph Scott, the archetypal leading men of the day.)

Maupin, the undisputed literary genius and gay icon, is the creator of the *Tales of the City* novels, which recount the adventures of that infamous group of residents at 28 Barbary Lane, and their friends. The first of these had recently begun its serialisation in the *San Francisco Chronicle*. The British publication, *Gay News*, observed (1978):

> Like Trollope's Barsetshire, Maupin's San Francisco is an imaginative creation that is immediately recognisable. His larger than life characters have the compulsive attraction of soap opera heros and heroines and his plots – Dickensian in complexity – move from one cliffhanger to another. The whole potent brew is mixed with equal measures of wit and pathos – which constantly move the reader between laughter, excitement and tears.

Maupin and Rock had met in San Bernadino during the tour of *John Brown's Body* in 1976. Ironically they were introduced by Jack Coates and Coates' new lover, champion diver Steven Del Re, of whom more later. According to Maupin – on the face of it, physically not at all Rock's type – it had not taken Rock long to fall for him and the pair had embarked on a brief affair, which had begun in Rock's suite at San Francisco's Fairmont Hotel. Years later (quoted in

Patrick Gale's *Armistead Maupin*, Absolute Press, 1999) the writer would recall their 'first time' – of how, after rolling around with him on the floor, Rock had pulled out a small leather case embossed with his initials:

> He had a personalised Rock Hudson poppers case! And I completely lost my hard-on. I was so overwhelmed at the notion that I was about to go to bed with Rock Hudson. Not to mention the fact that I'd just seen the baby's arm hanging between his legs. And we sat on the couch together and he put his arm around me and said, 'You know I'm just another guy like any other guy?' And all I could say to this was, 'No, you're not. And I'm Doris Day.'

The great observer, Maupin is widely thought to have based his Barbary Lane characters on real-life acquaintances, and his books poignantly cover those all-important years from San Francisco's hedonistic pre-AIDS seventies through to the less intoxicating, self-conscious, safe-sex nineties. Central to the plot are the transsexual landlady Anna Madrigal, and Michael Tolliver, the indefatigable 'Mouse', who is perpetually in search of the big romance of his life. This comes in the form of hunky gynaecologist Jon Fielden, whom many believe could not have been based on anyone but Rock.

When the *Tales of the City* novels were adapted for a British television series in 1993, Fielden was played by William Campbell, a very tall, smoulderingly attractive young actor whose 'Hudson connection' had occurred eight years previously when he had portrayed Steven Carrington's lover in *Dynasty*. In one *Tales of the City* scene, Fielden visits one of the many bathhouses favoured by Rock: sauntering smugly through the steamy corridors he cruises the dozens of muscular studs who are lusting after him, before disappearing into one of the cubicles to have sex with a mysterious stranger who, Hudson-style, is later unceremoniously dumped when Fielden realises that he is becoming too fond of him.

Maupin is also widely believed to have based another of Mouse's lovers on either Rock or *Maverick* actor James Garner, though in more recent interviews the writer has maintained that the closeted actor referred to in the novels as 'Blank Blank', was actually an amalgam of all the closeted gay stars in Hollywood.

A few weeks after the 'Beauties' party – which also features in *Tales of the City* with Rock described, though not by name, as 'Truly magnificent, a lumbering Titan in this garden of younger, prettier men' – Rock began shooting his first television mini-series. *Wheels* was a ten-hour epic drama based on the 1971 best-selling novel by Arthur Hailey. His co-stars were Anthony Franciosa, Blair Brown, Ralph Bellamy and Lee Remick. Rock played Adam Trenton, a wheeling and dealing, adulterous automobile executive from Detroit. When *TV Times'* Douglas Thompson visited the set, Rock told him:

> He's not the usual hero and he's very complex. Married to the boss's daughter he's ambitious, mercenary, loving. He's manipulative, fair, dishonest. Honest, too. He's whatever's necessary. He badgers, pushes, pleads, blackmails to save his company. At the same time things are happening in his personal life which affect his relationship with his wife and their two grown-up sons.

Rock also maintained that *Wheels* was the most complicated production he had ever worked on, on account of the length of the script – in order to keep the 100-strong cast 'on their toes', the producer had elected to shoot most of the scenes out of sequence . . . and no one was more surprised than Rock, following his 'five years' hard labour' as Stewart McMillan, at how truly exciting television could be now that he had found his niche. 'Because mini-series have a limited run, they're better written and the effort is stronger,' he told Thompson. 'I'd like to do more. I don't want to do big movies any more.'

While shooting *Wheels*, Rock made frequent visits to an adjacent lot to watch another Hollywood legend famed for his 'good guy' roles – Gregory Peck – filming *The Boys from Brazil* (1978), one of the rare occasions Peck played a villain. Rock was amazed by his portrayal of an evil Nazi, and only wished that he could have been offered such a meaty role, instead of the 'dross' constantly flung his way by studios that were afraid of taking risks. He told *Photoplay*'s Vernon Scott:

> I don't think the public would have difficulty accepting me as a menace. I killed and scalped John McIntire in *Winchester '73*, then there was *Pretty Maids All in a Row*. I'd love to play more villains. There are a lot of anti-hero roles these days and I'd welcome a chance at some of them. There must be a reason Peck and I haven't been offered villain parts. Maybe it's because no one thought we could play them with conviction. I imagine personal appearance has something to do with it. A sinister appearance does give an actor a better chance to play a mean guy . . . but sinister facial characteristics certainly aren't mandatory. Ernest Borgnine and Charlie Bronson started out as villains and eventually wound up playing good guys. Sometimes it's to everyone's advantage for an actor to play against type. Playing straight leading men is boring, boring, BORING! I'd love to play the heavy, the guy who can swear or smack the leading lady without losing his status as hero.

The latter admission was in reference to the scene in *Wheels* where Adam Trenton hits his wife (Remick) – something Rock initially refused to do, concerned that parallels would be drawn with Phyllis Gates' allegations that he had physically abused her. He told Vernon Scott:

> Hitting an actress across the face was a first for me. Lee was pleading with me to slap her hard so she could give a good reaction. I couldn't manage it until the close-up, and even then the slap wasn't very hard, though that's what we had to settle for.

Rock had just begun working on the series when, in the October, he received a call from his mother's Newport Beach home informing him that she had suffered a stroke. Rock had not seen Kay for almost a year – he later said he had put a little distance between them because Kay had been terminally ill for some time and he had been unable to bear watching her suffer. By the time he and Tom Clark arrived at Newport Beach, however, it was too late.

Kay's death affected Rock badly – probably due to a combination of his guilt and becoming suddenly aware of his own mortality and the fact that he, who had once had the most beautiful men in the world positively flinging themselves at him had, one way or another, resorted to buying the affection of his lovers, Tom Clark included. And as his relationship with Clark started to disintegrate, once again Rock's only solace came from out of a bottle.

Thankfully, this period of self-loathing was brief. In June 1978, Rock joined a New York-based theatre group for a five-month tour with another musical comedy, *On the Twentieth Century*. His co-star was Dean Dittman, the oversized, fun-loving actor who had portrayed Daddy Warbucks in a stage production of *Annie*. Rock had hated it, but he and Dittman would become close friends, and it was Dittman who persuaded him to look for a more permanent base in New York. Rock bought a luxury apartment on the Beresford, near Central Park.

Initially, *On the Twentieth Century* did well at the box office, though by the time the tour reached Chicago, the production was losing money hand over fist and there was talk of its closure. Rock solved the dilemma by performing without pay, and the tour staggered on to Los Angeles, where it managed to recoup its losses. Rock celebrated the premiere here a little too enthusiastically: driving home to the Castle, he fell asleep at the wheel and crashed into a palm tree. Fortunately he was unhurt, but the incident does appear to have brought him to his senses so far as his drinking was concerned.

On the negative side Rock, who had spent his entire professional life trying to keep his sexuality a secret, entered a period where he virtually advertised not just the fact that he was gay, but that in his search for ultimate sexual titillation he had sunk to the very depths of what many might have called depravity. In July of the same year Armistead Maupin, now a regular visitor to the Castle, invited Rock, Mark Miller and George Nader to San Francisco to attend a special performance of his ultra-camp play, *Beach Blanket Babylon*.

The weekend turned into a gay-club bender and opened even

Rock's experienced eyes – though if he was initially shocked, this would not prevent future visits to any number of establishments that catered for all ages and absolutely every taste, no matter how extreme. Armistead Maupin recalled to Patrick Gale (*Guardian*, June 1999):

> Rock was the perfect name for him. At fifty, his butt was solid. He was very charming and looked you straight in the eye – Rock Hudson in a red alpaca sweater, looking like a tourist from the Midwest.

The quartet's first port of call was the Black and Blue Club, the notorious leather bar, which had motorcycles suspended from the ceiling and a not so very discreet backroom that was partitioned off from the main cruising area by corrugated metal sheets, behind which upon the stroke of midnight when the doors of the club were closed to all but its bona-fide members, couples and groups in full bondage gear could participate in the dusk-to-dawn 'fuckathons' advertised in local contact magazines. The whole heaving, sweaty scenario was captured for posterity in the drawings of Tom of Finland (1920–91), a cult figure among gay S&M enthusiasts, whose illustrations of ultra-macho, phenomenally endowed Titans such as Rock is supposed to have been, are known throughout the world. Tom's subjects – including Rock – would eventually be 'brought to life' in his company's porno-flick, *The Wild Ones* (1994) directed by Durk Dehner and starring Zak Spears.

One finds it hard to imagine a famous movie star such as Rock, who would have had to be extremely discreet and limit his sexual activities to his home turf, even thinking of indulging in some of the heavy S&M activities depicted in Dehner's film. The action begins with Dehner's recreation of the opening scene of Marlon Brando's *The Wild One* (1953), save that this particular group of buddies are riding their Harley-Davidsons en route for the Eagle Club. And it ends with the Hudson character (Spears, whose Midwestern drawl uncannily resembles Rock's) getting his lover to 'fire' pool balls out of his anus.

Rock was, however, almost tempted into joining in with the fun at the South of Market Club – a slightly upmarket den of iniquity, for obvious reasons nicknamed the 'Glory Holes' – part of which comprised a series of plywood booths where customers 'made contact' by pushing their penises through the holes in the partitions. But if the recipient had no knowledge at the time who was pleasuring him from the other side, the scores of mostly masturbating men assembled on the balcony overlooking the booths were able to observe and applaud every movement.

One of the numerous celebrities whom Rock met at the Glory Holes was Freddie Mercury, the flamboyant front man of the British rock band Queen, yet another tragic victim of the AIDS virus. Although Rock and Freddie were definitely not each other's type – just as Rock adored muscular blonds, according to his close friend David Evans (quoted in my biography of the singer, *Living on the Edge*), so Freddie had a penchant for what he called 'nice, well-built people with a good lot of meat on them' – they enjoyed a certain rapport, which did not exclude a little harmless, mutual voyeurism from the balcony. Both were also offered exclusive membership of the club, but much to the relief of their respective entourages, declined.

Another Glory Holes regular – and sadly yet another AIDS casualty – was John Kobal, the founder of the famous photographic collection, who was briefly part of the 'Hudson gay-scene clique'. Invited to spend the weekend at the Castle, Kobal seems to have failed to have entered the hallowed portals of Rock's bedroom, though Rock did consent to a 'tell-all' interview. He later requested Kobal not to publish the piece, not happy with the way the young man had compared him with 'tall, dark and handsome, sensitive matinée idols' Cary Grant, Tyrone Power, Clark Gable and Robert Taylor – all closeted gay actors.

'To be honest, the interview was like pulling teeth,' Kobal wrote in his introduction to the much-abridged feature, which instead of appearing in *Hollywood Reporter* was held back and finally published in *Films & Filming* three weeks after Rock's death in 1985 – by which time the muckrakers had done all they could to sully his memory and Kobal sensed he would only be fanning the flames of discontent by adding what Rock had said about his secret gay life.

Instead, all Rock's fans got was another run-of-the-mill résumé of his career, though one which ended somewhat portentously now that he was no longer around:

> I don't even think of my career any more. That's a point of view of people looking in from the outside. I do the jobs as best I can, and if it all finished tomorrow I'd probably go back to school and learn to do something else – maybe a landscape gardener would be interesting. That's something I'd really like doing. Making films sometimes isn't all that pleasant, you know.

The British tabloids, meanwhile, frequently more spiteful and unfeeling than their American counterparts when it comes to flushing out sensationalist tittle-tattle, began searching for a way of outing Rock without getting sued. Astonishingly, despite his new-found 'freedom' amongst the heavy San Francisco and Los Angeles gay scene, he was still managing to cover his tracks even when trailed by Hollywood *agents provocateurs* – journalists posing as homosexuals, some of whom, then as today, would have gone as far as having sex with their quarry just to get an exclusive even though they were straight. Rock never fell into this trap, though he did make the mistake of showing one British journalist – Paul Callan of the *Daily Mirror* – his most recent piece of needlepoint embroidery. He told Callan how he had taken up the hobby some years before because he had grown tired of watching TV day after day.

Although Callan does not appear to have been deliberately intent on interrogating Rock about his personal life, this was too good an opportunity to miss out on, so he asked him outright if the rumours about his sexuality were true. Outraged – and with fists clenched, it is said – Rock managed to extricate himself from a decidedly sticky situation:

> Bullshit! I've heard that rumour for years and I just don't care about it. I know lots of gays in Hollywood. Some have tried it on with me, but I've always said, 'Come on, you've got the wrong guy!' As soon as they know that, it's okay!

Rock's belated taste of public hedonism did not affect his work. In 1980 he played himself in *The Patricia Neal Story*, and this was followed by another television mini-series, *The Martian Chronicles* (1980), co-starring Gayle Hunnicutt, Roddy McDowall and Barry Morse. The locations were filmed at Anchor Bay, in Malta. Rock played an officer in a space programme who, renouncing the military, relocates to Mars with his family.

He was interviewed for *Screen International* and the anonymous reporter, having seen him 'canoodling' with a young man in a Valetta gay bar, confronted him with the old chestnut. Why was he still a bachelor? Rock could have asked the reporter why he had been in the bar in the first place, but levelled instead, 'Because I prefer being so. There's more variety, less problems. However, I do have a favourite actress – though it's not fair to tell you who she is!' A local newspaper followed up on this by assuming that this fictitious female could only have been Gayle Hunnicutt, and when cornered Rock was of course perfectly content not to deny this. The gay bar, he said, had 'reluctantly tempted' him through its doors because it had sold a brand of American beer that the straight bars did not stock.

During the summer of 1981, Rock appeared in another television mini-series. *The Starmaker* centres around a celebrated Hollywood producer who utilises his position as a means of seducing any number of would-be stars, mostly by giving them bit parts in erotic films – ironically, apart from Suzanne Pleshette and Melanie Griffith, most of the starlets who played these are forgotten today. And for a man who had spent his entire career fighting to hide his sexuality there was an all-important first – a brief but brave bedroom scene with another man, played by Jack Scalia, an up-and-coming young actor who would soon feature prominently in Rock's life.

Rock hated working on this series even more so than he had *McMillan*, as he explained to his friend Joan Mac Trevor:

The whole thing was filmed far too quickly. The scriptwriters weren't interested in the development or even the probability of the characters. My own character wasn't a man but a big, stupid marshmallow – grinning all the time, never once losing his cool. He didn't curse or throw chairs across the room like producers do, like I wanted to do! He was just too perfect for his own good, like something out of a comic book!

A thoroughly discreet, warm-hearted woman, Joan Mac Trevor had many times been party to Rock's most profound confidences, and even after his death when she could have earned a tidy sum divulging these to the world, she remained tight-lipped. 'Of course I know lots of homosexuals,' Rock told her at this time, 'and yes, I have taken them out to clubs such as La Cage aux Folles, in Venice [Hollywood]. But who would be interested in knowing that, now?'

When Mac Trevor included this admission in her deeply moving obituary, *Rock Hudson: Le courage jusqu'au bout*, published by *Ciné-Revue* in October 1985, many thought that Rock had actually wanted her to tell the world that he was gay, and effectively end all the speculation. For some journalists, however, there were such traits as loyalty and honesty.

Rock's fans were next treated to him on the big screen in the film adaptation of Agatha Christie's *The Mirror Crack'd* (1980) – a star-studded, high-camp romp filmed in England and set adjacent to the sleepy English village of St Mary Mead, home to the celebrated sleuth Miss Marple (Angela Lansbury). His co-stars were his most prestigious in more than a decade: Kim Novak, Tony Curtis, Edward Fox, Geraldine Chaplin . . . and close friend Elizabeth Taylor.

It is a gem of a production. The action takes place in coronation month, June 1953, when a bunch of Hollywood eccentrics take over an old country mansion to make a film about Mary, Queen of Scots. There is the loudmouthed producer Marty Fenn (Curtis), whose egocentric wife, Lola Brewster (Novak), has been miscast as the ill-fated monarch . . . 'Mary, Queen of Sluts' someone cattily refers to her as she swans into the village fête, overdressed and posturing. Playing Mary's arch-enemy, Elizabeth I, and making her movie comeback is faded icon Marina Gregg (Taylor), whose womanising husband Jason Rudd (Rock) has been hired to direct.

The off-screen rivalry of these female protagonists within the film, however, is far more virulent than any Tudor court cat fight. In a repartee worthy of Crawford and Davis in *Whatever Happened to Baby Jane?* (1962) (and which Rock said brought to mind his location experiences with Julie Andrews), Lola never ceases to remind Marina which of them is the greatest star, and that she once had an affair with the utterly charming Jason – while Marina hammers home what a tart Lola has always been. Marina goads, 'In that wig you could play Lassie. What are you supposed to be, a birthday cake? Too bad everybody's had a piece!' To which Lola quips, 'Chin up, darling – both of them!' Then she coos to her former beau, 'Jason, darling. I'm so looking forward to working under you again!' The plum line, however, allegedly put in by Taylor herself, comes from Marina when she is with Jason in their room. Gazing at her reflection in the dressing-table mirror while he looks on, po-faced, she sighs, 'Bags, bags, go away. Come right back on Doris Day!'

Much of this bitching stops when Heather Babcock (Maureen Bennett), one of the guests at the cast party, dies after quaffing a poisoned cocktail, which Miss Marple – always one step ahead of the man in charge of the investigation, in this instance her nephew, Chief Inspector Craddock (Fox) – concludes must have been meant for Marina, who gave Heather her drink after she spilled her own. The killer has actually been seen doctoring the drink by Jason's personal assistant, Ella (Chaplin), a hay-fever sufferer, who is subsequently silenced by a fatal dose of Prussic acid, secreted into her nasal spray.

For a while, Lola is the chief suspect. Years ago she had tried to kill Marina, but the bullet missed and someone was paid to keep the scandal out of the press – and while making the film, Marina has already received death-threat letters, and once someone slopped arsenic into her coffee. Then, thanks to the wily Miss Marple, the penny drops when she learns that Marina's hugely successful career ended years ago when she suffered a series of breakdowns following the birth of a baby that came into the world brain-damaged, on account of Marina having contracted German measles . . . a disease passed on by an admirer during the war, who kissed her after being given her autograph.

By sheer coincidence this fan was Heather Babcock: Marina has killed her, then made it appear that someone was trying to bump her off. The film ends with Jason being made aware of this – and the doting husband, avowing that Marina has suffered enough in life without the added rigours of a murder accusation, does the humane thing by slipping poison into her nightcap. Marina, however, knows he has done this and chooses to die by her own hand, Camille-like, in an anteroom on a chaise-longue. 'She's given the performance of her life,' Miss Marple soothes, as the credits prepare to roll.

Because of its glittering pantheon of stars, the Kent location of *The Mirror Crack'd* was a fiercely guarded secret, though Rock's journalist friend, David Castell, was allowed on to the set. When Castell complimented him on how distinguished he looked now that he had a few faint wrinkles and greying hair, Rock replied with good humour, 'I'm at what they call a difficult age. I'm no longer a young man, but I'm not old enough to play grandfathers. In ten years' time there'll be dozens of good parts for me. Just now they are thin on the ground.' How sad that this prophecy would not come true.

There was some cause for concern when Rock returned to Hollywood. He had complained several times of feeling unwell while in England, and during the flight home he was taken ill, developing a raging fever before the plane landed but insisting on being driven straight to the Castle all the same. Here, his doctor – celebrity physician Rex Kennamer, recommended some years earlier by Montgomery Clift – admitted him at once to the UCLA Medical Centre where, according to Rock, a specialist diagnosed nothing more serious than flu. This was Rock being somewhat economical with the truth, as Tom Clark – incurring Rock's wrath by going behind his back – confided to Joan Mac Trevor, who should have been interviewing her favourite movie star for *Ciné-Revue*, and who only published her piece when convinced by Clark that Rock had given his permission, which does not appear to have been the case:

For six months now Rock has been suffering from atrocious pains in his chest. He knows he has a heart problem, yet chooses to ignore this. Rock wants to make his television comeback at whatever price, and is prepared to play games with his life to get there . . . I've tried to get him to see a doctor, but he won't listen to me. He just shrugs his shoulders and says it's

indigestion. Then he tops himself up with hot milk and whisky
to kill the pain. He's thrown himself heart and soul into this
new project. It's as if his life depends on it. He wants to be
Hollywood's Number One again. He told me only the other
day, 'I'm Rock Hudson. I'm a star and people had better
understand that!' He's obsessed. He needs his publicity like an
alcoholic craves booze. He would rather die than walk into a
room and no one recognise him.

Within 48 hours of his indisposition, Rock was back on his feet, and
he who had sworn never to do another potentially long-running
television series after *McMillan*, had only too quickly changed his
mind when offered 'a large pot of gold' for the project Tom Clark
had spoken of – *The Devlin Connection* (1982), about a father and
estranged son detective team.

As with his partner in *McMillan and Wife*, Rock was permitted to
choose his own 'son', and NBC are said to have advised him not to
pick one with whom he had had or might wish to have an
'incestuous' relationship. Rock plumped for Jack Scalia, one of his
love-interests from *The Starmaker*. Scalia lived with his wife not far
from Rock's New York apartment and, as had frequently happened
in the past, Rock had been interested in a man but wary of making
the first move – in this instance because he had been told that Scalia
was 'rampantly heterosexual' and in no way capable of becoming
amorously interested in another man, not even one famed for
seducing even the so-called straightest of individuals. Rock had had
Scalia checked out just the same and had come to the conclusion that
if he could not become another notch on the Hudson bedpost, then at
least he was possessed of an 'impressive pedigree'.

Born in New York, Jack Scalia was a tall, ruggedly handsome
beefcake-type in his late twenties with a gravely voice that Rock said
sent shivers down his spine. The son of Brooklyn Dodger Rocky
Tedesco, he had been raised in one of the city's roughest
neighbourhoods and had soon learned how to look after himself in a
situation. In 1971 he had followed in his father's footsteps, signing
up with the Montreal Expos, but during his second season as a
pitcher with the team, a serious arm injury had put paid to his

baseball career. After spending years drifting from one dead-end job to another he had taken up modelling, successfully treading the catwalks of Milan, San Francisco and Paris before returning to New York where, in 1980 while at the top of his new profession, Scalia had taken another change of direction by enrolling for acting lessons.

There seems little doubt that Rock fell in love with Jack Scalia – despite his dark, almost swarthy complexion – though whether he actually got around to expressing his feelings is not known. Early on in their friendship the young man is said to have reminded Rock that he was one hundred per cent heterosexual, but Rock appears to have either not believed or not wanted to believe this – and to have possibly misread Scalia's gestures of 'filial affection', which the actor recalled for Sara Davidson:

> From the first, Jack kissed Rock on the cheek and hugged him, 'because that's the relationship I had with my own father. I could feel, sometimes, Rock was awkward with it, but he got used to it.' . . . Jack came to feel he and Rock were similar in temperament. They both were Scorpios, born in November; both were secretive and private.

The Devlin Connection began shooting in Hollywood in September 1981. Rock had personally arranged somewhere for Scalia and his wife to stay and the couple socialised with Rock and Tom Clark. Also, Rock and Scalia frequently went out on the town together – dispensing with his earlier vow never to be seen alone or photographed with another man.

While the second episode of the series was being filmed in Malibu, Rock and Scalia received a visit from Mark Rowland of *Playgirl*, which for over a decade had been titillating America's female population – and more than a few males – with tasteful photospreads of some of the world's most attractive men. Almost all of these had posed naked – some, like Burt Reynolds and Henry Kissinger, had gone as far as their public positions and reputations as family men had allowed, while actors such as teen idol Fabian, George Maharis and Flash Gordon star Sam Jones had insisted upon appearing full frontal. *Playgirl*'s photographer, Alison Morley, had rather hoped to snap 'father and son' in all their glory, or as much of it as they might allow, but when Rock learned of this – and that the magazine had been tipped off that he and Scalia might have been sharing the same trailer and having an affair – he refused to be interviewed and is further alleged to have 'briefed' Scalia before allowing him to see Rowland, who reported:

> Shirtless, he reveals the rippling, muscular torso of a well-conditioned athlete (which he is), but his facial features are lean and surprisingly delicate. 'Rock and I are similar sorts,' Scalia reveals. 'We're both cut-ups and like to joke and tell stories. He's really become like a father figure to me. You know, when I was a kid, if one of the gang would put on airs and graces or act stuck-up, we'd always say, "Hey, who do you think you are, Rock Hudson?" And now I'm here!'

The series, however, was plagued with problems from the outset. Rock disliked the producer and dismissed the scripts as tacky, and there were no requisite 'token fucks' as had happened with *McMillan and Wife*. After just three episodes had been filmed, Rock began searching for a loophole that might get him out of his contract, though it was a cruel twist of fate that intervened at six in the morning on 30 October 1981, when Tom Clark found him sitting in his kitchen, deathly pale and clutching his chest.

Clark sensed that there might be insufficient time to wait for an ambulance, and drove Rock to the Cedars-Sinai Hospital, where a heart specialist ordered an ECG and informed him that there was no evidence to suggest that he had had a coronary. Rex Kennamer was dissatisfied, however, and arranged further tests, which revealed that Rock had blocked arteries, almost certainly caused by his excessive smoking and high-cholesterol diet. But even at this stage Rock refused to heed his doctor's advice, as Tom Clark explained to *Ciné-Revue*'s David Duffy a few weeks later:

> Those last few weeks leading up to his illness were a real nightmare for Rock, but he was so obstinate. He told me, 'I've got to make this comeback work. I've got to prove I'm still a

great star!' It was a vicious circle because his worrying over this so-called comeback only aggravated the chest pains he'd been having for the last six months, since his housekeeper found him wandering around in the middle of the night, not even knowing where he was. So he began drinking hot toddies to ease the situation, and the worse the pains became, the more he drank. Even when Rock's doctor told him how bad things were, he bellowed, 'You can't keep me [in hospital]. At least allow me to work tomorrow – just ten minutes are all I need to wrap up this last scene!' To which Dr Kennamer responded, severely, that ten minutes was all that it would take to kill him. That's when Rock decided to listen.

Rock was re-admitted to the Cedars-Sinai at once for triple bypass surgery, and on 1 November, the eve of his operation, he summoned his closest friends to his bedside and called several more on the telephone, who had been unable to make it at such short notice. Rex Kennamer had put the fear of God into him, he said, and he was convinced that he was going to die. For two hours the group drank and chain-smoked, until a worried nurse contacted Kennamer and he ordered everyone to leave. Rock was moved to another room, and the one he vacated was fumigated.

Rock's tenacity astounded the medical staff. During the six-hour operation the team of surgeons found more arterial damage than they had anticipated, and he was not expected to survive. The hospital switchboard was jammed with calls from well-wishers, and during the next 24 hours Rock received 50,000 letters and cards. Yet in less than a week he was on his feet, stomping impatiently around his room and pestering the doctors to allow him home. Jack Scalia visited him regularly, and later said how proud he had felt when Rock had held his hand and let go of his reserve – bursting into tears, then just as quickly pulling himself together again. His pre-occupation, of course, was with getting back to work. He told a bedside press conference:

Staying healthy's no fun at all. No drinks, no cigarettes, no excitement. But I'm sticking with it and feel better than I have in twenty years! Now that I'm no longer a sex symbol I can go ahead and act. The best years are still to come. I'm actually looking forward to growing old and playing good parts!

It was all a façade, for within hours of returning to the Castle in the middle of November, he was smoking heavily again. He also refused to keep to Rex Kennamer's low-cholesterol diet – for years his favourite treat had been a huge daily plateful of chicken gizzards – though he did cut down on his alcohol consumption on account of the medication he had been prescribed, pills that brought about intermittent periods of blackest depression and that also played havoc with his already sky-high libido. At 56, Rock was probably not exaggerating when he told friends that he had reached a stage where he was quite capable of having sex with as many as five different men in a 24-hour period!

Rock's first public outing following his hospitalisation took place early in December 1981 when, accompanied by Elizabeth Taylor, he attended Natalie Wood's funeral. The actress, a friend of long-standing, had mysteriously drowned off Catalina Island, though at this time – taking into consideration her lifelong fear of water – there was considerable media speculation as to whether Wood's death had been accidental, suicide, or even murder. As such, the press were far less interested in Rock than they might ordinarily have been.

In the spring of 1982, six months after his bypass, Rock and Jack Scalia resumed working on *The Devlin Connection*. During the long break between filming, however, the producer and most of the crew had been seconded elsewhere, robbing the series of all continuity when the new team was recruited. Rock later said that everyone had been fumbling in the dark and that he had been truly relieved when NBC pulled the plug after an unlucky thirteenth episode and cancelled the second series.

By this time, too, Rock's relationship with Tom Clark had completely disintegrated, and the pair were sleeping in separate rooms. In addition to this, Rock received news that his father had died. In his eighties and suffering for some time from senile dementia, Roy Scherer had been living at the Motion Picture Home for several months since the death of his third wife, Edith. Rock, who had been paying him $200 a month for longer than he cared to remember, had insisted that Scherer spend his last days here, though he had hardly seen him since the day he had walked out on his family. The old man, however, had kept wandering off and had finally been handed over to relatives in Oregon, where he had died. Rock paid for the funeral and sent flowers, but he did not attend and for the rest of his life would rarely mention his father again.

10

The Sleeping Prince

'I welcome my birthdays. Relish them, as a matter of fact. I have confidence now and can look forward to trying new things. I don't think fifty was a crucial age. Forty was, and thirty-nine because I was facing forty. But lately everything has fallen into place for me.'

Rock Hudson

During the autumn of 1982, Rock met the most controversial of all his lovers – Marc Christian (surname MacGuinnis, which he subsequently dropped), a tall, strikingly handsome, overtly muscular 29-year-old fitness enthusiast. In one interview, Christian said he had been a musicologist with the Institute of the American Musical in 1982; in another that he had worked for the Record Institute. He is also said to have told Rock, initially, that he was a fitness instructor and standing six foot two inches and almost as solidly built as Rock, he certainly looked the part. In addition, Christian's knowledge of music and recording techniques are said to have been exemplary.

Much also has to be said for Christian's obvious animal magnetism and innate charisma: borne out by the fact that when he won Rock over he had not just the then almost requisite moustache favoured by seriously butch gay males, but – horror of horrors so far as Rock was concerned! – a beard, an 'appendage' that soon came off once he and Rock began dating, earning the clean-shaven, almost ethereal-looking Christian the nickname 'Sleeping Prince'.

Exactly where and when the pair met is also unclear. Christian himself has cited at least three different locations in interviews over the years: at a fund-raising rally for Gore Vidal's Senate campaign (which had actually concluded the previous June), at another unspecified political event, and at the Brooks Baths – arguably the more likely of the three, for Rock is quoted in his biography as telling George Nader, 'He kept waving his dick at me until I finally noticed him. The rest is history.'

On the face of it, *where* the couple met might have been of little consequence, were it not for what would later transpire in the Los Angeles Court House, itself an indication of Christian's mysterious, complex persona. As Sara Davidson also observed, 'What's disturbing is that people don't usually forget the way they met their lovers, particularly important ones. They are asked how they met and tell the story again and again; it becomes a piece of shared history.' Equally odd, Christian – a self-confessed bisexual – was living with a woman, 62-year-old Liberty Martin, a Libby Holman-type with a penchant for much younger, gay men.

Rock and Christian's affair took off like wildfire. Initially they met discreetly at Liberty Martin's apartment. Then Christian began spending weekends at the Castle. Rock had found a way of adding his name to the payroll, for with infinite patience and expertise Christian had taken on the task of remastering and logging Rock's vast collection of 78rpm records, using a costly and then little known technique which reduced surface noise – though on a weekly salary of $400 he was netting considerably more than the other household staff, who had been on the same low wages (but treated like Hollywood royalty by Rock) for years.

On top of this, Christian was provided with a car and a personal fitness adviser, and Rock paid for him to have his teeth fixed. Taking another leaf out of Henry Willson's book he called veteran actress Nina Foch, to whom he had grown close since she had played a murderess in the penultimate *McMillan*. Foch had cut down on film work and was currently running a small drama school. Rock was seemingly convinced that his new lover possessed all the requirements to hit the big time as a movie star – something that would not happen – he was enrolled for a series of lessons.

In addition to all these expenses, when Christian informed Rock that his father was terminally ill and that all that was keeping him alive was his dream of restoring his 1959 Chevrolet Nomad station wagon – Rock agreed to pick up the tab. Over the next year or so, Christian would run up a repair bill of over $20,000, several times the vehicle's value.

Needless to say, such favouritism caused considerable resentment amongst Rock's employees, making it difficult to separate truth from hearsay, while sifting through the events of the next two years and beyond.

Not long after Rock had taken up with Marc Christian he was interviewed by the distinguished columnist Donald Zec, one of the few media people he felt he could trust and be open with. Referring to his recent heart surgery, rather than the rumours that had been buzzing around Hollywood that Rock may have been suffering from pancreatic cancer brought about by his drinking, Zec recalled, 'Maybe he had a clue that all was not well inside that fine, bronzed torso that had, in the earliest days of his great career, earned him the title of Baron of Beefcake.'

Rock spoke of his fear of failure, during these formative years:

> I was always inhibited. It wasn't just ordinary shyness – it was paranoia, probably the most painful sickness I ever endured in my life. I was so scared I wouldn't make it, I just worked my arse off, always looking over my shoulder.

He spoke of his bitterness, not over his failed marriage, but of the way he believed Phyllis Gates had sullied his name:

> She cited mental cruelty, which is what you say when you can't think of anything else. A lot of people speculated – still do. Well, let 'em. The more they do, the more I like it!

Zec asked Rock if, in view of his never having remarried, he was offended by the whispering campaign concerning his sexuality. Zec was well aware that Rock was gay and to please him helped him to concoct the answer to this question. No doubt both men were laughing their sides sore:

> Of course it offends me! I've heard it about almost everybody here in Hollywood. In the old days when I went out with an actor, the studio insisted we had to take a couple of girls along. Actresses lunch together and nobody calls them lesbians, but God help actors who do the same! But if people want to think that way, let 'em. What am I supposed to do to prove myself – take some broad up on to the stage and invite everybody to watch?

And lastly, he recalled almost with indifference his recent hospitalisation and brush with death:

> I said to myself, either I wake up or I don't. Whichever it is, terrific! My life, like this house, has been a mixture of pleasant and unpleasant memories. I'm happy to settle for that!

The final rupture with Tom Clark occurred in September 1983, when he and Rock flew to New York. Rock had been pencilled in to play one of the two flagrantly effeminate leads in a forthcoming British stage production of *La Cage aux Folles* (1984), and for once no longer seemed to care what the media's reaction might be. His part was to have been the one immortalised in Edouard Molinaro's 1978 film by Ugo Tognazzi, the owner of the gay nightclub that puts on transvestite revues and who secretly lusts after the 'maid' – a pretty black youth who spends much of his time on stage wearing nothing but a pair of spray-on hot pants – and whose lover is a cloying neurotic scene-queen who dresses like an ageing, slightly mad Bette Davis.

Rock's friend, Claire Trevor, took him to see the Broadway revival of the show, and though he did not give the producer an immediate decision, he very seriously considered the part over the coming months – until a British publicist sent him a clipping from *Him Monthly*, then the country's most popular gay magazine. In this, the not always subtle but immensely revered journalist Kris Kirk had composed a fun feature entitled *New Year Gay Alphabet*, and under the letter 'L' had written:

> L is for *La Cage aux Folles*, the musical, which is whispered to be opening in London in the New Year. Normally, you could count me out, but ROCK HUDSON playing a faggot? This I must see . . .

Rock is alleged to have considered suing *Him Monthly* for 'implying between the lines' that he was gay, but soon changed his mind upon the realisation that the likes of Kris Kirk had been getting away with murder for years in their acerbic columns. These were usually published in magazines with suggestive titles such as *Bona* and *Gold*, which folded after a few issues, leaving other magazines free to unleash an incontrollable backlash of 'gay-Rock' anecdotes, real and invented.

Meanwhile, just two days after arriving in New York, Rock told Tom Clark that he had booked himself on the next flight back to Los Angeles. Three weeks later, when Clark returned to the Castle hoping for a reconciliation, the pair had a violent quarrel, during which Rock hit him and ordered him out of the house. Clark left, but refused to give up on what he claimed were the ten best years of his life: he flew back to New York and moved into the Beresford apartment, where he waited for Rock to cool down.

On 31 October 1983, Rock flew to Israel to shoot what would be his last film, *The Ambassador* (1984), with Robert Mitchum. Before leaving Hollywood, he installed Marc Christian at the Castle – full-time, and not just as his regular 'wife', but it is said to ensure that Tom Clark would not get back in while he was overseas. He returned home at the beginning of January, and his friends have commented that around this time he was observed to have lost weight, but that he looked better for it as, prior to his bypass operation, he had been getting a little podgy around the middle. For the time being Rock attributed the weight loss to the night-sweats he had suffered in Israel on account of the intense heat. And in any case he was still tipping the scales at a robust 210 pounds.

As had happened in London during the run of *I Do! I Do!*, Rock, accompanied by Marc Christian, began 'doing the rounds' of all the gay establishments in Hollywood – bars, clubs, saunas, restaurants – which he had refused to patronise before for fear of evoking a scandal. Times and public attitudes had changed, he said, besides which it made him feel great that, at 58, he could be seen on the town with a devastatingly handsome, thirty-year-old stud who had eyes for him alone. Little did he realise that his lover was cheating on him so soon in their relationship. Mark Miller told Rock – and later the Los Angeles court – that on one occasion while Rock had been filming in Israel, he had gone into one of the bedrooms at the Castle to search for a photograph for a publicist. He found Christian asleep in the bed with a young man, Keith Johnson.

Neither, apparently, was Johnson the only one. In March, Rock was asked to present the Best Actress Award to Shirley MacLaine at the Oscars ceremony. He wore an old tuxedo that he had last worn several years earlier and such was his weight loss, the audience did not observe that it had to be tucked in at the back with dozens of pins. His elderly gardener, Clarence Morimoto, stated at the subsequent court case that during Rock's absence Marc Christian sneaked a man into the Castle, apparently the first of many. Morimoto recalled that he had entered his employer's bedroom to water the plants and seen Christian with Marty Flaherty, the handyman. Both had been naked from the waist up, caressing in the bed. Not that Rock would condemn him for this, for after the Oscars ceremony he himself spent the night with a young Canadian boat-builder, Pierre B—, whom he had picked up in a Long Beach Bar and moved into his hotel suite.

Rock, in common with most of his lovers, had never been faithful during any of his relationships. Even so, when he suspected that Christian might have been seeing other men behind his back, he too was relegated to the guest room. Christian himself later said that *he* had taken the initiative to move out of Rock's room because of Rock's excessive sweating, which, he thought at the time, was caused by Rock's heavy drinking.

Why Rock allowed Marc Christian to stay on at the Castle when he obviously had begun to tire of him (according to subsequent evidence submitted for the trial over his estate) cannot be readily determined.

It has been suggested that he both loved and loathed the loquacious charmer with equal passion, that he had allowed himself to be caught up in an impossible-to-live-with, impossible-to-live-without situation, and that he was too weak to effect a remedy either way, as had happened during his final agonising months with Tom Clark.

To some friends Rock boasted that Christian was the kindest, most understanding and above all lustiest lover he had ever known – only to denounce him to others as cold and devious, and possibly even a gold-digger. The truth may lie somewhere in the middle – the fact that at times Rock was reported to be overwhelmingly tetchy and conceited, as many movie legends almost invariably become once their careers have started to wane – and if so Christian should have realised this and offered him the support he so obviously craved . . . or just moved on.

Also to be considered is the fact that, due to cautious investments in property and his own film production company, Rock Productions, Rock was a very wealthy man, and as such could have lured virtually anyone into his bed. Hollywood was teeming with opportunists eager to take advantage of him and help him spend his money. From a professional angle, many might have been willing to declare the commodity to be getting past its sell-by date, but as an amorous conquest Rock Hudson was still essentially easy pickings.

One man who had recently entered Rock's affections and who was reputedly not out for all he could get was Ron Channell, a 28-year-old actor–singer and fitness instructor from Tampa, Florida. He had been visiting the Castle since October 1983 to supervise Rock's workouts – probably the first time anyone had used the gymnasium. The pair had met at the Sports Connection, a health club catering for both gays and straights, and where the former could go in search of partners and not arouse suspicion. Rock was taken aback, however, when Channell informed him that there would never be anything physical between them because, like Jack Scalia, he was straight.

He was sufficiently fond of Channell to nickname him 'Speed' after the character he had played in *Iron Man*. Whether there actually was anything sexual between Rock and Ron Channell is not known. Rock was certainly frustrated at not being able to jump into bed with a man he was mad about. For whatever reason, Rock contacted Pierre B——, the lover who had escorted him to the Oscars ceremony. The pair went off to Mexico, where they spent a short vacation at the home of Pierre's father. Rock later told friends that he had been unwilling to have sex with the handsome boat-builder, giving them the impression that he was 'saving himself' for Ron Channell, should he decide to change his mind and let Rock sleep with him.

However, Pierre told Dean Dittman (according to Sara Davidson), that *he* had refused to have sex with Rock for no other reason than he had been put off by Rock being the same age as his father. Given Rock's predilection towards hunky blonds – and the fact that he and Pierre had slept together before going to Mexico – one finds it hard to believe either account. It seems that Rock loved Channell in such a way as he could not have loved Marc Christian, whom Channell later claimed to be just another employee at the Castle until Rock's friends enlightened him.

Over the next year or so, on all of Rock's trips abroad, Channell was almost invariably his only travelling companion. Marc Christian was never taken anywhere important or introduced to any of the Hollywood luminaries who dropped in at the Castle. Neither was he invited to Dean Dittman's almost nightly supper parties because Dittman and most of Rock's inner circle could not stand him.

On 15 May 1984, Rock flew to Washington, where he had been invited to a presidential dinner with Ronald and Nancy Reagan at the White House. Photographs of the event appeared in newspapers around the world and one – ironically, the same one that was autographed by the Reagans and sent to the Castle one week after the bash – revealed a large mole on the side of Rock's neck. Mark Miller urged Rock to make an appointment to see Dr Kennamer, who in turn sent him to see dermatologist Dr Letantia Bussell, and a biopsy was taken. On 28 May, Dr Bussell called Rock with the results: the mole, which had been there for the past year, was Kaposi's sarcoma – a type of skin cancer that mainly men with AIDS often develop, although it is not exclusive to the disease – and Rock was told, point-blank, that he most probably had AIDS. This was confirmed a few days later by a Dr Frank Kramer, a plastic surgeon and skin specialist who carried out a second biopsy to see if the mole could be removed.

Rock's initial reaction to this devastating news, according to Dr Kramer – speaking to Sara Davidson – was to put on a brave face and say something along the lines of, 'Fine, but I'm going to lick this thing and if I don't – well, it's been a good life!' Privately, of course, he must have been mortified and it would have taken a while for the news to sink in. In these early days of HIV, little was known of the disease or how it could be transmitted. Such was the hysteria in some circles that many believed it could be passed from one person to another as innocuously as by touching, drinking from the same glass, or even by being in the same room as the sufferer . . . though of one thing there was *no* uncertainty: those with full-blown Acquired Immune Deficiency Syndrome, dubbed by the media as 'The Gay Plague' and by homophobes and Bible-bashers as 'The Wrath of God', did not survive.

Rock shared his tragic secret only with Mark Miller, George Nader – and later with Dean Dittman, his most trusted confidants who would help him through his alternating fits of fear, anger, shame and denial. Marc Christian was told absolutely nothing, and over the coming months would be left to speculate as to why Rock was seemingly fading before his very eyes. On the face of it this appears insensitive, if not downright malevolent. As Rock's most recent live-in lover, whether they were still having sex or not – unlikely, if the animosity between them was as all-consuming as Rock's friends have claimed – Christian had a moral right to know if his health was being put at risk and, equally important, that he himself was a danger to others if he was sleeping around and not using protection.

Rock, however, had a legitimate reason for keeping Christian in the dark: Christian had already threatened to expose his 'affair' with Ron Channell to the press, besides their own, and had they got their hands on the AIDS story, the media would have shown absolutely no mercy. However, Rock did send out several anonymous letters to young men with whom he had been intimate over the last three months, one of which ended up on the desk of a well-known Los Angeles handwriting analyst . . . just as Rock had feared it might, which was why he had dictated it to George Nader, and why each letter had been worded differently in the event of them all ending up in unscrupulous hands, so that no one would ever suspect they had been written by the same person.

So far as is known, not one of these men subsequently contracted HIV, and the one who sent his letter to the analyst (identified to me by a *People* magazine journalist in May 1992 as P— M—) claimed that Rock was the only man he had ever had sex with, which begs the question why he wanted the handwriting analysed in the first place. Unless, as the journalist suggested, P— M— was merely trying to verify that it genuinely was Rock's handwriting so that he could sell it as a piece of invaluable Hollywood memorabilia in the event of Rock's death:

> This note shall remain anonymous. Since we have had sexual contact where semen has passed between us, it's only polite to tell you that I've discovered I have AIDS. That's why I suggest you have tests, the way I've done, to make sure you're okay. Good luck.

Even more desperate to conceal the details of his illness than he had his sexuality, Rock consulted his lawyer and attempted to ensure that his all-important image would remain intact beyond the grave – by having the words 'cirrhosis of the liver' typed on his autopsy report. He was confident that he would get away with this and though nothing had yet appeared in the press, he was aware of how the media were speculating that he had cancer or anorexia, on account of the noticeable change in his appearance. His weight was now down to 195 pounds.

On 7 June, just two days after sharing his secret with Mark Miller and George Nader, and accompanied by Miller and Rex Kennamer, Rock went for a consultation with Dr Michael Gottlieb, an immunologist and at that time one of America's leading AIDS specialists who was based at the UCLA. In the summer of 1981, Gottlieb and several colleagues had published a paper, one of the earliest studies of HIV, on behalf of the Atlanta Center of Disease Control. Of the six patients detailed in his report, all were self-confessed promiscuous homosexuals, each one had suffered irreparable collapse of the immune system, most had gone on to contract pneumonia and all had died or were close to death. Although the term 'AIDS' was yet to become a household word, within weeks of this report the American press, most especially in the San Francisco area, had begun referring to 'a new form of cancer' that was exclusive to the gay community. This ignorance, combined with media castigation beyond the realms of human decency, rapidly spawned mass public hysteria.

Gottlieb outlined the then-known, frequently speculated facts about the disease – that aside from being transmitted by shared infected needles or blood transfusions, it could only be passed on by way of anal sex, and that the passive partner was the one most likely to be stricken with the virus if tearing of the rectal tissue took place, enabling the active partner's infected semen to enter the blood-stream. Then, according to what Rock told his friends – as if the prognosis was not grim enough – when he asked if his condition was terminal, Gottlieb's response was reputed to be, 'I would get my affairs in order, if I were you'.

Early in June 1984, in the midst of his anguish and confusion, Rock received an invitation to attend the Deauville Film Festival, scheduled to open at the French resort on 31 August. This year they were featuring a George Stevens retrospective, including *Giant*. While Rock was deliberating over this, he learned through Dean Dittman that a pioneer in AIDS research, Dr Dominique Dormont of the Hôpital Militaire de Percy, just outside Paris, had recently developed an experimental serum, HPA-23, which though not thought to be an actual cure for AIDS, had in a number of tests proved to have delayed some of the worsening effects of the disease.

Dr Gottlieb suggested to Rock that he had nothing to lose and Rock asked Mark Miller to make the necessary arrangements. Deauville would provide him with the ideal cover, and Rock got his agent, Dale Olsen, to contact *Ciné-Revue*'s Joan Mac Trevor and inform her how much his client was looking forward to the event, but that Rock might not make it to the opening night because of another commitment. Rock then spoke to his favourite journalist over the phone, and once he had attempted to dispel her concerns for his health, he informed her that during this particular trip, certain conditions would apply:

I'm better, now. Tremendously well. And I'm happy! Happiness is the best cure for illness and old age. But I'm only going to Deauville to honour a man who is the greatest magician [George Stevens] the film world has ever known. I'm not going for myself, so there'll be no press conferences and no photographs. I'm getting too old for that sort of thing!

Rock made a slight amendment to this rule a few days later when he learned that *Ciné-Revue*'s editor-in-chief, Gérard Néves, was in the country visiting the Los Angeles Olympic Games. Calling Néves, he told him, 'You'd better come over for dinner. I'll be celebrating my sixtieth birthday in November, so maybe you can do a piece about what it's like to be growing old gracefully here in Hollywood!' Néves later confessed that he had been well aware that Rock would be 59 next, and later speculated – correctly, perhaps – that Rock must already have had an inkling that he would not see sixty.

Néves went along with the charade, and turned up at the Castle with a photographer. Just weeks earlier he had seen Rock on the television and, apart from a few grey hairs, had thought he looked good for his age. One year later, in the same publication, he would reveal his shock at seeing him in the flesh:

I had such trouble recognising him. Indeed, were it not for his great height I wouldn't have known who he was. He looked so thin and pale – giving me the impression that he'd lost ten kilos in the space of a few weeks. He also seemed to have some difficulty speaking, though his easy approach and kindly attitude helped take my mind off his strained face. Dale Olsen had warned us that Rock would probably not allow us to photograph him, but when I asked, he took me by the arm. He tried to crack a joke, though he had immense trouble hiding his illness from me. 'Fine,' he said, 'but first allow me to make myself a little more presentable!' He was *adorable*!

The various facts that Rock volunteered concerning his health and personal life would only be published posthumously – no problem for Néves, who as *patron* of *Ciné-Revue* did not have a superior breathing down his neck and pressing for an exclusive, though the following year (after Rock's untimely death) he must have felt more than a little ill at ease, recalling what he had told him back in August 1984:

> Life doesn't have to end at sixty. I've always wanted to play a happy-go-lucky sexagenarian opposite other oldies such as Liz, Doris, Gina and Bob [Mitchum]. What a wonderful family we'd make! Okay, so not so long ago I was staring death in the face, and I'm not going to look up to heaven before lighting my next cigarette. But I *am* living wisely, and my doctor reckons that if I take things easy and don't work too hard, I should see my centenary. So, without missing out on too many of life's pleasures I'm heading for 17 November 2024 [sic]. And do you want to know the secret of my second youth? Well, it must have something to do with my being surrounded by men. *Women* put too much of a strain on the heart!

Much of Rock's tête-á-tête with Néves, however, centred around his personal impression of the world's perception of modern Hollywood, as opposed to the so-called 'Golden Days' of the studio system:

> It's significant to say that stars such as Richard Pryor, Dan Aykroyd and Scott Baio are enormously popular here in America, but totally unknown in Europe. Similarly, Dolly Parton, Burt Reynolds and Gene Wilder are unable to make a successful crossover because the humour over there is so different to ours. They know nothing about country music in Finland, and the French aren't interested in baseball. Programmes such as *Dynasty*, *Dallas* and *Hotel* are, on the other hand, international and popular everywhere. It's the same with scripts. Nowadays people are only interested in their so-called intellectual quality, so most of the storylines are boring. Bob Mitchum never questioned the profundity of the characters he played. Liz always accepted that her movies were diversions, not speeches for the defence. And look at today's

directors! Few are blessed with any kind of personality, yet they *think* they're geniuses. Steven Spielberg's an exception, I suppose. But who apart from him has *truly* brought anything of value to the cinema in recent years?

It was around this time that Rock received a call from Esther Shapiro, an associate of television soaps magnate, Aaron Spelling. Shapiro and her husband Richard were co-producers of the hugely successful *Dynasty* series, and she was anxious that Rock should augment her already impressive cast. Rock said that he would think about it, and promised Shapiro that he would call her as soon as he returned to Hollywood. Since the aborted *Devlin Connection* he had sworn – 'and meant it' – that he would never appear on television again. Also, or so he told friends, he was not particularly enamoured of starring in a glossy saga where the plots were flimsy, hard to believe in and, more often than not, were centred around the feuds and extensive wardrobes of the show's female rivals.

Dr Gottlieb had warned Rock of the dangers of travelling long distances, in case he should suddenly fall ill, but he said that for what Dr Dormont might have to offer, such risks would be well worth taking, provided he was accompanied by a responsible person who would be capable of handling the situation, should the worse come to the worst.

Mark Miller had coerced Marc Christian into having a complete medical check-up by telling him that, as a Hudson 'employee', this was essential for insurance purposes. Although the clinic attended by Christian had not possessed the facility to conduct HIV tests, the young man had been certified A1 fit in every other respect. Rock, however, had absolutely no intention of taking Christian to Paris. Mark Miller should have gone, but Rock's treatment was expected to take a minimum of eight weeks and he did not wish to leave the ailing George Nader behind for that long. So at the last minute, Rock asked Ron Channell to accompany him, though the young man was told nothing about the real reason behind the trip to France – so far as he was concerned, this was just another working holiday.

On 20 August, Rock flew to New York – alone, for a secret

meeting with his lawyers to amend his will. Tom Clark's name was removed, and George Nader was named first beneficiary, followed by Mark Miller. A few days later Ron Channell joined him, and on 27 August the pair flew to Paris by Concorde. Rock's treatment was scheduled to begin the next day, and after breakfast he left Channell in their suite at the Ritz – telling him he had a script-reading appointment with a French producer – and took a taxi to Percy. Dr Dormont carried out a few preliminary tests, informed Rock that he was 'not in too bad a state', and proposed two alternative courses of treatment. The first would require daily injections of HPA-23 over a fourteen-week period; the second a course of 120-minute infusions, one each day for a week, followed by a week's respite, until the procedure had been repeated four times; Rock opted for the latter. Throughout this time, Ron Channell is said to have suspected nothing, not even when he observed the large bruises on Rock's arms left by the intravenous needles.

The effects of the HPA-23 were debilitating: bouts of nausea, extreme fatigue, loss of balance and appetite. Rock, however, quickly adapted to his new regime and after his first week in Paris reported back to his friends at the Castle that he was feeling much better. He then met up with Dale Olsen – who had also been kept in the dark about his illness – and during his week off from the Hôpital Percy he, Olsen and Channell drove across to Deauville.

Rock had made it clear before leaving Hollywood that he would not be interested in meeting the media. Even so, a cameraman slipped through the net of security and snapped him in the hotel bar – leafing through a copy of *Ciné-Revue* that one of the staff had asked him to sign – and later having a drink in the same bar with Jacqueline Cartier, the respected journalist from *France-Soir*, whom he had agreed to meet socially. The first photograph – Rock looks gaunt and has big bags under his eyes – appeared in the following week's issue of *Ciné-Revue* and so incensed Rock when he spied it on a Paris newsstand that he threatened to sue, dropping the action only when Gérard Néves convinced him that he had been totally unaware of the press embargo.

Rock's treatment continued and, according to Dr Dormont's subsequent report, he appeared to be responding well to the infusions. He was also still managing to keep his visits to the Hôpital Percy secret, even from Dale Olsen, despite unflattering comments from reporters who always seemed to be one step ahead as he and Ron Channell 'did Europe' – Nice, St Tropez, Barcelona – during his weeks off when he was not 'discussing business'. Wherever Rock went, there was persistent reference to his weight loss and haggard appearance.

Rock may have been willing to stay in France, but there were those who could not wait for him to return to Hollywood, where there was renewed pressure from the producers of *Dynasty*, urging him to join the cast before the end of October so that his character would fit in with the storyline the scriptwriters were currently working on. Indeed, they were so eager to have him that Esther Shapiro made a special 24-hour trip to Paris to see him. The pair took tea at the Ritz, and Shapiro's offer was more encouraging than Rock had anticipated: initially, he would play wealthy ranch owner Daniel Reece in six episodes, but if ratings turned out to be satisfactory – and Shapiro assured him they would be – he would appear in three more, and a possible spin-off series. His fee had already been fixed at $2.5 million! Needless to say, Rock must have somehow put the worries about his health to the back of his mind and signed the contract, there and then.

A few days later, Rock began his fourth and final series of HPA-23 infusions, and in the middle of the week Dr Dormont ran a number of tests. Rock was told that he still had AIDS, but that the virus had been curtailed. He was warned that it would return, but that there was a good chance that it would be kept under control, providing he returned to the Hôpital Percy on a regular basis, leaving no more than four weeks between infusion courses.

Rock weighed up the situation. His career had always come first, even before health and personal happiness, and at 58 – an age when he had begun denouncing himself as 'all washed up' – a potential *McMillan*-sized triumph was to all intents and purposes waiting around the next corner. He informed Dr Dormont that his *Dynasty* schedule would keep him occupied until February 1985, paid his, in those days, costly medical bill and on 7 October – convinced that he was cured – he and Ron Channell flew back to Los Angeles.

When Rock arrived back at the Castle, Marc Christian had gone away for the weekend. It would appear that Christian had had no communication whatsoever with Rock during his absence and had thought that the trip would be no longer than two weeks. It is possible he had gone away to avoid a confrontation with Ron Channell whom, he had been told, had replaced him in Rock's affections.

11

The Last Sunset

'Hudson loved his stardom and surrendered much to hold on to it. He called himself Charlie Movie Star as a self-deprecating joke, but creating that persona and preserving it for 35 years was a remarkable performance that deserves a little respect and appreciation.'

Angie Errigo, journalist

Much had happened, concerning San Francisco's vibrant gay community, during recent months. In May 1984, following weeks of arguments, the city's director of public health had issued a decree 'forbidding all sexual activity between individuals where the transmission of AIDS is likely to occur' – a move that had even been supported by some gay groups and had led to pressure being put upon the mayor, Diane Feinstein, to close the city's bath-houses, orgy rooms and glory holes. By the end of August, most of these had been assigned to history, as had others in gay villages around the country.

Rock was now 'tickled' to see footage of demonstrators on the television news, just wearing towels and chanting, 'Out of the Tubs and into the Shrubs!' – a statement to the fact that if they could not meet partners and have sex in what they considered to be appropriate surroundings, then they would begin 'hitting' parks and public toilets, which is of course what happened. Rock was not so amused, however, when rebel gay organisations started canvassing famous former patrons of the shut-down establishments for support – threatening to name names if they did not comply. According to friends, at the trial over his estate, it later emerged that for weeks he was terrified of answering the phone or of leaving the Castle.

At the end of October, Rock began working on *Dynasty*. He was extremely nervous about meeting the cast on account of the drastic change in his appearance, but when he walked on to the set for the first time, they and the crew applauded him as if he were royalty. Rock was no prima donna: there would be no arguments over what he was asked to do, or the numerous takes, despite his extreme fatigue. He was equally interested in fraternising with the extras as he was with the major stars, several of whom are said to have snubbed these 'underlings' and treated them with disdain. He became particularly fond of John Forsythe and Linda Evans, who played Blake and Crystal Carrington, and Joan Collins, who portrayed much-married resident superbitch, Alexis, no doubt one of the most exciting characters ever to appear in an American soap. Some of the younger male actors, on the other hand, Rock did not care for.

Rock's scenes in *Dynasty* are, unquestionably, the most heart-rending of his entire career. Occasionally, he has to break a line in the middle and gasp for breath, and in one scene when Crystal gives him a gentle, playful shove he is hard put not to lose his balance. It is obvious that he is deteriorating rapidly between episodes, fading before our very eyes. Yet everything he does remains utterly natural and charming, in complete contrast to the frequently over-the-top, lacklustre amateurism of most of his colleagues, who, when called to play opposite him, were auto-matically demoted to second-rate hams.

Daniel Reece, the millionaire owner of the Delta Rio stables, is in love with Crystal Carrington, and is ultimately revealed to be the father of her wayward niece, Sammy Jo (Heather Locklear) – who is enamoured of Crystal's gay stepson, Steven Carrington (Jack Coleman). When Daniel enters the scenario, Steven is the lover of Luke Fuller – played by William Campbell, who some years later played the Blank-Blank character reputedly based on Rock in the television adaptations of Armistead Maupin's *Tales of the City*.

Rock must have found this indirect link to an ongoing gay story line daunting, but also amusing, particularly the line pronounced to him by Sammy Jo, 'I never would have married Steven if I'd known he was gay, no matter how much money he had.' He was also tickled by the repartee between Alexis and her third husband, the dishy Dex Dexter (Michael Nader). Prior to Daniel's arrival on the scene, he and Dex have been 'war buddies', and there is now some talk of them heading off to Libya to sort out an international crisis:

> ALEXIS: I'm talking about a certain Mr Reece. Darling, I hope you don't have any imminent plans to go off adventuring with him again? From what I've heard about your exploits, they can be quite dangerous – and I'd hate to spend a fortune on a widow's wardrobe again!
> DEX: Alexis, I have absolutely no intention of getting involved with Mr Reece . . . How did you find out about all that, anyhow? Nobody's supposed to know.
> ALEXIS: Sombody knows, and somebody talked . . .
> DEX: Well, that somebody ought to have kept his mouth shut.

When not required on the set, Rock spent much of his time resting or doing needlepoint in his trailer. His almost constant fatigue resulted in him having problems remembering his lines, though in this respect he was not the only one. On one occasion the show's assistant director, Connie Garcia-Singer, flew into a panic when she was unable to rouse him, though by the time she had summoned help Rock was on his feet, begging her not to worry. There was a further problem with make-up, which was why Rock personally hired Universal's Jack Freeman, an artist who had first made him up for *Come September* in 1960. Speaking to *American TV Guide* in October 1985, Freeman recalled the differences between then and now:

> Then, it was just a matter of keeping the suntan on him. But here, he'd lost a great deal of weight. His colouring was very pale. I did what I could to make him look better, but it was evident that he wasn't really well or strong. Yet his face would

light up at times and he'd look wonderful and he didn't seem at all worried about his condition. When he sat in the make-up chair, he'd never look in the mirror and he was a little impatient. I'd have to go as fast as I could. But his humour was always up. Rock had a great sense of what I call *noblesse oblige*. He wanted to make sure that every actor, no matter how nervous or inexperienced, had his moments . . . At times another actor would keep making mistakes, so Rock would make a mistake too, so that the actor wouldn't be the focus of everyone's attention. I think he never forgot how hard it was for him the first time, and he wanted everybody to enjoy working as much as he did.

Only once did Rock's indefatigable good humour fail him – when he insisted upon doing his own stunts and the producer, Irving Moore, would not let him. Interviewed for the same publication as Jack Freeman, Moore – who seems to have known the truth, remembered one scene in particular:

It was very tough. Reece was supposed to be brought into a cell, thrown on the floor, then slammed up against the wall. Rock wanted to do it all himself, but of course we couldn't allow it. We picked up the scene with a stunt double after Rock hit the floor. I think it gave him a boost to be able to get in there and do something physical.

Rock's biggest dilemma during *Dynasty* came when the script called for him to kiss his on-screen mistress, Crystal, for his doctors had cautioned him that the AIDS virus could be transmitted through saliva and Rock had several open sores inside his mouth. For over a week after reading the script he deliberated what to do: whether to refuse to perform the kiss, which would have robbed the plot of its passionate twist, or whether to tell everyone *why* he could not kiss Linda Evans. The latter, of course, would not only have guaranteed his removal from the show and therefore necessitated a costly, last-minute rewriting of the plot, but inevitably the world's press would have got hold of the story, however Rock tried to hide it. Rock therefore decided that the kiss would have to take place, but that it would not be open-mouthed. The scene was filmed, and nothing more was said about it until July 1985 when thousands of Linda Evans fans accused him of deliberately putting her life at risk.

By the end of 1984, Rock's social and sex life had all but ground to a halt. The 'old-timers' – Rock's celebrity friends – had begun avoiding him, allegedly because of their resentment of Marc Christian. There were no parties held at the Castle and few invitations to attend others elsewhere. According to his very closest friends, Rock had become celibate, ashamed that his seemingly limitless libido and addiction to sex had contributed to his moribund state and shortly after his fifty-ninth birthday, Rock told Mark Miller, 'No sixtieth. I'm leaving town next year.'

There were two exceptions: a Christmas Eve knees-up at the home of Martha Raye, one of his *McMillan* co-stars and the only woman he had trusted to confide in about his condition, and a visit to the Golden Globes in January 1985, when he arrived linking arms with Liza Minnelli and Elizabeth Taylor.

Rock's deterioration was rapid. By March 1985 his weight had dropped to 180 pounds – an impressive weight for most men, but not for one whom people had frequently been willing to swear stood six-and-half-feet tall and who had, without an ounce of fat, once tipped the scales at 225 pounds. The loss, Rock told Marc Christian, was the result of overzealous dieting and recurring influenza. He could hardly keep anything down, was suffering almost constantly from diarrhoea, and had developed agonising impetigo. On some days he slurred his speech, as had happened while filming his last *Dynasty* episode when the script girl, thinking him to be suffering from a hangover, had arranged for him to read from cue cards.

He was urged to return to Paris for another course of infusions at the Hôpital Percy, but would not hear of this, complaining that Paris would be too cold at this time of year. By way of a 'compromise', to stop everyone nagging at him, he flew to Hawaii for a week's vacation with Ron Channell, who astonishingly still does not appear to have been told what was wrong with him. A few weeks after this, he and Mark Miller spent several days at Miller's and George Nader's Palm Desert retreat, sightseeing and reminiscing over times long past. Nader would later define this as Rock's way of saying goodbye.

At the end of May, Marc Christian's sister, Susan, was married and Rock told the press that the wedding reception would be taking place at the Castle, as he would have done for any other member of his staff. The previous year he had thrown a surprise ruby wedding party for Christian's parents, declaring how his lover's family was his family too. Yet only days after this second bash – at which he himself was not present – Rock is said to have hit the roof upon receiving a $10,000 bill from the garage that had been restoring Mr Christian's car. Rock had already shelled out $20,000 on repairs, and he now returned the bill, declaring that it was no longer his responsibility – a move interpreted by his friends that he and Christian were definitely no longer an item. Christian later accused the garage-owner of 'kiting' the bill by charging Rock twice for the same parts – the owner reciprocated by informing Rock that besides Mr Christian's station wagon, he had been unwittingly contributing towards the repair of Liberty Martin's car. Who eventually settled the bill, or indeed if it was ever paid at all, is not known, though the incident appears to have been the last straw so far as Rock's patience with Christian was concerned and he didn't speak to him for several days.

At the end of June, Rock received a telephone call from old pal Doris Day, now semi-retired at her home in Carmel. Doris had been invited to make a television programme, *Doris Day's Best Friends* – her first in years – and naturally she was anxious that Rock should participate. The show's producer had already set up a press conference to attend the event on 16 July, and *Life* magazine had arranged to do a photo-spread and cover feature of what was being hailed 'the biggest show business reunion of the decade'. There was even talk of the pair making another film together.

Rock's friends and his doctors urged him not to do the show because he looked so terribly ill. He now weighed 170 pounds, and on occasions could hardly stand on his feet. He refused to listen, however. Well aware that he was offering his swansong, on 15 July he flew out to Carmel.

The actual filming of the show went well, though Rock turned up late, wearing old clothes, and with unkempt hair and moustache. At one stage he stumbled, and he trembled noticeably when Doris put her arms about him and called him her best buddy. Doris was so shocked by his appearance that she wanted to cancel the show until he was feeling a little stronger, but Rock would not hear of this. When asked point-blank what was wrong with his client, Dale Olson merely repeated to the press what Rock had told Marc Christian about the recurring bouts of flu. For the moment the AIDS word would not be printed: to the layman, Rock's sunken eyes, hollow cheeks and ghastly tinge indicated that he must have been suffering from cancer, possibly of the liver.

Rock's contribution to *Doris Day's Best Friends* was a skit on *Pillow Talk* and opens with the familiar split screen: two old pals chatting on the phone while she arranges roses in a vase and he is at home, preparing to leave for the show. Doris expresses her delight that he has consented to appear, but now tells him that the budget cannot allow for him to fly, therefore he must catch the bus. He does, turning up in an old banger that she goes to meet in a country lane. They then drive off in a buttercup-yellow convertible similar to the one Rock had owned when living with Jack Navaar. Finally, in Doris' garden, surrounded by her dogs, they talk over old times. The tableau is intended to be hilariously funny, but Rock looks so feeble, gaunt and prematurely aged that one finds it near impossible to watch this last image of him without shedding tears.

It has never been established if Rock actually told Doris Day about his illness, or if she worked it out for herself. She has steadfastly refused to speak about this period of Rock's life, and she was still biting back the tears when she brushed off the politely persuasive Gloria Hunniford at the end of 1994 in a British television interview honouring her seventieth birthday. 'It was shattering,' she told Hunniford, 'but enough of that. Let's think of him with laughter, because he was *so* funny.'

On 20 July, four days after leaving Carmel, and under considerable pressure from those friends who loved him most, Rock flew to Paris – again accompanied by Ron Channell, who by now had been let in on his dreadful secret. At Orly a limousine had been booked to take them directly to the Hôpital Percy. So far as everyone back home was aware – save Mark Miller and George Nader – Rock was travelling to Geneva to be treated for anorexia. Doctors there, the press had been told, had developed an experimental serum, which thus far had not been approved by the US Federal Drugs Administration. The car, however, did not turn up, and when Rock collapsed in the airport lounge an ambulance was summoned and he was transported to the Hôpital Americain, at Neuilly, on the city peripheral.

The next morning, a hospital spokesman issued a brief statement:

It is my sad duty to announce that Mr Rock Hudson is suffering from acute metastatic liver disease. The chances of recovering from this are not good.

Ron Channell relayed this news to Mark Miller, and the next day Miller flew to Paris. And on 23 July, following a tip-off from their Paris correspondent, *Daily Variety* ran a brief exclusive:

The whispering campaign against Rock Hudson can and should stop . . . The Institute Pasteur has been very active in its research of AIDS. Hudson's dramatic weight loss was made evident to the national press last week when he winged his way to Carmel. His illness was no secret to close Hollywood friends, but its true nature was disclosed to very few.

For a few days at least, the *Daily Variety* piece was dismissed by Rock's fans as just another exercise in tabloid scandalmongering. Its writer, Army Archard, had quoted the correct location but the wrong clinic, but more importantly a French hospital specialist had disclosed the exact nature of his illness, and the word AIDS had not even been mentioned.

For several days, Rock appeared to be rallying. Meanwhile the Hôpital Percy, who as pioneers in the treatment of AIDS patients could hardly deny that some of these were famous, was besieged by scores of reporters who had been tricked into believing that Rock was still there. One of these, probably suspecting the truth about Rock's illness, leaked the news to a male nurse at the Hôpital

Americain. This caused confusion amongst the doctors, who asked Rock to leave the hospital – their official line being that the establishment was not licensed to treat infectious diseases and it led to mass panic.

Neither was Rock allowed back to Hôpital Percy. Though Dr Dormont was permitted to treat day-patients on an experimental-only basis, Percy was a military hospital where civilians other than ex-military could not be admitted for overnight stays. Nancy Reagan (but *not* her husband, as was stated at the time) personally intervened: Rock was allowed to stay on at Neuilly, though its administrators insisted upon a '100 per cent truthful' statement being given to the media. The statement was read out by Rock's French press agent, Yanou Collart on 25 July:

> Mr Rock Hudson has Acquired Immune Deficiency Syndrome, which was diagnosed over a year ago in the United States. He came to Paris to consult with a specialist in this disease. Prior to meeting the specialist he became very ill at the Ritz Hotel, and his personal business manager, Mr Mark Miller, advised him from California to enter the American Hospital of Paris immediately. The physicians at the American Hospital conducted a series of diagnostic examinations of Mr Hudson. At the time they suspected, but did not know, about Mr Hudson's AIDS diagnosis. They were informed of this by Mr Miller upon his arrival in Paris. All our prayers are with Mr Hudson, and we wish him the best.

Collart later said that she had had to coerce Rock into giving his permission for the statement to be read out, that if it had been left to him, the world would never have known the truth about his illness, certainly not then. He is also thought to have insisted upon the clause explaining that he had collapsed in his suite at the Ritz – that the great star could not have suffered the indignity of being taken ill in a modest airport lounge. Also, it is very unlikely that anyone would have insisted upon him being conveyed to the Hôpital Americain – then, as now, all stricken celebrities were more often than not treated there. The announcement coincided with the photographs of Rock that had been taken at Carmel – in particular an unposed head-and-shoulders shot taken from a larger photograph with Doris Day, in which he really does resemble a corpse – being wired to press offices around the world. Terry Sanderson, writing in his acclaimed *Gay Times* mediawatch column, rightly criticised this particular aspect of the Hudson smear campaign:

> The most pervasive image in the papers was that picture of Rock Hudson – gaunt and enfeebled. Day after day the same sunken-eyed, hollow-cheeked face looked out from the headlines . . . and the floodgates opened once more. Poor Rock Hudson. The vultures swooped in to pick at his bones before he's even dead . . . All the old clichés were wheeled out: 'Living A Lie', 'Secret Torment', 'Bizarre Lifestyle' and so on. Oh, how they wallowed in it.

Everyone who saw this picture, even before hearing the statement from the Hôpital Americain, knew at once that Rock was seriously ill, but it took the British tabloids to actually declare that he had AIDS. Over the next few days the public were fed the most lurid resumé of Rock's personal life. Very dubious 'exclusives' were acquired from suspicious sources – insiders, talent scouts, long-time friends, prominent doctors, who were, of course, unnamed and in almost every instance no more than editorial invention, the oldest trick in the book.

In a stream of bile equalled by that which followed the death of Freddie Mercury six years later, the tabloids fought to see which of them could come up with the headline that vilified him the most. Anti-gay supremo John Junor, of the *Sunday Express*, called the *Dynasty* kiss a deliberate attempt by Rock to give Linda Evans AIDS. Junor concluded:

> There is rightly much public sympathy for Mr Hudson. Might there not have been more if when suspecting, as he must have done, the nature of the ailment from which he was suffering, he had not gone out of his way – as do homosexuals who offer blood – to place other and innocent people in danger?

This particular statement deeply offended the British gay community, the majority of whom were taking active steps to curb the spread of the disease and who, like John Junor, knew only too well, on account of the unprecedented wealth of medical facts being broadcast by the media, that HIV could not be transmitted by kissing. This time in his *Gay Times* column, Terry Sanderson was unafraid of going for the jugular:

> *Innocent*? What is Rock Hudson supposed to be guilty of? As far as the vile Junor is concerned, he is guilty simply of being gay.

Only a select handful of journalists were similarly brave enough to defend him, the most sympathetic being Donald Zec, who observed in the *Sunday Mirror*:

> It is a sad and painfully embarrassing twilight for one of Hollywood's best-loved legends . . . Not since Humphrey Bogart's staggering courageous battle with cancer, years ago, have we seen so devastating a disintegration of a star. His Hollywood chums wince if not weep at what they see. I felt the stab of it, too, recalling the lively and pretty forthright character who invited me to his Beverly Hills mountain home for a talk not that long ago . . . Rock Hudson, lying stricken in a Paris hospital, is not fighting to sustain an image, but for his life. But if I know anything about this likeable and modest character, he won't be whimpering at the stakes mounted against him.

Phyllis Gates, meanwhile, told a New York press conference that her long-threatened book about their troubled marriage was close to completion. The book, she vowed (as reported by the *Sunday Mirror*'s June Walton) would reveal all: Rock's lack of sexual interest in her when she had believed herself to have been the love of his life; how a psychiatrist had advised her to try 'straightening' him out by attempting to seduce him in frilly underwear; and how they had only wed in the first place to prevent the Hollywood press from exposing Rock as a wildly promiscuous homosexual.

Rock was defended by several close, gay-friendly colleagues in a follow-up feature published by *People* magazine. Arlene Dahl, Rock's co-star in *Bengal Brigade*, proclaimed, 'Phyllis was *not* the love of Rock's life. It was simply an arrangement!' And Mamie Van Doren hit out, 'In Hollywood we *all* knew Rock was gay, but it never made the slightest difference to us!'

Rock is alleged never to have been told about Phyllis' proposed book, but he was delighted by the level of support he received from the American gay press – surprisingly, perhaps, considering how he had upset some of the more militant publications by never declaring his sexuality. Some drew attention to the fact, not entirely true, that the Reagan administration was *so* homophobic that one of the country's biggest stars, a man who had earned millions for the box office, had been forced to travel abroad and spend an estimated $350,000 of his own money on medical treatment that had been denied him at home. Others praised Rock for his immense courage.

'It's a hell of a way to come out, lying in a hospital bed and knowing how everyone's talking about you,' observed Vito Russo, the author of *The Celluloid Closet* (HarperCollins, 1981). And Brian Jones, the editor of San Francisco's *Bay Area Reporter*, whose staff had frequently 'rubbed shoulders' with Rock in some of the city's bathhouses, was but one of the many who regarded Rock Hudson as a modern-day Christ-like saviour put on this earth to suffer so that others might live and learn. Within days of Phyllis' press conference he defended:

> Rock Hudson's illness may be an important factor in changing public attitudes. Yesterday, most Americans didn't know anyone with AIDS. Today they do, for they feel they know their movie stars. This could represent a tremendous shift in public perception – that even nice people get AIDS.

Rock's friend Armistead Maupin, told the *San Francisco Chronicle*:

> Actors in Hollywood, until now, have abided by rules which keep the identities of gay actors secret. These rules state that if

you keep quiet, everyone will lie about it for you. All
Hollywood will know. But the public – *never*!

Years later Maupin told the *Guardian*'s Patrick Gale (June 1999)
he would still be castigating himself for 'outing' Rock: the fact that
he had told the journalist from *The Chronicle* of how the 'secret
game' Rock had been playing all his adult life had finally and
tragically caught up with him, and that this had resulted in the
world learning that he was gay. But Maupin had nothing to
reproach himself with, he has always spoken of Rock with the
utmost respect and would never have done anything intentionally
malicious. However, the fact that the tabloid hacks could not see
beyond the physical image of homosexuality as opposed to the
idea that one man could actually love another just as whole-
heartedly and tenderly as he might a woman was hypocrisy of the
worst kind.

A Boeing 747 was chartered to fly Rock back to Los Angeles on 30
July, and he was transferred by helicopter, gravely ill, to the UCLA
Medical Centre, where visitors were counselled before being
ushered into the sickroom so that they would not let him see how
shocked they were by his appearance. They were further warned not
to tell him what was being written about him in the press, though he
was shown the cover of the 12 August issue of *Newsweek,* half of
which was taken up by the Carmel photograph and a single word,
AIDS. The report began:

> It is the nation's worst public-health problem. No one has ever
> recovered from the disease, and the number of cases is doubling
> every year. New fears are growing that the AIDS epidemic may
> spread beyond gays and other high-risk groups to threaten the
> population at large . . .

The first person Rock asked for was Tom Clark, but unfairly or not
he flatly refused to see Marc Christian. Though Clark had been
removed from his will – and Rock was far too ill to change it, now –
his former lover would hardly ever leave his side from now on, and

was Rock's greatest comfort during his last weeks. Martha Raye and Roddy McDowall also spent a lot of time with him.

Meanwhile the snubbed Marc Christian flew to Paris shortly after Rock's admission to the UCLA Medical Centre. Like the rest of the world, he had first learned that Rock had AIDS by way of Yanou Collart's announcement on the television news, and he was understandably devastated. He was also bitter, most of all because Collart had disclosed how Rock had been diagnosed over a year ago. 'I began to sweat, then I passed out,' he later said at the court hearing. 'I just thought, "Oh, my God. I'm a dead man."'

Christian was met at Orly airport by Steven Del Re, Jack Coates' lover, who had been diagnosed HIV positive before meeting Coates, and who had since developed full-blown AIDS and begun attending the Hôpital Percy. The same age as Christian, he had been on the same treatment programme as Rock, but unlike Rock had kept up his infusions and was reported to have begun showing signs of slight improvement. Del Re escorted Christian to the hospital, sat with him while Dr Dormont tested him for HIV and enlightened him on every known aspect of the disease.

Distressed as he is said to have been, however, Christian did not refuse when his new friend asked him to accompany him to the South of France while awaiting his test results and the pair shared a hotel room at Mougins, near Cannes. Christian subsequently told, under oath (see Appendix I), how Mark Miller laughingly told him over the telephone, 'Throw a rubber on your dick and have sex with Del Re. If you've got AIDS from Rock, it wouldn't matter now if you had sex with Del Re.'

Back at Percy, Christian was told by Dr Dormont that though his test had proved negative, he should not build up his hopes: the prognosis (then) was that the HIV virus did not always show up in preliminary tests and that he would have to be re-tested every eight weeks until the hospital was satisfied that he was clear. Christian also received little comfort when Dr Dormont added that the last test he had carried out on Rock, at a time when it had been only too obvious that he had developed full-blown AIDS, had shown no traces of the virus.

Christian flew back to Los Angeles on 10 August severely deflated. No sooner had he entered the Castle than Mark Miller served him with his marching orders – declaring that Rock himself had given the instruction. The young man was understandably sceptical, and refused to budge until Rock had personally asked him to leave. According to Christian, when he went to see Rock in the hospital, he was told to stay put.

During his first two weeks in hospital, Rock received over 30,000 letters, get-well cards and gifts from his fans and, though these were appreciated, there were considerably less than there had been after his bypass operation, no doubt because many hypocritical former admirers no longer wished to be seen supporting him now that the truth was out. There were also hundreds of telegrams from show business pals and colleagues, and many from luminaries who had never met him. Madonna, Ava Gardner and Marlene Dietrich were but three who expressed profound admiration of his courage. No one gave a damn about his sexuality any more, as if they had in the first place. They just wanted the impossible, for him to be well again.

Elizabeth Taylor is thought to have been the one who put Rock in touch with the Shanti Foundation, a Los Angeles organisation which had set up a telephone hotline for AIDS sufferers who did not wish to be seen visiting their centre. Even this was mocked by the tabloids who dubbed it 'Hudson's Hotline of Death'. But Rock's personal message to his fans, published in newspapers worldwide, earned him tremendous respect, even from some of his harshest detractors:

> I'm not the first actor to get AIDS, but I'm the first to go public. At least in saying I have it, I might help others who are going through the same hell, and that might push the scientists a bit harder to find a cure. And of course, everyone is going to immediately assume *how* I got AIDS. Do you think people would accept that I got it from a blood transfusion when I had heart bypass surgery three years ago? I don't want all my fans making their own conclusions. That would only make everything I've done in my life a sham.

Tom Clark moved back into the Castle at once, and on the evening of 24 August, Rock was discharged from the UCLA Medical Centre: the doctors had told him that nothing more could be done to save

him, or even to prolong his life. His homecoming was akin to that of
the warrior returning doomed from the battlefield, with weeping fans
joining the hundreds of reporters, photographers and cameramen
outside the Castle gates. He was the first major celebrity to have been
diagnosed as suffering from AIDS – the pop stars Jobriath Boone
and Klaus Nomi had already succumbed to the disease, but these
were unknown outside their limited circles – and suddenly Rock,
who had dreaded the repercussions of his sexuality being revealed to
the world, was hailed a martyr by the gay community. Only the
unimportant homophobes would revile him from now on.

Elizabeth Taylor visited him almost every day, despite the fact
that some days he could keep nothing down, and the stench of the
sickroom was overpowering. Rock's greatest champion always
managed to stay calm while she was with him but the press reports
and photographs suggest she went to pieces the moment she left.
Others found themselves incapable of witnessing his suffering.
Claire Trevor told *Ciné-Revue*'s Joan Mac Trevor:

> It was horrible, just seeing him waste away like that, and I
> didn't want my lasting image of Rock Hudson to be his looking
> like that. To me it seemed more decent to call him, rather than
> go to the house.

Rock received a telephone call from Nancy Reagan, who announced
how much she and Ronald were looking forward to visiting the
Castle. He was hardly surprised, however, when the President's
advisers strongly voiced their disapproval, declaring that such an
'unconventional' meeting could never take place for fear of
offending the so-called moral majority. Rock reacted to this with a
statement of his own, brief and to the point, delivered by Tom Clark
to reporters clustered around the gates of the Castle:

> Reagan is yet to actually say the word AIDS in public. He and
> his people are so afraid of the Far Right. Fuck them all!

Despite the efforts of Rock's friends to evict him, and Rock's own
apparent refusal to have anything to do with him, Marc Christian

stayed on at the Castle, always keeping out of everyone's way . . . the lover who, through no fault of his own, had suddenly become the enemy, castigated by this jealous bickering bevy of over-protective nursemaids – Miller, Nader, Clark and the household staff – each of whom believed he held a divine right to help Rock through his final days and make what remained of his life as peaceful as possible.

On 4 September, Rock was visited by Sara Davidson, a Los Angeles novelist who had been given the daunting task (having first been vetted by Rock's lawyers, Mark Miller and the William Morris Publishing Co) of working with him as ghostwriter for the auto-biography he had been planning for years, but for obvious reasons never got around to starting. Everyone involved, of course, was well aware that Rock might not have sufficient time left to complete the project, and with this in mind Rock had instructed Miller to complete the commission, if need be, telling him, 'You know the whole story. You'll have to do it for me.' Davidson herself was told at the outset, 'So much bullshit has been written about me. It's time to set things straight.' Rock also stipulated that his share of profits from the book should be donated to his recently set up Rock Hudson AIDS Research Foundation.

The announcement of Rock's 'kiss and tell' sent huge shock waves throughout the entire film community, as Tom Clark explained to Joan Mac Trevor:

Rock had met countless people during his career, and there were some of these with whom he'd had 'special' connections. Hollywood is very nervous today. These people are married with grandchildren. They're terrified of Rock's revelations destroying their peace of mind. Rock and his editors have had lots of fun since he decided to write this book. They wanted to call it *Hollywood Dictionary* because it names everyone, from A to Z, who influenced his life. And some of these people have doubtless forgotten that they didn't always treat him kindly.

Mac Trevor also disclosed in her *Ciné-Revue* feature of 1985 how the wife of a 'very famous actor' had turned up at the Castle and offered a large donation to Rock's charity providing he remove any references to him from the book. Troy Donahue also offered to buy Rock's silence. Mac Trevor, however, was convinced that Rock never had been and never would be a malevolent man:

> I've known him virtually since the day he arrived in Hollywood. Rock has always been honest and upstanding. He is not writing this book to settle any scores. He's too nice to be leaving this world in a vengeful manner, though I do have to say that no one's going to have much to gain by appearing in his memoirs . . .

Initially, Rock was alert and coherent in his recollections, but as his condition worsened over the next few weeks, he soon started to tire. According to Mark Miller, such fatigue caused his mind to wander. Sara Davidson recalled too how daunting a place the Castle was:

> It was one of the most bizarre scenes I'd ever witnessed: the old lover and the new lover brushing elbows in the hall, the old lover reclaiming his place while the new one refused to give ground. Friends gathering in the living room, laughing and telling stories while the movie star lay dying of a terrible disease – the plague of our time. The eighty-year-old gardener eating ice cream in the kitchen. The butler in his towel. What was I getting into?

Rock Hudson: His Story cannot under any circumstances be even loosely regarded as Rock's autobiography – indeed, most of his comments, anecdotes, observations and opinions come from other sources, most especially Mark Miller and George Nader. Because of this – the fact that these were his most trusted confidants who for three decades had done their utmost to conceal his and their own sexuality – some of Rock's other friends would feel that he had been deceived, if not downright insulted. Most importantly they would believe that, had Rock been in a sounder state of mind, he would never have entertained the idea of *anyone* letting the world in on the most intimate secrets of his love life.

Such was Rock's confusion during these last weeks that he is quoted (by Tom Clark) as having asked Marc Christian, while pointing to Sara Davidson, 'Who is she? Is she one of the nurses?' However, given the fact that most of those who confided in the author did so without any axe to grind and with the utmost respect – the book positively bustles with a lively, frequently bitchy gay banter – it ultimately represents an honest, fairly rounded and at times intensely upsetting, portrait of the man behind the mask. Davidson sums up this, for her, somewhat unorthodox approach by writing in her introduction:

Mark and George were cautious, censoring what they said, but at the end they held little back. We became collaborators, trying to crack a puzzle they had been grappling with for three decades.

Meanwhile, on 19 September, Elizabeth Taylor and Shirley MacLaine, who had already raised a great deal of money for AIDS charities, organised a benefit dinner for Rock in Los Angeles. The pair had confidently announced, prior to sending out the invitations, that they would achieve their $250,000 target – the amount that Rock himself had donated to his foundation – but such was the response that the event realised five times this amount, though some of Elizabeth Taylor's gay actor friends who gave generously insisted upon anonymity and did not show up on the evening. Armistead Maupin's announcement, earlier, had served as a veiled warning, forcing them to keep a suitable distance for fear of being exposed by the press.

The guests included Gregory Peck, Burt Reynolds, Ricardo Montalban and Linda Evans. Burt Lancaster presided over the dinner and read out the speech that Rock had written, hoping that he might be well enough to attend and deliver himself:

People have told me that the disclosure that I have AIDS has helped make this evening an immediate sellout, and it will raise $1 million in the battle against AIDS. I have also been told that media coverage of my own situation has brought enormous international attention to the gravity of the disease. If this is helping others, then I can at least know my own misfortune has some positive worth.

Only once during this dreadfully anguished period could Rock's closest friends be accused of failing in their duties to protect him from the indignations of the outside world . . . when they allowed him to be taken advantage of by a group of religious fanatics. Tom Clark recounted the story of how, on 21 September, he had been alone with Rock – who was bedridden and attached to an intravenous drip – when a woman had knocked on the door and announced that she had brought a message to Rock from God. Clark, apparently, had tried to get rid of her – how she had managed to get through the security gates is not known – but when, several hours later she had still been there, he had foolishly welcomed her into the house and taken her upstairs to see Rock. And, standing at the foot of his bed, she had told him, 'God has asked me to tell you you're not going to leave us yet. The cancer will leave your body and you are going to be just fine'.

This charade persisted for over a week with Clark, his judgement clouded by grief, allowing Rock's room to be transformed into an extended deathbed scenario worthy of Pirandello. Religious medals and pictures sent in by fans were hung from the walls and bedposts – and despite being a lapsed Catholic, he received visits from ultra-clean-cut singer and born-again Christian, Pat Boone, accompanied by his wife Shirley and their three daughters. One of these, pop star Debbie, had outraged gay groups in 1979 by giving an interview to *Playgirl*, said to have been almost as popular with homosexual readers as female ones, in that it was the only one openly available on newsstands that featured photographs of naked men sporting erections. Debbie had gaffed by telling journalist Elliot Mintz:

I could more easily sit and have a discussion with a homosexual than a killer, because somebody who has the potential to kill is more frightening to me. But I feel that God does not necessarily regard a killer any differently than a homosexual . . . He's looking at a killer or a homosexual and saying, "You're out, you're never gonna make it!"

That being gay could be equated as sinful as murder in some people's eyes – and in view of some of the inexcusably vituperative comments being aimed at AIDS victims by religious zealots – was for Rock and every single one of those who genuinely cared about him the supreme insult.

Another guest, not welcomed by Rock's entourage, was Susan Stafford, an actress friend of Rock's who for several years had hosted the television quiz, *Wheel of Fortune*, but who was now an intern minister. It was she who organised for a Catholic priest, Father Tom Sweeney – himself a television personality, and also adviser on the mini-series, *The Thornbirds* – to visit Rock. He, Stafford and the Boones knelt around Rock's bed, praying and chanting in tongues.

What happened next, reported by the tabloids and collated by John Parker in *The Trial Of Rock Hudson*, makes for grim reading. On the evening of Tuesday 1 October the Boones turned up at the Castle for a laying-on-of-hands ceremony. Pat Boone placed the Bible on Rock's chest – he was down to 98 pounds and could scarcely breathe – while his wife and their fellow converts chanted some more. Boone next gave instructions to Tom Clark to place Rock's everyday clothes next to him on the bed, vowing that a miracle would occur during the night – that when completely cured, Rock would get up and put these on. When Clark discovered him the next morning – fully dressed and in apparent agony – he hit the roof and, not before time, ordered the Boones out of the house.

Many people, this author included, condemned this unfortunate final episode as ill-timed and extremely sick. Though it probably did not hasten Rock's end, it certainly did little to make his last moments comfortable. By 8.45 a.m., less than one hour after his nurse had changed him back into his pyjamas, Rock was gone.

Epilogue

'He's gone. But the most important thing is that he was here –
that he was a wonderful guy while he was here.'
Michael Nader, *Dynasty* co-star

The news of Rock's death was announced in a national radio
broadcast at 9.11 a.m., less than half an hour after he died. Within ten
minutes of this, seemingly every television camera crew, reporter
and photographer in Hollywood had flocked to the gates of the
Castle, where even the most hackish amongst them would be taken
aback by the subsequent speed of events. A few managed to get into
the grounds, only to be ejected by the crack team of security men
provided by Elizabeth Taylor.

While making her public statement, Elizabeth Taylor was near
inconsolable, and for months would refuse to refer to Rock in the
past tense. She told the press on the day of his death, 'I love him, and
he is tragically gone. Please God he has not died in vain.' Doris Day
said from her Carmel home:

> This is when our faith is really tested. All of those years I
> worked with him I saw him as big, handsome and
> indestructible. I'm saddened by this and all I can do is uplift
> myself. Life is eternal. I hope we'll meet again.

244

The 'official' statement from the White House, delivered by one of the advisers who had apparently talked President and Nancy Reagan out of visiting the Castle, was branded the height of hypocrisy by Rock's friends, whose feelings were obviously running high at the time:

> Nancy and I are saddened by the news of Rock Hudson's death. He will always be remembered for his dynamic impact on the film industry and fans all over the world will certainly mourn his loss. He will be remembered for his humanity, his sympathetic spirit and well-deserved reputation for kindness. May God rest his soul.

The press were politely requested not to pester the *Dynasty* cast, which of course only had the opposite effect – their comments are mostly unworthy of mention. Eric Eston of *American TV Guide* was an exception, and kindly refrained from publishing his piece until six months after Rock's death. Even so, some of his former co-stars were reticent to pay him homage: it was as if the nature of his illness had made them feel ashamed of knowing and speaking about him. Eston observed that they:

> . . . spoke only in the presence of the show's publicist who, in the case of Linda Evans, cut the interview short when she sensed the star was growing understandably uncomfortable when reference was made to the infamous kiss.

Only days before, the kiss had been mocked in a television sketch by the acid-tongued comedienne Joan Rivers, and because of the palaver, the Screen Actors Guild had recently introduced a temporary measure forbidding open-mouthed kissing on the screen.

Jack Coleman, the straight actor who had played gay Steven Carrington – who, in a hasty rewriting of the *Dynasty* script, was about to be 'turned' rampantly heterosexual, while plans had been made for his on-screen lover to be killed in a European wedding fiasco – was conspicuous by his absence, as was the homophobic actor who had asked for Rock to be fired from the production.

The ones who mattered, however, were unafraid of speaking out in his favour. John Forsythe remembered Rock's 'playful good humour and gentle spirit.' He added, referring to the shows prima donnas of both sexes:

> Some actors crave love, and as a result they get nothing in return. Other actors don't push it. He was one that didn't push it, and everybody warmed to him.

Michael Nader agreed with this:

> Rock was just a real down-home kind of guy. He used to come in comfortably dressed – not that showy type of rag-magazine glamour. We've had other people on the show who've not been so comfortable . . . And he did work with us. It was a real nice session for this show to go through.
>
> As far as the disease is concerned, there's no need for discussion. The country has it, the world has it. But in terms of him it was hard watching, knowing that this guy was gone – just as he was reaching a maturity level where he could really get the recognition he deserved as an actor.

And Rock's favourite, Heather Locklear, tearfully recalled:

> I had just two scenes with him, and he was such a gentleman. He was very quiet, kind of shy. In one scene he had to throw me down and he said, 'Now, you just tell me if it's too rough.' Everything was for me! I was thinking, 'What do you mean? Throw me across the room. I don't *care*!' He was just a very, very nice man. It was such an honour to work with him.

The media reaction towards Rock's death could not have been more inhuman and undignified. The *Globe*, almost on a par with *Confidential* and The *National Enquirer* with its sordid, frequently implausible exclusives and woefully misguided observations, repeated its earlier 'defence' of Rock by declaring that he had not been gay upon his arrival in Hollywood – but that Henry Willson had made him this way. A further implication, harking back to the earlier comment by the *Sunday Express'* John Junor, was that as homosexuals were traditionally supposed to be woman-haters, Rock had deliberately kissed Linda Evans on the mouth during the *Dynasty* episode while knowing he had AIDS.

The ungagged British tabloids were worse. The *Star* called Rock's life 'but a sordid sham', and quoted Phyllis Gates as having said of their marriage, 'He would go for days sullen, not speaking, and my life was very miserable. He hit me when I asked why he wouldn't talk to me.' The *Sun*, denouncing him as 'The Hunk Who Lived A Lie', repeated Elizabeth Taylor's timeworn confession of how, while shooting *Giant,* she had failed to successfully woo Rock because he had been head-over-heels in love with James Dean. The piece went one step further with its 'exclusive admission' that though he had wanted to, Rock had been incapable of making love to any of his screen goddess co-stars – prevented from doing so by the dreadful infliction known as homosexuality. And always, *always* the Carmel photograph.

The *Hollywood Reporter*'s Arthur Knight, one of the few journalists with anything remotely sympathetic to say about him, urged his readers to make donations to the American Foundation for AIDS Research instead of sending flowers to his funeral, and ended his obituary, 'It's the sincerest possible tribute to a brave and gracious man.' And the most prosaic, heartfelt statement came from Rock's friend, Joan Mac Trevor, who had visited the Castle 24 hours after his death. She drew attention to the fact that, while his fans and friends could support one another during their grief, no one had given much thought to Rock's similarly bereft pets:

The star's blue Mercedes is still in the garage, and a cat scrambles up on to the roof, looking for the master who left so suddenly on his final journey. No one can explain to Rock's favourite animal that his buddy will never come home to stroke him like he used to do, hours on end next to the palm-shadowed pool, surveyed by the statues which adorn the terrace. But the cat understands all, through instinct and affection – driving away from the house I catch sight of him in the setting sun, looking lost, orphaned of the tenderness which came from a great man of the cinema.

Among the first to arrive at the Castle were Shirley Boone and the woman who had introduced herself to Tom Clark as Eleanor. Boone sank to her knees beside the bed, while the other prostrated herself on the floor and chanted in tongues, as before. At 10.45 a pair of undertakers' assistants wearing masks and gloves collected Rock's body – not in a hearse, but in a van with clear glass windows – an 'arrangement' that had been hastily made between the funeral parlour and a photographer who was hoping to snatch an exclusive shot of the corpse. Rock's friends prevented this from happening by taping towels over the windows, though this did not stop the farce that followed – the vehicle was purposely too small so that Rock's feet ended up sticking out of the back doors, and he made his final exit from his home with Tom Clark straddled across his body, desperately trying to hold the doors shut while the sea of jostling press tried to jerk them open. Then, instead of driving to a chapel of rest, the van headed straight for the crematorium, where Rock's body was placed in a large cardboard box bearing his name, and unceremoniously and shamelessly rolled into the oven.

The ever-loving Tom later told Sara Davidson:

I saw the box catch fire. I stood there watching it, then they closed the doors and I left. It was the hardest thing I ever had to do, but I did it and there weren't any photographs taken.

On 19 October 1985, Mexican music emanated from the grounds of the Castle as the celebration of Rock's life, organised by Tom Clark and Elizabeth Taylor, took place. His last wish was that he should have a rowdy send-off, 'with lots of laughter and good food'. A huge marquee had been erected and three hundred or so guests invited. It was Elizabeth who determined that the most fitting service for a lapsed Catholic should be a Quaker one – she had been in London in July 1966 when Montgomery Clift had died, but had wept on watching footage of his funeral at the Friends Cemetery in Brooklyn's Prospect Park, and so had Rock. Elizabeth also insisted that Rock's closest friends take the podium and share their most intimate memories of the buddy they had lost. A lot of these were funny, and some are said to have turned the air blue.

Phyllis Gates was conspicuous by her absence. George Nader had called her personally and begged her to come, declaring how six months before his death Rock had confessed that he had only truly loved two people – herself and Lee Garrington. She politely declined Nader's invitation, and later observed in her memoirs, 'It would have been hypocritical of me to appear at a memorial for the man I hadn't seen since we parted in the divorce court in 1958.'

In a serious moment the eulogies were read by Carol Burnett and Tab Hunter. The next day – it was George Nader's sixty-fourth birthday – Rock's ashes were scattered at sea, off Catalina Island, by Tom Clark. Because of the nature of his death Rock's assets had been temporarily frozen, so his friends and the household staff had clubbed together to pay for the ceremony.

It was over – or so everyone thought.

Appendix I

Marc Christian vs the Rock Hudson

Estate

The hearing of Marc Christian McGuinnis vs Mark Miller and Rock's estate ran for seven weeks. Its transcripts, housed at the Los Angeles Superior Court, amount to more than thirty A4-sized volumes containing some 4,000 pages. These were studied exhaustively and edited by John Parker in his excellent *The Trial of Rock Hudson* (Sidgwick & Jackson, 1990), to which further reference should be made by the Hudson enthusiast. The following represents a summary of events as reported daily by the media.

At the end of October 1985, Marc Christian left Rock's house. The house and its contents were put up for auction, with a minimum expected purchase price of $5 million. However, in the age of AIDS hysteria, the house stood empty for eighteen months and raised just half this amount. Rock's New York apartment – deemed 'cleaner' because he had not lived there while ill – brought in $2 million.

On 2 November, one month after Rock's death, Christian and his lawyer, celebrity advocate Marvin Mitchelson, announced their intention to sue the Hudson estate, Mark Miller, Rock's business manager Wallace Sheft, and two (never named) doctors for 'in excess of $10 million'. This quartet, they alleged, had deliberately conspired to endanger Christian's life by keeping the nature of Rock's illness from him while he and Rock had continued to have unprotected sex.

That Christian should have been desperately concerned for his health predicament is understandable, having witnessed first-hand the rapid deterioration of a gargantuan man to almost one-third of his usual body weight. Surrounded by friends and loved ones Rock had received the very best round-the-clock medical attention, something Christian knew he would never be able to afford should he himself be stricken with AIDS in the future. Also, Christian appears to have had few relatives or friends of the same caring nature as Rock's entourage. And although he did have health insurance, there was no way of knowing if he would be able to claim on this. After Rock's death, several of his closest allies – including Mark Miller, George Nader and Susan Stafford – are known to have promised to support him financially should the worst befall him. However, Christian did not feel he could rely on these people.

Initially, Marvin Mitchelson had attempted to negotiate a 'palimony' settlement with Rock's lawyers and Wallace Sheft. This had backfired, setting in motion a series of tit-for-tat reprisals. Told that there had been no cash and made to relinquish the car that Rock had given to him as a gift, the young man had absconded with Rock's massive record and video collection. He claimed Rock had given him this, along with several cameras and VCRs, a computer, and Rock's favourite needlepoint rug. Sheft had then ordered all the locks at the Castle to be changed.

The so-called 'Rock Hudson Trial' captured the world's head-lines, each session of the hearing revealing yet another personal, and frequently prurient, aspect of Rock's sexuality, ensuring that if he had been afforded little dignity during his last weeks, in death there would be absolutely none. The wholesome, boy-next-door reputa-tion nurtured by Rock and the studios for four decades was destroyed in one fell swoop. If many Americans did not know – even in the late eighties – what homosexuals got up to in bed, and there apparently were many who did not, they certainly would now!

Before the hearing, there was a veritable circus of public debates, in-depth newspaper confessions, and chat-show appearances by a very brave Marc Christian that Mitchelson hoped would gain his client invaluable mass support as 'unpaid ambassador for the wronged partners of AIDS victims'. This support would be essential to their winning arguably the most astonishing legal battle in show-business history.

Shortly before the proceedings opened on 6 January 1989, it emerged that Marvin Mitchelson was himself about to face charges

of tax evasion. Christian replaced him with another tough-talking
Los Angeles lawyer named Harold Rhoden, ironically the man
Mitchelson had hired for his own defence. Rhoden's first move had
been to approach the Hudson estate and declare that his client would
be willing to accept an out-of-court settlement of $1 million. This
had been vociferously refused.

And so the case came to court before judge Justice Bruce R
Geernaert and a carefully selected jury of seven men and five women
of mixed race, religion, profession and, so far as Rhoden had been
able to determine, all were non-homophobic and wholly unshockable.

The trial opened with Christian's allegation that Rock, well aware
that he had AIDS, had duped him into having 'turn-and-turn-about'
anal sex on an alleged 160 occasions. Mark Miller, having also been
aware of Rock's illness, was accused of deliberately conspiring with
his boss to endanger Christian's life. As a result Christian was
allegedly 'petrified' that he could die. Though he had tested negative
for HIV on several occasions, specialists had repeatedly warned him
that there was still no certainty of knowing if or when the virus might
show up.

According to the counterclaims by the defence, Marc Christian
was a blackmailer who had persistently cheated on Rock, and their
relationship had ended long before Rock had developed AIDS.
Christian had forced Rock into allowing him to live at the Castle
after their split by threatening to expose him to the press.
Additionally, they claimed to have substantial evidence that
Christian had worked as a prostitute. Christian had also aggrieved
the defence by canvassing public support by telling his story on
television chat shows. The jury were also asked to consider the fact
that, at the time Marc Christian was 'worried' sick while awaiting Dr
Dormont's test results, he had gone off to the South of France with
another AIDS patient.

On 8 January Marc Christian made his first appearance on the
witness stand – a polite, well-dressed and, the press observed
unanimously, strikingly handsome man of 35 who unflinchingly
replied to the most intimate questions about his personal life and

sexuality. No, he was not a gigolo. Yes, he was bisexual – prior to Rock there had been a serious girlfriend before Liberty Martin, and around twenty other male and female partners. Christian enlightened the court that he was not suing the Hudson estate because of his exclusion from Rock's will, but quite simply because Rock and Mark Miller had deceived him. He maintained that he and Rock had been deeply in love – later, he would furnish the jury with several intimate letters from Rock to prove this. He added that he and Rock had been 'sexually active', up to five times a week, from April 1983 until February 1985 – nine months after Rock had been diagnosed with AIDS – and that during this period both of them had been monogamous, inferring that only Rock had put him at risk from the virus. He explained, tremulously, his reaction to the news of Rock's diagnosis in a television report, and that it had been 24 hours before anyone had contacted him from Paris. Christian claimed that afterwards Mark Miller had defended his own actions by saying, referring to his and Rock's 'secret', 'I've lied for thirteen months and I'm sick of it. The Movie Star told me not to tell you.'

Christian took the stand again the following day, and explained the events that had taken place following his own return from Paris, when Mark Miller and George Nader had turned up at the Castle and ordered him to leave, and how he had refused, declaring that he would only take the instruction from Rock himself. He added that when he had subsequently tried to call Rock at the UCLA Medical Center, Miller had refused to let him speak to him. Neither had he been allowed to see Rock because Miller had not included his name on the visitors' list. This situation had only been rectified when Christian, desperately trying to see his friend, had been arrested by hospital security guards. According to Christian, Rock had then asked him to stay on at the Castle.

Miller's alleged persecution of Christian had nevertheless continued. The young man explained how Miller had threatened him, saying, 'If this goes to court, we'll smear you. We're going to call you a male hustler, a street hooker. And if that doesn't work, we'll call you a drug addict.' Christian's defence then read out the accusation levelled by Rock's former business manager, Wallace Sheft: the plaintiff had solicited for gay and straight sex while Rock had been shooting *The Ambassador* in Israel, and upon learning of this, Rock had ended the relationship. This was denied. Harold Rhoden begged the jury to focus their attention on his client's mental state because, despite having at least four HIV tests, given the lack of knowledge about the incubation period of the disease – which could be anything up to fifteen years – Christian still did not know whether he was going to live or die.

Robert Mills, in his two-day cross-examination, implied that if the disease's incubation period was so lengthy, then Marc Christian could just as easily have passed it on to Rock, in which case the estate should be suing him. Christian responded that of the fifteen men he had had sex with between 1979 and 1982, so far as he knew none had developed AIDS. Mills moved on, criticising him for his chat-show appearances, then asked about the sexual relationship between Christian and Rock, demanding to know where they had had sex while Rock's ex, Tom Clark, had still been living at the Castle. Christian told him they had had sex at Liberty Martin's apartment, at Miller and Nader's house, and in various hotels and motels – though he was unable to name any of these. When asked why they had never used condoms, his response raised a titter, 'Because there was no fear of pregnancy.'

Mills further queried the sheer number of times Rock and Christian had had sex – not strictly 160 times in eight months but, taking into consideration Rock's absences from home (Deauville, Florida, Washington, New York, Hawaii), 160 times in just five months. Christian's reply to this was a cocky, 'Rock wanted me to make up for lost time.'

As to Mills' assertion that there was no evidence that Rock and Christian had been intimate after Rock's diagnosis, Christian affirmed that a friend, Wayne Bernhard, had seen them 'naked and embracing' on a chaise longue on the Castle patio in June 1984, when all the guests had left after Christian's birthday party. When reminded that Christian had not mentioned this in his pre-trial deposition, his excuse was that Bernhard had only told him what he had witnessed during the hearing's weekend recess. Bernhard would later verify his story on the witness stand, and insist that Rock and Christian had actually been having sex, certainly during the few seconds that he had observed them before rushing into the house, acutely embarrassed. Bernhard told the court, 'It was like walking in on your parents when they are making love.'

Mills next questioned Marc Christian's validity in Rock's affections, wanting to know why Rock had never taken him on any overseas trips, seemingly always preferring the company of Ron Channell. He also asked why Christian had not been Rock's escort for the state dinner with the Reagans at the White House – something that should have been blatantly obvious, though Christian's replies were plausible: he had been unwilling to leave Hollywood because he had wanted to be close to his dying father.

On 20 January, Harold Rhoden began his interrogation of Christian's supporting witnesses. Liberty Martin, now 66, spoke of her first meeting with Rock at the end of 1982, and of how – as his friendship with Christian had intensified and his relationship with Tom Clark had started falling apart – Rock had begun visiting her apartment more frequently, though at one stage he had felt guilty that he might have been taking Christian away from her. She also spoke of how she had comforted Christian, her former lover, after he had watched the television news report and learned of Rock's diagnosis, and of how she had persuaded Mark Miller to finance Christian's trip to Paris for tests at the Hôpital Percy. She fiercely denied Rhoden's suggestion that she had offered Rock an ultimatum: unless he allowed Christian to stay on at the Castle, she would personally expose him to the press. The truth was, she added, that the *National Enquirer* had once offered her $100,000 or $200,000 – she was not sure which amount – for such a story, but she had firmly turned the offer down.

The second supporting witness was Gregory Rice, who claimed he had heard Mark Miller threatening Christian with the drugs hustling smear campaign, should he go public about his affair with Rock. Jeanne McGuinnis, Christian's mother, next attested (in a statement dismissed by Robert Mills as 'inconsequential') to Rock's great generosity regarding the parties he had thrown at the Castle for herself and her family. Choking back her tears, she spoke of her son's distress, upon learning that Rock had AIDS.

The most surprising of Christian's supporting witnesses was Mark Miller himself, who near-perjured himself by confessing to his knowledge that Rock and Christian had never shared the same bedroom at the Castle. In an earlier statement he had averred that they had, for three months. Miller also managed to get himself into a muddle as to whether Rock had or had not ordered him not to tell Christian of his illness. According to Miller's pre-trial deposition, Rock had said, 'It's my disease. Let me handle it my way.' Now, Miller denied he had ever said such a thing – only to add a moment later that he had! He then began digging a deeper hole for himself when Harold Rhoden confronted him with the fact that, being ignorant of Rock's condition, Christian could have spread the disease amongst other sexual partners and inadvertently 'caused the deaths of thousands'. Miller's response was to tell the court of Rock's confession to him, two days before being diagnosed, that Christian was safe because they had never engaged in anal sex – and that in any case, by then they had no longer been intimate because Rock had 'moved on' to Ron Channell.

Harold Rhoden then grilled Miller over Christian's alleged blackmailing of Rock, and promptly got him into another fix. Basically, Rhoden wanted to know how Christian could possibly have been threatening to expose Rock to the press while at the same time being allowed to share his bed – a valid point. On top of this, he was curious as to how Miller could have been so in touch with the goings on at the Castle when he was not residing there full time.

On 24 January, one of the first witnesses was Tony Rocco, a young actor friend of Christian's who had worked as an extra in *Dynasty*. Rocco had submitted a pre-trial deposition to Robert Mills, who declined to call him to the stand. Harold Rhoden, however, had subpoenaed him on suspicion that Mills had bribed him into committing perjury, should he be asked to give evidence. Rhoden declared that he had it on good authority that 'in exchange for a piece of the action, around $250,000,' Rocco would tell the court that Christian had been sleeping around at the time of his affair with Rock, and that Christian had informed him that he had been aware of Rock's AIDS diagnosis before the public announcement. To try and substantiate the claim, Rhoden called a back-up witness, Kevin Short, in whom Rocco had allegedly confided his plan. The court learned little from his cross-examination other than that Rocco and

Short had once been lovers, that Christian liked attending gay softball matches, and that he had ignominiously asked Rocco of Rock, 'Could *you* get it up for that old fart?'

On 25 January Ron Channell was called to give evidence. He told the court that, despite the alleged intensity of the Hudson–Christian relationship, he had never seen Christian until February 1984 – and even then he had assumed him to be an employee. He added that whenever he and Rock had socialised with friends, Christian had never tagged along and that during his and Rock's trips overseas, so far as he knew, Rock had never contacted Christian by letter or phone, or even mentioned his name. Under further cross-examination, Channell denied that he and Rock had been lovers.

After the quietly retiring Ron Channell, the court – particularly the public, who had queued for hours for seats in the gallery – was treated to some pretty eye-opening facts from members of Rock's all-gay former household staff, all of whom were urged by Robert Mills to do their utmost to blacken Marc Christian's name. Clarence Morimoto, Rock's octogenarian gardener, told of how, during one of Rock's absences, he had gone into the master bedroom at the Castle to water the plants and seen Christian naked on the bed with Marty Flaherty, Rock's part-time handyman. James Wright, the middle-aged English butler who had been in Rock's employ since 1978, explained how Christian had moved into the house on 5 November 1983, and that he had entertained several young men there while Rock had been away filming in Israel – an admission he claimed he had accidentally left out of his pre-trial deposition. There were gasps of horror from the gallery when Wright described the state of the bedsheets: 'I saw some grease stains and empty yellow packages – I think people call them poppers – in the bed, and a towel on the floor. I think they call the towel a trick-towel. There were skid-marks from sex-grease on the sheets, and other brown stains.' Wright then spoke of how he had observed first-hand the rapid disintegration of the union while at the same time witnessing Rock's growing affection for Ron Channell. Lastly, under cross-examination from Harold Rhoden, he firmly denied the allegation that he himself had 'plucked teenage boys from the streets' and brought them back to the Castle for his own personal pleasure.

There was hilarity from the public gallery when Susan Stafford took the witness stand. She glossed over her lengthy friendship with Rock and confessed how Marc Christian had made a pass at her on the very day Rock had died. Harold Rhoden next quoted her as having said she had once made a pass at the Pope on a visit to the Vatican! Stafford dismissed this as having been a joke. But what really brought hoots of derision from the entire court was Rhoden's next allegation that this 'acknowledged, born-again Christian' had not only stripped naked at one of Rock's parties, but had had sex with two AIDS sufferers before being exorcised of the disease by a priest. Christian had a fit of giggles upon hearing this and had to be cautioned by the judge.

Next on the stand was Richard Lovell, a theatrical agent. Lovell had been summoned to speak of a dinner party held at the Castle in the spring of 1984, the sole purpose of which had been to find Christian acting work, inferring that Rock had wanted him not just out of the house, but out of his life. Rock was alleged to have told Lovell, 'He's interested, and I'd like to find something for him to do in order to get rid of him.' Lovell, however, was attacked by both sides in the dispute. Robert Mills then posed the question, 'What did you do in terms of the interview?' While Harold Rhoden asked him more directly, 'Mr Lovell, isn't it true that when he came into your office, you asked Marc Christian to have sex with you?' Lovell vehemently denied this.

There was some very serious probing when Mark Miller once again took the stand, introduced to the jury by his defence counsel, Andrew Banks. Miller spoke of his first meeting with Marc Christian, in October 1983, prior to Rock's trip to Israel, when Rock had introduced him as his 'housesitter'. Like butler James Wright, Miller described Rock's exhilaration early on in his relationship with Christian, and how quickly this had deteriorated. He explained how he had seen Christian in bed with other men, and that upon Rock's return from Israel, Christian had frequently spent nights away from the house and that he had once 'hit on' a straight guest at a Dean Dittman soirée.

Of Christian's supposed blackmailing of Rock, when he had threatened to sell the Hudson–Channell story to the press, Miller claimed that Rock had said, 'He has letters. Give him anything he wants – money.' Miller's assertion that Rock had stopped having sex with Christian once Ron Channell had appeared on the scene was challenged by Harold Rhoden, who repeated what he earlier told Miller: Mark Miller could not have known this because he had not been living at the Castle around the clock. Miller's reaction was to say proof was not necessary – that everyone knew that for much of the first half of 1984, Rock had been on some trip or other, almost always with Ron Channell.

This admission made many assume, rightly or wrongly, that Rock and his fitness instructor had been more than good friends, and that Channell had denied the fact because he had not wanted the public to know that he had been physically involved with an AIDS victim.

According to Miller, on 5 June 1984, Rock told him that he had AIDS, and had made him swear to tell no one – not even long-time partner George Nader, though he had later permitted this. The court learned that Miller had accompanied his 'employer' to a number of AIDS specialists, and that Rock had said of Marc Christian, 'I could have gotten it from him. I want him out of the house.' On the subject of Rock's final hospitalisation at the UCLA Medical Center, Miller reeled off a mental list of those who had been allowed inside the sickroom – Christian's name had not been among them. When asked whether, in his opinion, he had thought that Christian should have been told about Rock having AIDS, bearing in mind that he had almost certainly been exposed to the virus, Miller repeated what Rock had told him – that he and Christian had never had anal sex, just oral. Allegedly Rock had said, 'I'm finished with Marc, I'm moving on to Ron Channell,' adding that there would be no risk of Channell getting AIDS because he had 'struck out' (levelled) with him. Channell again repeated that he was heterosexual, and that he had been unaware of Rock's diagnosis until their last trip to Paris – not that this prevented both sides in the dispute from speculating yet again on the kind of relationship he and Rock had shared, particularly as the court was told that Mark Miller had also been attracted to Channell.

Harold Rhoden interrogated Miller about this, and the $2,000 Rolex watch he had given Channell (he claimed on Rock's behalf) shortly before Rock's collapse in the Paris airport. Rhoden told the court of a reputed conversation between Christian and Miller wherein the latter, intent on seducing Channell by way of the costly gift, had said that Rock's money would turn Channell gay – 'The Movie Star's money will turn any farmboy queer – if it doesn't, then I don't know what would.' Miller denied ever saying this.

It was only at this stage in the hearing that the real reason for its being held in the first place was discussed – the alleged conspiracy to prevent Marc Christian from finding out that Rock had AIDS, and his own fears of contracting the disease. Particular emphasis was placed on Christian's pre-trial deposition, part of which read:

> I do not know whether [Rock] did it because he was *non compos*, or whether he wanted to kill me and take me down with him, but he wilfully withheld the information and slept with me.

The court was told that between July 1985 and March 1986, but not since, Marc Christian had been tested HIV negative by five different specialists, all using differing techniques, but that despite this and on account of its uncertain incubation period, there was still no way of knowing that he was not carrying the virus. Evidence of this was provided by Dr Jeffery Laurence of New York's Cornell Medical Center, one of the country's foremost authorities on AIDS. Laurence briefly explained the history of the disease, now said to be in its eighth year and still very much a mystery. The court learned of the grim conclusion, announced at the 1988 Stockholm AIDS Conference, that in some patients the virus could avoid detection by every known method of testing by entering the victim's body through anal or vaginal tearing during intercourse and subsequently not always passing into the bloodstream where a test would pick it up. Harold Rhoden emphasised that if this was the case, his client had every right to feel worried.

As the hearing headed towards its fourth week, the major players in this acrimonious drama were merciless with their further allegations – as if Rock's name had not been sullied enough. Wayne Bernhard repeated what he had seen taking place on the chaise longue at Marc Christian's birthday party – though by this stage of the hearing there was some doubt as to whether Rock had actually been present at the event – mere weeks after being diagnosed with AIDS. James Dodds, another part-time handyman at the Castle and subpoenaed as an 'adverse' witness, explained how he too had assumed that Rock and Christian had still been lovers in the late spring of 1984. Dodds then dropped a huge bombshell: once the estate had been turned over to George Nader, Mark Miller had promised that a percentage of the Hudson estate would be shared out between Dodds, Dean Dittman, Ron Channell, Clarence Morimoto, Tom Clark and James Wright. The only condition was that they would be required to perjure themselves during this hearing and make sure Miller won his case against Marc Christian.

The most uncompromising witness of all, not surprisingly, was Marc Christian himself. Well-dressed as usual, quietly confident and composed, he politely denied every accusation Robert Mills flung in his direction. He had never sold his body for sex, nor slept with any other men at the Castle while Rock had been away. He had not met Rock at a bathhouse but at the Gore Vidal rally. He had not denounced Rock as 'an old fart', and he denied making a pass at Susan Stafford – arguing that she had made a pass at him, and confessed to him how she had propositioned the Pope during an audience at the Vatican.

Christian also denied trying to pick up a straight man at the Dean Dittman party, though he felt it his duty to inform the court that at one of these he had observed a number of 'street urchins' – boys of fourteen or fifteen – procured by Dittman to serve the food, which they had done clad in just their underwear. And if this was not shocking enough, Christian added, Mark Miller had subsequently suggested, several times, that maybe Christian should bring a few under-aged boys back to the Castle to 'spice up' his sex life with Rock – moreover that he had made this suggestion after Rock's AIDS diagnosis.

Under cross-examination from Miller's defence, Christian repeated this, and added that Miller had once told him how he and

George Nader frequently enjoyed sex with 'pretties' (under-aged boys), and that he and Rock should follow their example.

On 7 February, during the fifth week of the hearing, the lawyers for both sides in the dispute began analysing the wealth of evidence – mostly a mixture of unsubstantiated facts, gay parlance, changed statements, arguments and contradictory medical facts. Harold Rhoden asked the jury to question Mark Miller's integrity. Was he 'an honest man', or 'a pathological liar'? Both he and Rock Hudson were immoral men who had acted with extreme deviousness towards a 'boy' (Christian) whom Rock had knowingly exposed to AIDS. And was it not the moral and legal duty of the AIDS victim to warn those around him, even those he hated, of the dangers of HIV so that they would not pass this infection to others? And just how could one measure the mental anguish and enhanced fear that Marc Christian had already suffered, not knowing if or when he was going to die? Harold Rhoden told the court that representing Marc Christian – a homosexual who did not have AIDS but who might still get it – was a no-win situation. More than this, it was likened to 'representing a Jewish client in 1939 Berlin'.

He therefore urged the jury to take into account the intense media and public prejudice that had been aimed at the gay community in the wake of the AIDS epidemic, and begged them not to inflict any prejudices of their own while reaching their verdict. Homosexuals, Rhoden declared somewhat unctuously, had the same feelings for member of their own sex as heterosexuals had for members of the opposite sex. Rock Hudson, he concluded, had possessed no feelings for anyone but himself. Well aware that he had AIDS, he had persistently engaged in high-risk, unprotected anal intercourse with any number of innocent young men, caring not at all how many of these he might have infected or even killed. And as for Mark Miller – as the chief beneficiary of the Hudson fortune, along with partner George Nader – he naturally had made every endeavour to 'please the boss' by conspiring with him to keep Marc Christian in the dark regarding the possible death sentence he had inflicted on him.

Miller's defence, Robert Mills, argued each of these points concisely. Rock had had no obligation, moral or otherwise, to warn Marc Christian of any possible dangers to his health because by June

1984, when he had been diagnosed with AIDS, the pair had no longer been having sex. Yet even if they had still been lovers, Mills argued, had not Rock been given the 'all clear' by Dr Dormont?

Harold Rhoden hotly contested this, declaring that a man of Dr Dormont's high standing would never have said such a thing to a patient who had clearly already been at death's door. And even if Rock and Christian had no longer been lovers, Christian should still have been told the truth because, as Dr Laurence had explained while describing the intricacies of the disease, there was just as strong a possibility that Christian had been infected with the disease before June 1984 and the condition not yet shown up – medical evidence had already ascertained that the virus often lay undetected by regular testing.

Rhoden then addressed the jury's 'moral interpretation' of Marc Christian, should any of its carefully vetted members be secretly disgusted with his sexual practices. His client, Rhoden avowed, was not gay but bisexual, and there might come a time when he would want to marry and have children, and if so these children could be doomed before birth by this virus. Rhoden next set out to prove just how much Rock had loved Marc Christian, and to utterly demolish the opposition's claim that their sexual relationship had ended before Rock's diagnosis. He did this by reading out a number of romantic, passionate letters, which, Christian claimed, Rock had sent him from Israel at the end of 1983. One included the admission:

> To say I miss you terribly is true. I have comfort in knowing it's temporary, and fairly soon I will be able to hold you in my arms for ever . . .

Another letter referred to a long-distance telephone call, proving that there had also been verbal communication between the pair, something that Mark Miller had denied. And a third proclaimed, irrefutably, that Rock and Christian must have been head over heels in love:

> Babe, I miss you so much . . . I've been in love before, but nothing like the way I feel now. I'm consumed and obsessed by

you, but in a very warm and wonderful way . . . My heart feels like it's going to explode with joy. When I get home I'm going to hug you and never let you go. We're both going to starve to death because I will not let you go long enough to eat . . .

Rhoden then asked the jury to carefully consider the evidence provided by James Wright and Clarence Morimoto. In his pre-trial deposition Wright had denied seeing Christian in bed with another man yet in court he had cited several names and vividly described the soiled state of the bedsheets. Morimoto had named Christian's lover as Marty Flaherty – yet in a further statement he had been unsure who had been in the bed with him. Both, Rhoden proposed, had lied under oath because Miller had promised them a percentage of his inheritance.

Rhoden further attacked Miller's defence for bringing in Dr Jeffery Laurence, a costly AIDS expert, all the way from New York when money could have been saved by hiring an equally authoritative local man. And finally, there was the irreparable slur on his client's good name. Miller had called Marc Christian a black-mailer and whore. Who would employ him now? And who would want to or ever dare make love to him after what Rock Hudson had done? In short, his life had been ruined.

Robert Mills was no less scathing in his attack upon Marc Christian. His chief concern was that the major witness in this case – Rock Hudson himself – was only conspicuous by his absence, that only he could have verified and defended himself against the charade that had unfolded over the last weeks. Mills asked the jury to consider why, if Rock had loved Christian as profoundly as Harold Rhoden and Rock's love-letters had implied, Christian had never been taken anywhere of importance, why he had been left nothing in his will – and why, when Rock had first been diagnosed, had he not turned to Christian for support instead of Mark Miller? More importantly, he demanded, would Christian still be suing the estate if his lover had been anyone other than the mega-rich Rock Hudson? He then asked the jury to ponder the fact that, if Christian was so mentally distressed, why had he not supplied the court with medical evidence to this effect?

Mills next challenged the authenticity of Rock's letters to Christian – whether they had been sent to him, or someone else. No names were mentioned in them: each began with the words 'Hi babe', or 'Hi honey', and Christian had not retained the envelopes. Though Mills did not specify Ron Channell as their recipient, the press assumed that he was implying this. Mills then cast his doubts over Christian's claim over the sheer number of times he and Rock had had sex. Just how, Mills demanded, when his partner had been dying of the disease, had Christian managed to get away with not contracting AIDS from him when they had been so sexually active? In short, he concluded, the court only had Christian's word that he and Rock had still been sexually involved between June 1984 and February 1985.

Andrew Banks, Mark Miller's lawyer, agreed with Mills on each of these points and concluded of Christian's defence, 'It's like Swiss cheese – it has so many holes in it, it's hard to believe.'

To assist the jury in reaching their verdict, in what he described was one of the most complex cases he had ever presided over, Justice Geernaert, with Mills' and Rhoden's assistance, drew up a document listing 37 questions, each relating to a particular aspect of Rock's relationship with Marc Christian and whether, aided by Mark Miller, Rock had conspired to put the young man's life at risk. Basically, this transcribed as:

1.   Had Rock had high-risk sex with Christian?

2–4. Had Rock given Christian the idea that he did not have AIDS, and had such representation been false?

5–7. Had Rock's misrepresentation been with the intent of coercing Christian to have high-risk sex with him, and would high-risk sex not have taken place had Rock told Christian the truth?

8–9. Had Christian been justified in relying on Rock's representation that he did not have AIDS, and as such had Christian suffered emotional distress upon subsequently learning that Rock had lied to him?

10–12. Had Rock concealed his AIDS status from Christian?

Had he been under a duty to reveal this status to him? And had he concealed his AIDS solely to coerce him into having high-risk sex?

13–15. Between 8 June 1984 and late-February 1985, had Christian been unaware that Rock was concealing his AIDS status from him, and because of this concealment had they had sex between these dates, as a result of which Christian had suffered emotional distress?

16–19. Had Rock behaved outrageously, purposely to cause Christian emotional distress, and had emotional distress occurred as a result of this outrageous conduct?

20–21. In knowing that Rock had AIDS had Mark Miller been aware that Rock and Christian had been engaging in high-risk sex, and had Miller denied between June 1984 and February 1985 that Rock had AIDS?

22–26. Had Miller lied to Christian, and had this lie been with the intent of coercing Christian into having high-risk sex with Rock, and was Christian unaware that Miller was lying and therefore willing to engage in high-risk sex, believing that Rock did not have AIDS?

27–28. Had Christian been justified in believing what Miller had told him, and had he suffered emotional distress as a result?

29–30. Had Miller conspired with Rock to hide the latter's AIDS status between June 1984 and February 1985 in order to coerce Christian into having high-risk sex?

31–32. Had Christian had high-risk sex with Rock between these dates, which he would not have consented to had he known the truth, and as a result of this had he suffered emotional distress?

33–36. Had Mark Miller behaved outrageously, as a result of which Christian had suffered emotional distress?

37.   What amount of damages should be awarded to Christian to compensate for the emotional distress caused him by Rock Hudson and Mark Miller?

The jury were instructed to study each question meticulously, and move on to the next question only when a minimum nine members had agreed upon 'Yes' or 'No'. They retired late on the afternoon of Thursday 9 February, and returned to the court the following Tuesday to query several points before retiring again. On Wednesday 15 February their foreman, Charles Garelick, announced the verdict: in a unanimous response to 23 of the 37 questions (and an average of 10–2 on the other fourteen). The jury had decided that Rock Hudson and Mark Miller had conspired to hide the truth of Rock's AIDS from Marc Christian, that Christian had been coerced into having high-risk sex, that subsequently he had suffered severe emotional stress, for which substantial damages should be paid. By a ten to twelve majority, these were fixed at a staggering $14,500,000.

The so-called 'Rock Hudson Trial', however, was not over – for the court now had to decide whether Marc Christian should be awarded 'punitive' damages – not from the Hudson estate, but from Mark Miller personally. The hearing was set for the next day, 16 February, and Harold Rhoden predicted that the outcome of this would set a worldwide precedent for future 'innocent victims' who, like his client, might be duped by unscrupulous partners into having unprotected sex. To set an example, Rhoden urged the jury to ignore Miller's declared assets of only $100,000, to find him guilty and force him to fork out a minimum $14,500,000 to equal the sum that had been awarded from Rock's estate.

The jury delivered their verdict the next day. Rhoden's demands had been way over the top. Even so, Miller was devastated to learn that he would be expected to pay Marc Christian $7,250,000.

The verdict, and Marc Christian's $21,750,000 'windfall', caused a furious reaction amongst leaders of the world's gay communities. Just as they had been winning their fight against public con-demnation of AIDS victims, a Los Angeles courthouse had cited the world's most famous casualty as a supreme example of 'fuck-em-and-be-damned' irresponsibility. Leading the outcry was Ben Schatz of the National Gay Rights Advocates, who fumed in his statement:

Since Marc Christian freely engaged in unprotected sex and never became infected, the amount he has been awarded seems hysterical. This decision could send a message that if people contract AIDS through unprotected sex then it's somebody else's fault and not their own.

Schatz was right. Henceforth, many AIDS sufferers would no longer be looked upon as victims of a malady that had caught them unawares, and which most of them were trying to combat by promoting and practising safe-sex techniques – but stigmatised and persecuted as selfish, cold-blooded killing machines – a persecution that persists in many homophobic circles to this day, and which is unlikely to change in the foreseeable future.

Needless to say, while Marc Christian was being fêted by the 'straight media' and making chat-show appearances, the opposition applied for a retrial: Robert Mills claimed to have acquired 'startling new evidence' that just weeks after Rock's death, when Marc Christian had supposedly been worried sick about getting AIDS, he had enjoyed a sexual relationship with an Orange County fitness instructor named Gunther Fraulob. Furthermore, Fraulob had furnished Mills with a sworn statement to this effect. Mills also claimed to be in possession of 'substantial evidence' that Christian had conversed with some of the jurors during the hearing.

In his announcement of 21 April, Justice Geernaert dismissed Robert Mills' application for a retrial, but reduced Marc Christian's compensatory and punitive damages to $5 million and $500,000 respectively, the latter on account of Mark Miller's financial status.

So far as is known, Marc Christian is alive and well, and living prosperously in Los Angeles.

Appendix II

How Did Rock Get Aids?

A Defence

It is now a known fact that there are three ways of contracting HIV: via infected blood as the result of transfusion or the sharing of syringes; by inheritance if either parent of a child has been infected; and, in a majority of cases, via unprotected sex. It is also a known fact that Rock Hudson was promiscuous, maybe no more so than many of his heterosexual contemporaries, and for no other reason than that he was a wealthy, hugely successful and, of course, inordinately good-looking man living in an equally glamorous, affluent community literally teeming with willing bed mates.

That Rock was gay and extremely sexually active throughout his entire adult life should not be regarded any differently than had he been straight. Like their heterosexual counterparts, until the real onset of AIDS during the early eighties, all that gay men had to worry about was contracting the mostly curable venereal diseases and, unless they were bisexual, they did not even have to agonise over getting their partners pregnant. Cary Grant, Robert Taylor, Montgomery Clift and Rudolph Valentino had been no less 'busy in the bedroom' than Rock. They did not have to worry about AIDS because in their day it had not existed – likewise in Rock's halcyon days as a leading man, when the bedroom traffic had been at its busiest. One must, however, point out that, promiscuous or not, Rock could still have ended up being one of the unlucky ones. Today, in a more sexually educated world, one would of course have expected him to be more responsible in taking the necessary precautions regarding safe sex.

The true gay revolution, certainly in the United States, began during the summer of 1969 with the death of Judy Garland and the

269

Stonewall riots in New York's Greenwich Village. Not unlike the blacks in *Something of Value*, tired of being oppressed and picked upon, gays had begun fighting back; not before time, gay pride had started taking hold. Rock was involved in the insurrection insomuch as, now in his forties, he was no longer the massive star he had been and certain risks could be afforded. For 25 years the fear of career assassination had confined him and countless others to the closet, and if he, Rock, could still not come out, at least there seemed no reason for his being quite so 'in' as he had been.

Like some of the more outrageous celebrities, Rock began frequenting some of the more colourful but less reputable clubs and watering holes wonderfully brought to life in the *Tales of the City* novels of his friend Armistead Maupin and the drawings of Tom of Finland. Unlike some of these, he is not on record as having actively participated in the goings-on at such extreme establishments as the Black & Blue Club – he just wanted to be in an environment where everyone licked his side of the stamp, without shame or reproach.

It is thought that Rock became HIV-positive around 1981, very definitely the pre-condom age and at a time when the condition was wholly unrecognised. Indeed, by the time he developed full-blown AIDS some three years later, society in general was still largely ignorant of the disease, or how to attempt treatment. Had Rock and all those poor souls who succumbed to an early grave been as sexually active today as then and purposely not employed safe-sex techniques, then many of us might be on the side of the bigots in declaring that they are only bringing it upon themselves and not worthy of pity. However, as Rock and his gay generation were unaware of the killer in their midst, they should not be adjudged as they were by moralists and religious organisations of the day, as well as the tabloids, to have been visited by the 'wrath of God' simply because they were considered immoral on account of sexual preference.

As there is no record of Rock ever being involved with drugs, other than for strictly medicinal purposes, it is generally assumed that he could only have acquired HIV status through sex, particularly as this side of him was cruelly and needlessly dragged through the court after his death, allowing the tabloid hacks full vent to spitefully educate their readers in every aspect of gay sex, paying especial attention to rich and vulgar terminology – but usually omitting to mention the word *love*.

In fact, this is not as clear cut as it would appear. Where gay sex is concerned, there are two high-risk areas: anal intercourse, where tissue tearing takes place to enable infected semen to enter the bloodstream – and oral sex, where the person executing the blow job has cuts or open sores to the mouth or gums. Rock is known to have enjoyed both giving and receiving, though so far as anal sex is concerned he is thought to have rarely been the passive (i.e. much more at risk) partner, something he blamed on his star status. Rock told several close friends (including Jon Epstein, the producer of the *McMillan* series, *see* quote, Chapter 6) how many of his lovers were, initially at least, *so* overwhelmed to be having sex with him that they were too nervous to achieve or sustain erections, and that subsequently he always 'ended up on top'. Given the fact, therefore, that most of Rock's trysts were one-night stands, one may only assume that he spent more time 'on top' than he would have liked.

Rock remains the biggest early star to succumb to AIDS along with Freddie Mercury, who died in November 1991. An interesting comparison (*Freddie Mercury: Living On The Edge*, Robson Books, 1996) is that, while Rock was almost always the active sexual partner, the opposite applies to Mercury and the intimates who travelled with his self-confessed 'gay as daffodils' court. Similarly, while none of Rock's lovers who died after him succumbed to AIDS, sadly there are few of the Queen frontman's who have not – suggesting that he may not have been joking when he told *Gay Times'* Kris Kirk, during a trip to London, 'I like to make sure the baby's been pulled out of the crib before I let it puke!'

The result of any inquiry is of course inconclusive. Prejudice and ignorance resulted in Rock's remains being treated almost like trash. Yet even had there been an autopsy, there would have been no way of discerning how or when he had become ill. There is, however, one other almost as likely source of infection – mostly overlooked by those blinkered members of our society who are incapable or unwilling to see beyond Rock's so-called unconventional lifestyle. *In 1981 he had undergone open-heart surgery*. Although the purpose of this essay is to neither condemn nor apportion blame, during his operation Rock was administered at least one blood transfusion from stock that had not been screened for HIV – nothing whatsoever to do with malpractice, but simply because the condition was in its infancy and virtually every health authority in the world was as yet unaware of its existence. The tennis player Arthur Ashe and the wife and child of *Starsky & Hutch* actor Paul Michael Glaser all acquired HIV in such an accidental manner, as did thousands of others on both sides of the Atlantic. Bearing in mind that Rock curbed his sexual activities soon after his operation when his health began to fail and upon learning that he had AIDS, he did begin to practise safe sex; also bearing in mind the aforementioned fact that none of his lovers have died of AIDS – there is therefore a strong possibility that he did not get AIDS from sex.

Appendix III

Filmography

The following represents Rock Hudson's complete output on celluloid, so far as is known given the large number of productions he appeared in during his first three years in Hollywood, before stardom beckoned, when he was largely unbilled. Some prints are of varying length: the times stated are of the ones most commonly seen on cinema and television screens.

Fighter Squadron [1948], UNIVERSAL, 96 minutes
Director: Raoul Walsh
Starring: Robert Stack, Edmond O'Brien, Henry Hull, John Rodney, Tom d'Andrea, James Holden, Walter Reed, Shepperd Strudwick
Rock, unbilled, played a Jewish fightor pilot, 5 lines.

Undertow [1949], UNIVERSAL, 71 minutes
(based on the novel *The Big Frame* by Arthur T Horman)
Director: William Castle
Starring: Scott Brady, John Russell, Dorothy Hart, Bruce Bennett, Peggy Dow, Gregg Martell, Daniel Ferniel, Robert Anderson
Billed as 'Roc Hudson', Rock played a plain-clothes detective, 5 lines.

One Way Street [1950], UNIVERSAL, 79 minutes.
Director: Hugo Fregonese
Starring: James Mason, Dan Duryea, Märta Torén, William Conrad, Jack Elam, King Donovan, Tito Renaldo, Basil Ruysdael
Rock, unbilled, played a truck driver, 1 line.

I Was a Shoplifter [1950], UNIVERSAL, 74 minutes
Director: Charles Lamont
Starring: Scott Brady, Mona Freeman, Anthony (Tony) Curtis, Andrea King, Gregg Martell, Michael Raffetto, Charles Drake
Rock, unbilled, played a store detective, 4 lines.

Winchester '73 [1950], UNIVERSAL, 88 minutes
Director: Anthony Mann
Starring: James Stewart, Shelley Winters, Dan Duryea, Stephen McNally, John McIntire, Charles Drake, Jay C Flippen, Will Geer, Millard Mitchell and Rock Hudson (as Young Bull)

Peggy [1950], UNIVERSAL, 78 minutes
Director: Frederick de Cordova
Starring: Diana Lynn, Charles Coburn, Charles Drake, Charlotte Greenwood, Barbara Lawrence and Rock Hudson (as Johnny Higgins)

The Desert Hawk [1950], UNIVERSAL, 77 minutes
Director: Frederick de Cordova
Starring: Yvonne de Carlo, Carl Esmond, Richard Greene, Jackie Gleason, George Macready and Rock Hudson (as Captain Ras)

Shakedown [1950], UNIVERSAL, 80 minutes
Director: Joseph Pevney
Starring: Howard Duff, Brian Donlevy, Peggy Dow, Lawrence Tierney, Bruce Bennett, Peggie Castle, Charles Sherlock
Rock, unbilled, played a nightclub doorman.

Double Crossbones [1950], UNIVERSAL, 76 minutes
Director: Charles T Barton
Starring: Donald O'Connor, Helena Carter, Will Geer, John Emery, Stanley Logan, Kathryn Givney, Rock, unbilled

Tomahawk (GB: ***Battle of Powder River***) [1951], UNIVERSAL, 82 minutes
Director: George Sherman
Starring: Van Heflin, Yvonne de Carlo, Preston Foster, Alex Nicol, Russell Conway, Jack Oakie, Tom Tully, Rock Hudson (as Corporal Hanna), Susan Cabot, John War Eagle, Ann Doran

Air Cadet (GB: ***Jet Man of the Air***) [1951], UNIVERSAL, 94 minutes
Director: Joseph Pevney
Starring: Gail Russell, Stephen McNally, Alex Nicol, Richard Long, Charles Drake, Robert Arthur, Rock Hudson (an 'Upper Classman'), Peggie Castle, James Best, Parley Baer

The Fat Man [1951], UNIVERSAL, 77 minutes
(Based on the radio show of the same title)
Director: William Castle
Starring: J Scott Smart, Clinton Sundberg, Rock Hudson (as Roy Clark), Julie London, Jayne Meadows, Teddy Hart, John Russell, Jerome Cowan, Emmett Kelly, Lucille Barkley, Robert Osterloh

Iron Man [1951], UNIVERSAL, 82 minutes
(Based on the novel by W R Burnett and a remake of *The Iron Man* (1931) with Jean Harlow and Robert Armstrong and *Some Blondes Are Dangerous* (1937) with Noah Beery Jr and Dorothea Kent)
Director: Joseph Pevney
Starring: Jeff Chandler, Evelyn Keyes, Stephen McNally, Rock Hudson (as Speed O'Keefe), Jim Backus, Steve Martin, Jim (James) Arness, Joyce Holden

Bright Victory (GB: ***Lights Out***) [1951], UNIVERSAL, 97 minutes
(Based on the novel by Baynard Kendrick)
Director: Mark Robson
Starring: Arthur Kennedy, Julia Adams, Peggy Dow, Will Geer, Jim Backus, James Edwards, Nana Bryant, Minor Watson, Richard Egan, Joan Banks
Rock, eighteenth billing, played a soldier.

Here Come the Nelsons [1952], UNIVERSAL, 76 minutes
(Based on the radio series *The Adventures of Ozzie and Harriet*)
Director: Frederick de Cordova
Starring: Ricky and David Nelson, Barbara Lawrence, Ann Doran, Rock Hudson (as Charlie Jones), Jim Backus, Gale Gordon, Paul Harvey

Bend of the River (GB: *Where the River Bends*) [1952], UNIVERSAL, 91 minutes
(Based on the novel *Bend of the Snake* by Bill Gulick)
Director: Anthony Mann
Starring: James Stewart, Arthur Kennedy, Julia Adams, Rock Hudson (as Trey Wilson), Jay C Flippen, Henry Morgan, Stepin Fetchit, Henry Morgan, Lori Nelson, Chubby Johnson, Royal Dano

Scarlet Angel [1952], UNIVERSAL, 78 minutes
(Based on a story by Oscar Brodney)
Director: Sidney Salkow
Starring: Rock Hudson (as Captain Frank 'Panama' Truscott), Yvonne de Carlo, Richard Denning, Whitfield Connor, Amanda Blake, Bodil Miller, Henry O'Neill, Dan Riss, Maude Wallace, Henry Brandon, Tol Avery

Has Anybody Seen My Gal? [1952], UNIVERSAL, 89 minutes
(Based on a story by Eleanor H Porter)
Director: Douglas Sirk
Starring: Rock Hudson (as Dan Stebbins), Charles Coburn, Piper Laurie, Gigi Perreau, Lynn Bari, Larry Gates, Skip Homeier, William Reynolds, Frank Ferguson, Natalie Schafer, James Dean

Horizons West [1952], UNIVERSAL, 81 minutes.
Director: Budd Boetticher
Starring: Rock Hudson (as Neal Hammond), Julia Adams, Robert Ryan, Raymond Burr, John McIntire, Dennis Weaver, Judith Braun, Frances Bavier, Jim (James) Arness, Rodolfo Acosta, Tom Powers

The Lawless Breed [1953], UNIVERSAL, 83 minutes
Director: Raoul Walsh
Starring: Rock Hudson (as John Wesley Hardin), Julia Adams, Hugh O'Brian, John McIntire, Lee Van Cleef, Glenn Strange, William Pullen, Michael Ansara, Dennis Weaver, Race Gentry

Seminole [1953], UNIVERSAL, 86 minutes
Director: Budd Boetticher
Starring: Rock Hudson (as Lieutenant Lance Caldwell), Anthony Quinn, Barbara Hale, Hugh O'Brian, Richard Carlson, Lee Marvin, Russell Johnson, James Best, Ralph Moody, Dan Poore

Sea Devils [1953], RKO RADIO, 91 minutes
Director: Raoul Walsh
Starring: Rock Hudson (as Captain Gilliatt), Yvonne de Carlo, Maxwell Reed, Bryan Forbes, Denis O'Dea, Gérard Oury, Michael Goodliffe, Jacques Brunius, Ivor Barnard, Arthur Wontner

The Golden Blade [1953], UNIVERSAL, 81 minutes
Director: Nathan Juran
Starring: Rock Hudson (as Harun), Piper Laurie, Gene Evans, Kathleen Hughes, George Macready, Steven Geray, Anita Ekberg, Edgar Barrier, Alice Kelley, Erika Nordin

Back to God's Country [1953], UNIVERSAL, 78 minutes
(Based on the novel by James Oliver Curwood)
Director: Joseph Pevney
Starring: Rock Hudson (as Peter Keith), Steve Cochran, Marcia Henderson, Hugh O'Brian, Chubby Johnson, Tudor Owen, Bill Radovich, Arthur Space, John Cliff

Gun Fury [1953], COLUMBIA 3D, 83 minutes
(Based on the novel *Ten Against Caesar* by Kathleen B George and Robert A Granger)
Director: Raoul Walsh
Starring: Rock Hudson (as Ben Warren), Donna Reed, Phil Carey, Leo Gordon, Roberta Haynes, Neville Brand, Lee Marvin, Ray Thomas

Taza, Son of Cochise [1954], UNIVERSAL 3D, 79 minutes
Director: Douglas Sirk
Starring: Rock Hudson (as Taza), Barbara Rush, Gregg Palmer, Bart Roberts, Morris Ankrum, Eugene Iglesias, Richard H Cutting, Ian MacDonald, Joe Sawyer, Brad Jackson, Lance Fuller

Magnificent Obsession [1954], UNIVERSAL, 108 minutes
(Based on the novel by Lloyd C Douglas and a remake of *The Magnificent Obsession* (1935) starring Robert Taylor, Irene Dunne)
Director: Douglas Sirk
Starring: Rock Hudson (as Bob Merrick), Jane Wyman, Barbara Rush, Agnes Moorehead, Otto Kruger, Gregg Palmer, Sara Shane, Paul Cavanagh, Judy Nugent, George Lynn

Bengal Brigade (GB: ***Bengal Rifles***) [1954], UNIVERSAL, 87 minutes
(Based on the novel *Bengal Tiger* by Hall Hunter)
Director: Laslo Benedek
Starring: Rock Hudson (as Jeff Claybourne), Arlene Dahl, Ursula Thiess, Torin Thatcher, Arnold Moss, Michael Ansara, Daniel O'Herlihy

Captain Lightfoot [1955], UNIVERSAL, 91 minutes
(Based on the novel by W R Burnett)
Director: Douglas Sirk
Starring: Rock Hudson (as Michael Martin, aka Captain Lightfoot), Barbara Rush, Jeff Morrow, Kathleen Ryan, Finlay Currie, Denis O'Dea

One Desire [1955], UNIVERSAL, 94 minutes
(Based on the novel *Tacey Cromwell* by Conrad Richter)
Director: Jerry Hopper
Starring: Rock Hudson (as Clint Saunders), Anne Baxter, Julie Adams, Benton Reid, Natalie Wood, William Hopper, Betty Garde, Barry Curtis

All That Heaven Allows [1956], UNIVERSAL, 89 minutes
(Based on the novel by Edna L and Harry Lee)
Director: Douglas Sirk
Starring: Rock Hudson (as Ron Kirby), Jane Wyman, Agnes Moorehead, Virginia Grey, Conrad Nagel, Gloria Talbott, William Reynolds, Jacqueline deWit, Charles Drake, Leigh Snowden
An extract from this film appears in Martin Scorcese's *Cape Fear* (1991).

Never Say Goodbye [1956], UNIVERSAL, 96 minutes
(Based on the Pirandello play *Come Prima Meglio Di Prima*)
Directors: Jerry Hopper and (uncredited) Douglas Sirk
Starring: Rock Hudson (as Dr Michael Parker), Cornell Borchers, George Sanders, David Janssen, Ray Collins, Casey Adams, Shelley Fabares, Frank Wilcox, Raymond Greenleaf

Giant [1956], WARNER BROS, 198 minutes
(Based on the novel by Edna Ferber)
Director: George Stevens
Starring: Rock Hudson (as Bick Benedict), Elizabeth Taylor, James Dean, Carroll Baker, Mercedes McCambridge, Jane Withers, Chill Wills, Sal Mineo, Dennis Hopper, Paul Fix, Rodney Taylor, Judith Evelyn

Four Girls in Town [1956], UNIVERSAL, 99 minutes
Director: Jack Sher
Starring: George Nader, Julie Adams, Marianne Cook, Gia Scala, Elsa Martinelli, Sydney Chaplin,
Rock, unbilled, played a guest.

Written on the Wind [1956], UNIVERSAL, 99 minutes
(Based on the novel by Robert Wilder and first filmed in 1935 as *Reckless* with Jean Harlow, William Powell, Franchot Tone)
Director: Douglas Sirk
Starring: Rock Hudson (as Mitch Wayne), Robert Stack, Lauren Bacall, Dorothy Malone, Robert Keith, Grant Williams, Robert J Wilke

Battle Hymn [1957], UNIVERSAL, 108 minutes
Director: Douglas Sirk
Starring: Rock Hudson (as Colonel Dean Hess), Martha Hyer, Anna Kashfi, Dan Duryea, Jock Mahoney, Alan Hale, Don DeFore, Carl Benton Reid, James Edwards, Richard Loo, Philip Ahn

Something of Value [1957], MGM, 113 minutes
(Based on the novel by Robert C Ruark)
Director: Richard Brooks
Starring: Rock Hudson (as Peter McKenzie), Dana Wynter, Wendy Hiller, Sidney Poitier, William Marshall, Juano Hernandez, Michael Pate, Robert Beatty

A Farewell to Arms [1957], 20th CENTURY FOX, 152 minutes
(Based on the novel by Ernest Hemingway and first filmed in 1932 with Gary Cooper, Helen Hayes, Adolphe Menjou)
Director: Charles Vidor (replacing John Huston)
Starring: Rock Hudson (as Lieutenant Frederic Henry), Jennifer Jones, Vittorio De Sica, Mercedes McCambridge, Kurt Kasznar, Alberto Sordi, Elaine Stritch, Oskar Homolka.

The Tarnished Angels [1958], UNIVERSAL, 91 minutes
(Based on the novel *Pylon* by William Faulkner)
Director: Douglas Sirk
Starring: Rock Hudson (as Burke Devlin), Dorothy Malone, Robert Stack, Jack Carson, Robert Middleton, Alan Reed, Troy Donahue, Robert J Wilke

Twilight for the Gods [1958], UNIVERSAL, 120 minutes
(Based on the novel by Ernest K Gann)
Director: Joseph Pevney
Starring: Rock Hudson (as David Bell), Arthur Kennedy, Cyd Charisse, Leif Erickson, Charles McGraw, Ernest Truex, Richard Haydn, Wallace Ford, Judith Evelyn, Celia Lovsky

This Earth is Mine [1959], UNIVERSAL, 125 minutes
(Based on the novel *The Cup and the Sword* by Alice Tinsdale Hobart)
Director: Henry King
Starring: Rock Hudson (as John Rambeau), Jean Simmons, Claude Rains, Dorothy McGuire, Kent Smith, Anna Lee, Ken Scott, Cindy Robbins

Pillow Talk [1959], UNIVERSAL, 105 minutes
Director: Michael Gordon
Starring: Rock Hudson (as Brad Allen), Doris Day, Tony Randall, Thelma Ritter, Nick Adams, Julia Meade, Allen Jenkins, Marcel Dalio, Lee Patrick, Mary McCarty

The Last Sunset [1961], UNIVERSAL, 115 minutes
(Based on the novel *Sundown at Crazy Horse* by Howard Rigsby)
Director: Robert Aldrich
Starring: Rock Hudson (as Dana Stribling), Kirk Douglas, Dorothy Malone, Joseph Cotten, Carol Lynley, Neville Brand, Regis Toomey, Rad Fulton

Come September [1961], UNIVERSAL, 112 minutes
Director: Robert Mulligan
Starring: Rock Hudson (as Robert Lawrence Talbot), Gina Lollobrigida, Sandra Dee, Bobby Darin, Walter Slezak, Joel Grey, Ronald Howard

Lover Come Back [1961], UNIVERSAL, 107 minutes
Director: Delbert Mann
Starring: Rock Hudson (as Jerry Webster), Doris Day, Tony Randall, Edie Adams, Jack Oakie, Jack Kruschen, Howard St John, Joe Flynn, Ann B Davis, Donna Douglas

The Spiral Road [1962], UNIVERSAL, 145 minutes
(Based on the novel by Jan de Hartog)
Director: Robert Mulligan
Starring: Rock Hudson (as Anton Drager), Burl Ives, Gena

Rowlands, Geoffrey Keen, Neva Patterson, Will Kuluva, Philip Abbott, Larry Gates, Karl Swenson, Edgar Stehli

Marilyn [1963], 20th CENTURY FOX, 83 minutes
(A documentary about the life and career of Marilyn Monroe)
Director: Harold Medford
Narrated by Rock Hudson.

A Gathering of Eagles [1963], UNIVERSAL, 115 minutes
Director: Delbert Mann
Starring: Rock Hudson (as Colonel Jim Caldwell), Rod Taylor, Leif Erickson, Mary Peach, Barry Sullivan, Kevin McCarthy, Henry Silva, Leora Dana, Robert Lansing

Man's Favorite Sport? [1964], UNIVERSAL, 120 minutes
(Based on the novel *The Girl Who Almost Got Away* by Pat Frank)
Director: Howard Hawks
Starring: Rock Hudson (as Roger Willoughby), Paula Prentiss, Maria Perschy, John McGiver, Charlene Holt, Roscoe Karns, James Westerfield, Norman Alden, Forrest Lewis, Regis Toomey

Send Me No Flowers [1964], UNIVERSAL, 100 minutes
(Based on the play by Norman Barasch and Carroll Moore)
Director: Norman Jewison
Starring: Rock Hudson (as George Kimball), Doris Day, Tony Randall, Hal March, Paul Lynde, Edward Andrews, Patricia Barry, Clint Walker

Strange Bedfellows [1965], UNIVERSAL, 99 minutes
Director: Melvin Frank
Starring: Rock Hudson (as Carter Harrison), Gina Lollobrigida, Gig Young, Edward Judd, Arthur Haynes, David King, Terry-Thomas, Howard St John

A Very Special Favor [1965], UNIVERSAL, 105 minutes
Director: Michael Gordon
Starring: Rock Hudson (as Paul Chadwick), Leslie Caron, Charles

Boyer, Walter Slezak, Dick Shawn, Larry Storch, Nina Talbot, Norma Varden

The Nurse [1965]
Narrated by Rock Hudson.

Blindfold [1965], UNIVERSAL, 98 minutes
(Based on the novel by Lucille Fletcher)
Director: Philip Dunne
Starring: Rock Hudson (as Dr Bartholomew Snow), Claudia Cardinale, Guy Stockwell, Jack Warden, Anne Seymour, Alejandro Rey

Seconds [1966], PARAMOUNT, 105 minutes
(Based on the novel by David Ely)
Director: John Frankenheimer
Starring: Rock Hudson (as Antiochus Wilson), Salome Jens, John Randolph, Will Geer, Jeff Corey, Richard Anderson, Murray Hamilton, Karl Swenson, Frances Reid

Tobruk [1967], UNIVERSAL, 107 minutes
Director: Arthur Hiller
Starring: Rock Hudson (as Major Donald Craig), George Peppard, Nigel Green, Guy Stockwell, Jack Watson, Percy Herbert, Norman Rossington, Liam Redmond, Heidy Hunt, Leo Gordon

Ice Station Zebra [1968], FILMWAYS/MGM, 148 minutes
(Based on the novel by Alistair MacLean)
Director: John Sturges
Starring: Rock Hudson (as Captain James Ferraday), Ernest Borgnine, Patrick McGoohan, Jim Brown, Tony Bill, Lloyd Nolan, Gerald O'Loughlin, Alf Kjellin, Murray Rose

Ruba al Prossimo Tuo (US/GB: *A Fine Pair*), [1969] NATIONAL GENERAL, 88 minutes
Director: Francesco Maselli
Starring: Rock Hudson (as Mike Harmon), Claudia Cardinale,

Tomas Milian, Leon Askin, Ellen Corby

The Undefeated [1969], 20th CENTURY FOX, 118 minutes
Director: Andrew V McLaglen
Starring: Rock Hudson (as Colonel James Langdon), John Wayne, Tony Aguilar, Roman Gabriel, Marian McCargo, Lee Meriwether, Merlin Olsen, Melissa Newman, Bruce Cabot, Ben Johnson, Michael Vincent

Darling Lili [1970], PARAMOUNT, 139 minutes
Director: Blake Edwards
Starring: Rock Hudson (as Major William Larrabee), Julie Andrews, Jeremy Kemp, Lance Percival, Michael Witney, Jacques Marin, André Maranne

Hornets' Nest [1970], UNITED ARTISTS, 110 minutes
Director: Phil Karlson
Starring: Rock Hudson (as Captain Turner), Sylva Koscina, Sergio Fantoni, Mark Colleano, Jacques Sernas

Pretty Maids All in a Row [1971], MGM, 97 minutes
(Based on the novel by Francis Pollini)
Director: Roger Vadim
Starring: Rock Hudson (as Michael 'Tiger' McDrew), Angie Dickinson, Telly Savalas, Roddy McDowall, Kennan Wynn, John David Carson

Showdown [1973], UNIVERSAL, 99 minutes
Director: George Seaton
Starring: Rock Hudson (as Charles 'Chuck' Jarvis), Dean Martin, Susan Clark, Donald Moffat, John McLiam

Embryo [1976], CINE ARTISTS, 104 minutes
Director: Ralph Nelson
Starring: Rock Hudson (as Dr Paul Holliston), Diane Ladd, Barbara Carrera, Roddy McDowall

Avalanche [1978], NEW WORLD PICTURES, 91 minutes
Director: Corey Allen
Starring: Rock Hudson (as David Shelby), Mia Farrow, Robert Forster

The Mirror Crack'd [1980], EMI FILMS, 100 minutes
(Based on the novel by Agatha Christie)
Director: Guy Hamilton
Starring: Rock Hudson (as Jason Rudd), Elizabeth Taylor, Tony Curtis, Edward Fox, Geraldine Chaplin, Kim Novak, Angela Lansbury, Dinah Sheridan, Wendy Morgan, Margaret Courtenay

The Ambassador [1984], CANNON FILMS, 97 minutes
Director: J Lee Thompson
Starring: Rock Hudson (as Frank Stevenson), Robert Mitchum, Ellen Burstyn, Donald Pleasence

Appendix IV

Television Features

McMillan and Wife [1971–6] UNIVERSAL STUDIOS
Devised by Leonard Stern
Starring: Rock Hudson, Susan Saint James, Nancy Walker, John Schuck
Produced by Paul Mason.

Author's choices

Terror Times Two [1972] 69 minutes. Directed by Ron Winston and starring Andrew Duggan, Martin E Brooks, Charlotte Stewart, Carl Esmond

Cop of the Year [1972] 69 minutes. Directed by Robert Michael Lewis and starring Edmond O'Brien, Lorraine Gary, Ken Mars, Michael Ansara, Paul Winchell

No Hearts, No Flowers [1972] 70 minutes. Directed by Gary Nelson and starring Sheree North, Scott Brady, Albert Salmi, Dick Van Patten

Blues for Sally M [1972] 72 minutes. Directed by Robert Michael Lewis and starring Keir Dullea, Edie Adams, Jack Carter, Tom Troupe, Don Mitchell

The Fine Art of Staying Alive [1973] 69 minutes. Directed by Edward M Abroms and starring Martin E Brooks, Henry Jones, Caesar Danova, Alan Hale Jr

Two Dollars on Trouble to Win [1973] 69 minutes. Directed by Gary Nelson and starring William Demarest, Murray Matheson, Jackie Coogan, Barbara Rhoades

Free Fall to Terror [1973] 71 minutes. Directed by Alj Kjellin and starring Barbara Feldon, James Olson, Dick Haymes, Tom Bosley, Edward Andrews

Death of a Monster . . . Birth of a Legend [1973] 70 minutes. Directed by Daniel Petrie and starring Roddy McDowall, Roger C Carmel, John McLian, Scott Thomas, Diana Webster

The Devil You Say [1974] 67 minutes. Directed by Alex Marchand and starring Keenan Wynn, Werner Klemperer, Barbara Colby, Rita Gam, Robert Hooks

Reunion in Terror [1975] Directed by Mel Ferberand starring Buddy Hackett, Salome Jens, Michael Ansara, Rosey Grier, Carole Cook

Mcmillan [1976–77]
Devised by Leonard Stern.
Starring: Martha Raye, Richard Galliland, John Schuck.
Produced mostly by Jon Epstein.

Author's choices
Dark Sunrise [1976] 69 minutes. Directed by Bob Finkel and starring Karen Valentine, Kim Basinger, Richard Lenz, Julie Adams, Dub Taylor

All Bets Off! [1976] 67 minutes. Directed by Jackie Cooper and starring Jessica Walter, Dane Clark, Werner Klemperer, Dick Haymes, Charles Drake

Coffee, Tea or Cyanide [1977] 67 minutes. Directed by James Sheldon and starring Julie Sommars, Jack Jones, Marisa Pavan, Leslie Charleson, Robert Webber

Have You Heard About Vanessa? [1977] 69 minutes. Directed by James Sheldon and starring Joan Van Ark, Trisha Noble, Peter Donat, Natalie Schafer, Roger Bowen

Philip's Game [1977] 68 minutes. Directed by Lou Antonio and starring Shirley Jones, Tony Roberts, Nina Foch, Lloyd Bochner, William Windom

Affair of the Heart [1977] 68 minutes. Directed by Jackie Cooper and starring Stefanie Powers, Larry Hagman, Barbara Babcock, John Kerr, Lloyd Nolan

Wheels [1978] Produced by Jerry London. Around 10 hours.
Based on the book by Arthur Hailey. Starring Rock Hudson (as Adam Trenton), Lee Remick, Tony Franciosa, Ralph Bellamy, Blair Brown

The Martian Chronicles [1980]
Produced by Michael Anderson in three parts.
Written by Ray Bradbury. Starring Rock Hudson, Maria Schell, Roddy McDowall, Barry Morese, Gayle Hunnicutt

The Starmaker [1981]
Produced by Lou Antonio.
Features Rock's only love scene with another man. Starring Rock Hudson, Ed McMahon, Suzanne Pleshette, Melanie Griffith, Jack Scalia, Terri Copley, Cathie Shiriff, April Clough, Kristian Alfonso

The Patricia Neal Story [1981]
Produced by Anthony Harvey and Anthony Page.
In a cameo role, Rock played himself.

The Devlin Connection [1982]
Produced by Susan Lichtwardt.
Starring Rock Hudson (as Brian Devlin) and Jack Scalia. Only 13 of a possible 24 episodes were filmed before Rock's hospitalisation with a heart attack.

Las Vegas Strip Wars [1984]
Produced by George Englund.
Starring Rock Hudson, James Earl Jones, Pat Morita, Sharon Stone

Dynasty [1984-85]
Produced by Aaron Spelling.
Rock played Daniel Reece in nine episodes, mostly directed by
Irving Moore.

Television Guest Appearances

I Love Lucy: In Palm Springs (1955)
Climax: The Louella Parsons Story (1956)
The Ed Sullivan Show (1956)
Sid Caesar's Hour (1956)
The Steve Allen Show (1958 & 1959)
The Big Party (1959)
The Jack Benny Show (1962)
Hollywood Squares (1974)
The Carol Burnett Show (1975)
Circus of the Stars (1980)
Doris Day's Best Friends (July 1985)

Theatre Productions

I Do! I Do! (1973–5) US tour, followed by London and Toronto,
firstly with Carol Burnett, then Juliette Prowse
John Brown's Body (1976) US tour with Claire Trevor, Leif
Erickson
Camelot (1977) US tour

Appendix V

Biopics and Documentaries

Rock Hudson [1989], KONIGSBERG/SANITSKY, 90 minutes
Director: John Nicolella
Producer: Renee Palyo. **Script:** Dennis Turner
Director of Photography: Tom Sigel. **Music:** Paul Chihara
Starring: Thomas Ian Griffith as Rock Hudson; William R Moses as Marc Christian; Daphne Askbrook as Phyllis Gates; Dianne Ladd as Kay Fitzgerald; Andrew Robinson as Henry Willson; Thom Matthews as Tim Murphy; Mathieu Carriere as Dominique Dormont and with Michael Ensign, Joycelyn O'Brien, Don Galloway

> A dramatisation of events in the life of the legendary Rock Hudson, based on books and magazine accounts, personal interviews and court records . . . Composite characters and re-sequencing of events have been used for dramatic purposes.

So reads the publicity for this outstanding and intensely moving biopic, but in truth there does not appear to be much of the usual rewriting of Hollywood history here: though most of the major protagonists in the Hudson saga were dead when the film was made, the producer and scriptwriter seem to have made little effort to conceal the true identities of Rock's earlier lovers other than to change their names. Relative newcomer Griffith is ideally cast as the educationally challenged, sexually voracious lead. *Falcon Crest* star Moses (whom Rock is alleged to have 'fancied' during a visit to the set to see the series' matriarch, Jane Wyman) comes across as affable, sincere and seductive – as Marc Christian is alleged to have been. It is said to have been a calculated guess on the producer's part, for so little was known about the real Christian, even after the infamous trial. Dianne Ladd, who had starred opposite Rock in *Embryo*, is less convincing as his mother, though Andrew Robinson (whom Rock had admired as the thug in Clint Eastwood's 1971 film, *Dirty Harry*) is first class in the role of the repugnant Svengali, Henry Willson.

The story begins three years after Rock's death, with Marc Christian being mobbed by reporters on the steps of the Los Angeles courthouse. 'Rock Hudson did a bad thing,' he tells them. 'But he was not a bad man.'

We are treated to a score or so stunning close-ups of the real Rock before his on-screen lookalike makes his appearance, striding confidently through the gates of the Selznick studio and into Henry Willson's office. 'Your pants are too short, your lapels are too narrow – but you're one hell of a package,' Willson says, his expression suggesting that this is one package he has every intention of unwrapping, while Rock just stands there, looking dumb.

Rock is taken on there and then, handed a slip of paper upon which Willson has scribbled his new name, and in the next scene he is seen stepping out of the Cadillac that has whisked him to his first Hollywood party – wearing excruciatingly tight denims and a cowboy shirt, and looking not much less handsome than the genuine article. Here, sticking out like the proverbial sore thumb, he is ogled and prodded like a stud bull at a cattle market, and introduced to Raoul Walsh, who quips, 'At least he'll make good scenery.'

In next to no time Rock is fluffing his lines in *Fighter Squadron*. On the set he falls for one of the extras, Tim Murphy, his first soul-mate in whom he confides about his dreadful childhood. Through Tim, over the next few years, his confidence in his abilities grows. The pair share an apartment, and of course it does not take long for the tongues to start wagging, and Henry Willson, the archetypal hypocrite, puts his foot down about them being seen together in public. Therefore, as Rock's career must always come before personal happiness, it is not long before Tim is packing his bags. 'You're so damned scared of being queer,' he laments, 'you're going to spend your whole life denying who and what you are. You can bury yourself if you want to, but you're not burying me!'

The split coincides with Rock's developing attachment to Phyllis Gates and the overwhelming success of *Magnificent Obsession*, and from this point the scriptwriter leans heavily on the Gates book, the fact that they fell in love like a 'regular' couple as opposed to being shanghaied into a fake union by Willson and the studio bigwigs. They buy their first home, have fun – and sex – on the set of *Giant*, and ultimately marry when *Confidential* begins pointing the finger of suspicion.

Henceforth, Rock's libido knows no bounds. He and Phyllis are in and out of bed with each shift of the camera angle, but the men are there too: the youth on the beach, the jealous gardener, the not so discreet pick-ups in gay bars, which almost lead to blackmail. And there is the infamous incident from Phyllis' book where Rock snaps after one 'queer' joke too many – slapping his wife in front of their friends and yelling that he is sick and tired of people telling him what to do.

The phoney marriage ends acrimoniously, but at least we are left with a Rock who is no longer gloomy and always looking over his shoulder. He makes *Pillow Talk* – an interlude that contains original Hudson–Day newsreel footage – and he buys the Castle. Finally, he fires the odious Henry Willson.

It's time I started living on my terms. I'll do the pictures I want to do, and from now on when I come in those front gates I'm gonna live the way I want to, *finally* live the way I want to!

And he does! The next scene is one of the legendary 'Grant and Scott' garden parties, with muscle-bound hunks (and more than a few genuine gay porn stars) decorating the Castle grounds, and one in particular who seduces Rock in the pool when the other guests have gone.

The scenario shifts to the sixties: miniskirts, the Vietnam War protests, the Kennedy and Martin Luther King assassinations, more movies with Doris Day, and *Seconds* with John Frankenheimer – who nurses him to sleep on his lap after he suffers a nervous breakdown on the set, from which he recovers to make the *McMillan and Wife* series. At this stage he is living openly with a (non-blond) young man named Sean (Tom Alexander). Then comes Rock's so-called downfall: the death of his mother; his bypass operation; his meeting with Marc Christian; *that* episode of *Dynasty*; his swansong with Doris Day; and the announcement that he has AIDS.

The final scenes are harrowing – sometimes almost too painful to watch and unnecessary to enlarge upon. All in all, a finely balanced and worthy portrait of a remarkable man.

Rock Hudson's Home Movies [1993], COUCH POTATO PRODUCTIONS, 60 minutes
Writer and **Director:** Mark Rappaport
Featuring: Rock Hudson and Eric Farr

Innovative at the time of its limited release, with the rapid growth of modern computer imagery this is now very much a curiosity, though strangely watchable. Rappaport evidently fantasised about getting close to the archetypal slab of American beefcake, and, through this strange film, successfully brought his fantasies to life. Unfortunately for Rappaport, he was a man in whom Rock would not have shown the least interest, and so he provided himself with a more attractive celluloid image – the seriously hunky Eric Farr.

Collaging footage of Rock's films and Rappaport's home movies of Farr (not Rock's, as the title suggests), the director's theory was to explore, in great homoerotic depth, the ironic set-up used in many of Rock's romantic comedies – the gay actor playing a straight man impersonating a gay man in order to get the likes of Doris Day into bed. Farr, an ethereal-looking model who spends much of his time effetely posing in a tight vest and flexing his muscles, more often than not gets in the way of the real Rock, whose own 'body shots' light up the screen. Void of acting experience and ability, Farr had little else to offer. Rappaport – aka Farr – highlights Rock's 'gayness' – which was not blatantly obvious at the time, as is suggested, otherwise Rock would not have survived 35 years in the closet – by freeze-framing certain gestures from his films: sly winks, curled lips and sneaked sidelong 'amorous' glances at homophobic co-stars such as John Wayne.

Rappaport, himself a purveyor of mostly forgettable films since the early seventies, wrote in *Film Quarterly*:

Rock Hudson was a prisoner, as well as a purveyor of sexual politics and stereotypes. He is a prism through which sexual assumptions, gender-coding and sexual role-playing in Hollywood movies and, therefore by extension, America of the 1950s and 1960s can be explored. In a sense, it is Hudson's sexuality that is the real auteur of his movies – just as his closetedness was the icon all America was worshipping.

Absolute rot, of course!

Such wishful thinking aside, the critics were divided in their opinions. Some denounced it as 'exploitative claptrap', others refused to review it at all, while *Premier*'s J Hoberman thought it a melodrama worthy of Douglas Sirk. 'The brilliance of *Rock Hudson's Home Movies* lies not just in the reanimation of its star,' Hoberman enthused. 'Rappaport invests "Rock Hudson" with a passion and pathos barely evident in his original imitation of life.'

The Wild Ones [1994], TOM OF FINLAND/RENEGADE PRODUCTIONS, 120 minutes
Writer and **Director:** Durk Dehner
Starring: Zak Spears, Bull Stanton, Blue Blake, Wolff, Steve Gibson, Clint Benedict and a host of gay porn stars

This XXX-rated movie centres around Rock's visit to San Francisco's Black & Blue Club, and is not for the squeamish! It was dedicated to the memory of *Kaka* magazine cartoonist Tom of Finland (1920–91), famous for his illustrations of leather-clad, phenomenally endowed macho men. The sequence that features the Hudson character (Spears) was filmed in the actual backroom of the equally infamous Eagle Bar.

Rock Hudson: Acting the Part [1999], A & E NETWORK, 45 minutes
Writer and **Director:** John Griffin
Narrator: Tim Bentinck

This documentary concentrates more on Rock Hudson's death and sexuality than on his career as an actor. Jack Larson and Robert Stack repeat the well-worn anecdotes such as Rock's fluffing of his lines in *Fighter Squadron* and Arlene Dahl (his co-star in *Bengal Brigade*, and once married to Fernando Lamas, with whom he had had a fling) tells us that she had suspected Rock of being gay because he chewed his fingernails!

Only 85-year-old Jane Wyman has anything worthwhile to say, regarding his fears over working in *Magnificent Obsession*, 'Rock was a sponge. He just sucked up everything and pigeonholed it and used it, when he could, and by the end of the picture he was a pro.'

Even so, despite this lack of input from colleagues who more often than not had 'disowned' him owing to the manner of his death, it is perhaps a case of being thankful for small mercies. Like the aforementioned biopic, this starts off with images (home-movies) of a hale and hearty Rock, before getting down to the nitty-gritty – in this instance film footage of his reunion with Doris Day in Carmel, which is so poor, even if he had not been seriously ill, this would have made him appear so.

Cut then to Armistead Maupin, who speaks of the authentic autobiography Rock never got around to writing, and Sara Davidson who expresses the difficulties she encountered putting the Hudson story together because of her subject's fondness for telling different people different versions of the same story: 'It was like walking on a spider's web, and there was no place I could put a foot that was firm.' Jack Scalia, his co-star from *The Devlin Connection* and his only on-screen male dalliance in *The Starmaker*, observes how Rock liked to tell stories, because this way he would never have to show people who he really was, and John Frankenheimer is of the belief that Rock identified with his 'reborn' character in *Seconds* because he was a reinvented personality who had destroyed his past to become Rock Hudson. Rock himself reiterates this fact during a September 1984 clip from the BBC's *Terry Wogan Show*: already beginning to show the ravages of AIDS, he confesses that he dislikes interviews, much preferring to have a character to hide behind.

There are brief anecdotes from a cousin who hardly knew him, yet who distinctly remembers how she and friends used to dress Rock as a girl, to such effect that no one else could tell the difference; and a classmate who swears the Rock he knew never aspired to becoming an actor. There are photographs of the young marine 'stripped for action' and camping it up with his Navy buddies, and an interview with former 'roommate' Bob Preble, who, we are persistently reminded, was very definitely straight and in his younger days sported stubble to prove the fact. Obviously, Preble had forgotten the magazine photo-spreads and the galaxy of witnesses to the fact that, chez Hudson in those days, there had been one bedroom and one bed.

According to Preble, Rock had told him that he had had sexual experiences with men during his military service because there had been no girls around. Preble then goes on to say how *Confidential* approached him for a story – though in the early fifties there was no such term as 'gay-bird'. And when Sara Davidson describes Rock's preferences in men – blond, blue-eyed, big – the producer, inadvertently or not (considering the stills for the documentary were mostly supplied by Rock's former handyman, Marty Flaherty, now head of the Rock Hudson Collection), risks a photograph of by far the most handsome of all Rock's men, Massimo, in near-naked glory.

Rock's marriage is lightly touched upon, though images of Phyllis Gates (who like Marc Christian steadfastly refused to participate) crop up throughout the documentary. Stockton Biggle believes that it was an arranged marriage, but Mark Miller states for the first time that Rock was a willing participant and a genuine bisexual who liked getting physical with women.

Armistead Maupin needlessly defends Rock against the by-now old-fashioned 'lily-livered degenerate' image of gay men:

> He was a man. He was an all-solid, god-like man. It seemed to confirm what I'd always felt about homosexuality – that it simply denoted a sexual preference, a sexual orientation, not necessarily effeminacy.

Maupin again voices his opinion concerning the world's perception of AIDS, of how angry he was that someone famous had to succumb to the disease to make the public aware of a condition that should have been acknowledged years before. Mark Miller (in another exclusive) declares how he believed Rock had got AIDS from a lover in New York (the date and timing suggestive of Pierre B—, the boatbuilder he had been involved with at the time of the 1984 Academy Awards) – according to Miller, the young man had confessed his HIV status in a warning letter to Rock, later that year.

There is fleeting footage of a confident-looking Marc Christian arriving at the Los Angeles courthouse, with the narrator pronouncing that, at the time of the lawsuit, Christian had tested HIV negative. We then witness some disgraceful media behaviour as Rock's body leaves the Castle in the van en route to the crematorium and one of the security men screams at the press to back off and show some respect. Meanwhile, Ross Hunter breaks down in front of the cameras and sobs, 'He was the best friend I ever had in the world!'

The documentary concludes with the succinct but emotionless narratorial epigram, 'Rock Hudson will be remembered as a great Hollywood leading man, a television detective, and one of the first celebrities to die of AIDS. His fans loved him for all of these roles.'

Bibliography and Interviews

Primary Sources

Castell, David. 'Rock of All Ages', *Films Illustrated*. April 1976.
—— 'Rock Around the Clock'. August 1980.
Davidson, Sara. *Rock Hudson: His Story*. Weidenfeld & Nicholson, 1986.
Davis, Professor Ronald L. Taped interview with Rock Hudson. Southern Methodist University of Dallas, Oral History Project No 276: pp 1–51. 24 August 1983.
Duffy, David. 'Les Raisons Secrètes du Terrible Mal de Rock Hudson', *Ciné-Revue*. January 1982.
Eston, Eric. '*Dynasty* Remembers Rock Hudson', *American TV Guide*. April 1986.
Errico, Angie. 'Rock Hudson: Ten Years After', *Premiere*. May 1995.
Feidan, Robert and Colaciello, Robert. 'Interview With Rock Hudson', *Interview*. February 1970.
Gale, Patrick. 'Armistead Maupin: How I Outed Rock Hudson', *Guardian*. June 1999.
Gates, Phyllis. *My Husband, Rock Hudson*. Angus & Robertson, 1987.
Gow, Gordon. 'Rock Hudson: Actors Always Try', *Films & Filming*. June 1976.
Hicks, Jimmie. 'Rock Hudson: The Film Actor as Romantic Hero', *Films In Revue*. May 1975.
Hudson, Rock. 'Rock Hudson: My Life Story', *Picture Show*. December 1953.
—— 'Interview', *Coronet*. June 1976.

Hudson, Rock. 'Interviews with Rock Hudson', *McCalls*. February 1967.

—— 'My Marriage', *Screen*. September 1971.

—— 'Rock Interview', *Chicago American*. February 1967.

Kobal, John. 'Interview with Rock Hudson' (circa 1975), *Films & Filming*. October 1985.

Lippe, Richard. 'Rock Hudson His Story', *CinéAction!* August 1987.

Mac Trevor, Joan. 'Rock Hudson: Deauville Rend Hommage à un Géant', *Ciné-Revue*. August 1984.

—— 'Rock Hudson: Hollywood à Peur du Testament Secret de Rock Hudson', *Ciné-Revue*. October 1985.

—— 'Rock Hudson: La Television est un Monstre du Temps!', *Ciné-Revue*. July 1981.

—— 'Rock Hudson: Le Courage Jusqu'au Bout', *Ciné-Revue*, October 1985.

Martin, Ken. 'Lunch with Rock Hudson', *TV Times*. October 1972.

Neves, Gérard. 'Le Courageux Combat de Rock Hudson', *Ciné-Revue*. August 1985.

—— 'Rock Hudson: Les Secrets de sa Nouvelle Vie à Soixante-Ans', *Ciné-Revue*. October 1984.

Oppenheimer, Jerry. *Idol: The Unauthorised Biography of Rock Hudson*, Bantam Press. 1987.

Osborne, Robert. 'Rock Hudson From A-Z', *Hollywood Reporter*. 1976.

Parker, John, *Five for Hollywood: Hudson, Clift, Taylor, Wood, Dean*, Lyle Stuart. 1989.

—— *The Trial of Rock Hudson*, Sidgwick & Jackson. 1990.

Reuter's reports on 'Marc Christian Versus The Rock Hudson Estate', to the *New York Times*, *Chicago Tribune*, *Globe*, etc., 1985–7

Sampson, Low and Marston. 'Give Me the Simple Life!', *Hollywood Album*. 1952.

Zec, Donald. 'Secret Torment of the Baron of Beefcake', *Sunday Mirror*. August 1985.

Secondary Sources

Anger, Kenneth. *Hollywood Babylon I and II*, Arrow, 1986.

Anonymous. 'Rock Hudson Gravely Ill', *Gay Times*. September 1985.

Anonymous. 'Rock Hudson: Dateline Malta', *Screen International*. October 1978.

Archard, Army. 'The Whispering Campaign Against Rock Hudson Should Stop', *Daily Variety*. July 1985.

Belsten, Mick. 'Rock Hudson: Health Report', *Gay Times*. September 1985.

Bret, David. *Freddie Mercury: Living on the Edge*. Robson Books, 1996.

Brooks, Tony. 'The Heart-throb who Lived a Lie', *Star*, October 1985.

Cleutat, Michel. 'Rock Hudson: Le Géant aux Pieds Nus', *Positif.* December 1985.

Christian, Marc. 'Rock's Boyfriend: Why I'm Suing for $10 Million', *National Enquirer*. November 1985.

Christian, Marc. Interview on French Television's *Stars à la Barre*. July 1989.

Considine, Shaun. *Bette and Joan: The Divine Feud*. Warner. 1992.

Dalton, David. *James Dean: The Mutant King*. St Martin's Press, 1987.

Day, Doris. *Doris Day: Her Own Story*. W H Allen, 1988.

Eames, John Douglas. *The MGM Story*. Octopus, 1976.

Ellis, Richard. 'Rock Hudson Is Dead', *Sun*. October 1985.

Forrest, Elizabeth. 'They're Running Hudson onto the Rocks', *Picturegoer*. Jaunuary 1954.

Harrigan, Brian. 'Rock Hudson: A Giant in Hollywood', *Video Business*. October 1985.

Holley, Val. *James Dean*. Robson Books, 1995.

Hoberman, J. 'Woolf in Potter's Clothing', *Premiere*. July 1993.

Jackson, John. 'Final Hours of Tragic Rock', *Daily Mirror*. October 1985.

Key, Ivor. 'Rock: The Agony is Over', *Star*. October 1985.

Knight, Arthur. 'Knight at the Movies', *Hollywood Reporter*. October 1985.

LaGuardia, Robert. *Montgomery Clift*. Arbor House, 1977.

McCann, Graham. *Rebel Males*, Hamish Hamilton. 1991.

Medved, Harry and Michael. *The Golden Turkey Awards*. Angus & Robertson, 1980.

Mills, Bart. 'Rock Hudson: The Programme is Terrible, Terrible!' *Guardian*. February 1977.

Mintz, Elliot. 'Interview with Debbie Boone', *Playgirl*, October 1979.

Morley, Sheridan. 'Solid Rock Hudson', *The Times*. January 1976.

Moseley, Ray and Charles Catchpole. 'The Hunk who Lived a Lie', *Sun*. October 1985.

Perrick, Eve. 'Spot the Film Star', *Daily Express*. November 1952.

Pickard, Roy. 'Rock Hudson: McMillan is Finished', *Photoplay*. June 1976.

Quinlan, David. *Quinlan's Film Stars/Film Character Actors*. Batsford, 1996.

Rappaport, Mark. 'Notes sur les Home-Movies de Rock Hudson', *Trafic*. October 1994.

Rees, Alex. 'Rock's Fit for a Hit', *Sun*. July 1982.

Rogers, Jenny. 'Rappaport: Re-imaging the Lives of Jean Seberg and Rock Hudson', *Femme-Flicke*. June 1997.

Rowland, Mark. 'Interview With Jack Scalia', *Playgirl*. October 1981.

Sanderson, Terry, 'In Defence of Rock Hudson', *Gay Times*. September 1985.

Scott, Vernon. 'A Slap in the Face from Rock', *Photoplay*. June 1978.

Seton, John. 'Rock Under the Surface', *Picturegoer*, November 1952.

Thompson, Douglas. 'Rock Hudson: Me – The Fonz of the Fifties?', *TV Times*. June 1978.

Various. 'Lawsuit Over Rock's Estate Exposes Scandal', *People*. November 1985.

Walton, June. 'Rock's Gay Life by his Ex-Wife', *Sunday Mirror*. August 1985.

Ward, L E. 'The Reel Rock Hudson', *Classic Images*. January 1989.

Webb, Mike. 'Rock Hudson: A Man's Frank Look at Himself', *Photoplay*. July 1969.

Wigg, David. 'Rock Hudson Sings!', *Daily Express*. March 1970.

Williams, Peter. 'I Saw Rock Wed Man', *News of the World*. August 1985.

Zec, Donald. 'Beefcake'/The 14-Stone He-Man', *Daily Mirror*. August 1952.

Index